Geraldine Farrar
Second Edition

Geraldine Farrar
Opera's Charismatic Innovator

Second Edition

Elizabeth Nash

McFarland & Company, Inc., Publishers
Jefferson, North Carolina, and London

Frontispiece: Geraldine Farrar as *Madama Butterfly*, 1916.

LIBRARY OF CONGRESS CATALOGUING-IN-PUBLICATION DATA

Nash, Elizabeth, 1934–
    Geraldine Farrar : opera's charismatic innovator / Elizabeth Nash — 2nd ed.
       p.   cm.
    Includes bibliographical references and index.

ISBN 978-0-7864-7067-9

softcover : acid free paper ∞

1. Farrar, Geraldine, 1882–1967. 2. Sopranos (Singers)—United States—Biography. I. Title.
ML420.F27N43 2012
782.1092
[B]   2012028614

BRITISH LIBRARY CATALOGUING DATA ARE AVAILABLE

© 2012 Elizabeth Nash. All rights reserved

No part of this book may be reproduced or transmitted in any form or by any means, electronic or mechanical, including photocopying or recording, or by any information storage and retrieval system, without permission in writing from the publisher.

On the cover: Geraldine Farrar portrays Joan of Arc as woman and soldier in *Joan the Woman* (1917), Cecil B. DeMille's first historical film.

Manufactured in the United States of America

McFarland & Company, Inc., Publishers
  Box 611, Jefferson, North Carolina 28640
    www.mcfarlandpub.com

With love and gratitude
to my mother and father,
Renee H. and Allan B. Nash,
for their unfailing support,
faith and encouragement

Acknowledgments

I am deeply grateful to the late Professor Emerita Camilla Williams of the Jacobs School of Music, Indiana University, for sharing her knowledge of Miss Farrar, which revealed fascinating aspects of her life unknown to me at the time of this book's first publication in 1981. Professor Williams became a good friend and wise counselor to me as Miss Farrar was to her. On January 29, 2012, she passed away at her home in Bloomington, Indiana.

For their generous assistance, I am much indebted to the late Dr. Oscar G. Brockett, University of Texas, Austin; to the late Edward N. Waters, Music Division chief of the Library of Congress; to Dr. James Norwood for his meticulous reading of the manuscript, suggestions and encouragement; to Reed Munson for his computer expertise; and to John Bishop for his photographic ingenuity.

My grateful thanks is extended to Curtis Licensing for permission to reprint copyright material from "*Coming Back and Looking Back*" story © SEPS licensed by Curtis Licensing, Indianapolis, IN. All rights reserved.

Contents

Acknowledgments vi
Preface 1
Introduction 5

CHAPTER ONE
The Early Years, 1882–1906 11

CHAPTER TWO
At the Metropolitan Opera, 1906–1908 34

CHAPTER THREE
At the Metropolitan Opera, 1908–1915 57

CHAPTER FOUR
Hollywood, 1915–1920 90

CHAPTER FIVE
At the Metropolitan Opera, 1916–1922 110

CHAPTER SIX
The Transition Years, 1922–1935 129

CHAPTER SEVEN
Retirement, 1935–1967 131

Appendix 1: Theory and Practice 135
Appendix 2: "The Art of Acting in the Movies Requires a Technique Unlike That of the Operatic Stage," by Geraldine Farrar 143
Appendix 3: Conversations on Geraldine Farrar with Camilla Williams, 1995–2011 150

Appendix 4: Operatic Roles 155
Appendix 5: Silent Films....................................... 157
Appendix 6: Select Discography 160
Appendix 7: Select Radio Broadcasts 162
Chapter Notes 163
Select Bibliography... 179
Index 183

Preface

"They may come and they may go but there is only one Geraldine Farrar to remain in the heart of the world."[1] Thus the theatrical director and producer David Belasco spoke of the American prima donna who was the Metropolitan Opera's most popular and glamorous diva from 1906 until 1922.

Her operatic impersonations united the arts of the singer and of the actress. Convinced that music must always serve the drama, this magnetic singing actress often sacrificed tonal beauty to dramatic effect. Nevertheless Farrar was a superb singer, possessing a beautiful lyric soprano voice, as evidenced in her numerous phonograph recordings.

During her sixteen-year reign at the Metropolitan, she performed 493 times in twenty-nine roles, the most popular of which were Giacomo Puccini's Madama Butterfly and Tosca, Engelbert Humperdinck's Goose Girl, Georges Bizet's Carmen and Ruggero Leoncavallo's Zazà. Her acting was noted for its intensity and realism. In 1906 she worked with the Japanese actress Fu-ji-Ko on Madama Butterfly which she created at the Metropolitan. In 1909 she studied Tosca with Sarah Bernhardt for whom the role was written. In 1920 she was directed by David Belasco as Zazà.

The renowned tenor Enrico Caruso was her frequent partner, guaranteeing sold-out houses. They were the most dynamic duo in the annals of the Metropolitan Opera. Aside from her popularity with the general operatic public, Miss Farrar developed a large following of devoted young women known as the Gerryflappers who attended all of her performances. Her farewell appearance at the Metropolitan aroused a frenzy of excitement concluding with a parade up Broadway to her home with cheering fans marching behind her flower-bedecked open touring car. Never before or since has there been such adoration for an American opera star. She was and remains America's first lady of opera.

Aside from her opera performances and concert tours, Geraldine Farrar was a star of the silent screen. From 1915 to 1920, she made fourteen films with Jesse L. Lasky, Samuel Goldwyn and Pathé. Jesse L. Lasky brought her out to Hollywood in order to attract the much desired carriage trade. Cecil B. DeMille featured her in *Carmen* and then in his first historical film *Joan the Woman*. They reveal DeMille's early use of spectacle and Miss Farrar's mastery of acting for the films under his guidance. Because of her desire to perform exclusively with her new husband, the matinee idol Lou Tellegen, she left Jesse L. Lasky in 1917 to join Samuel Goldwyn and later Pathé films. The scenarios and direction were inferior to those of the Famous Players-Lasky Corporation. Also Tellegen's good looks did not compensate for his lack of talent. By 1920, Miss Farrar's films no longer appealed to the public and she terminated her annual summer Hollywood contracts. Until her retirement from the Metropolitan in 1922, she again devoted her entire time to opera and concert engagements.

Geraldine Farrar has fascinated me since childhood, because I cannot remember a time when I did not want to sing in opera. My musical aspirations were encouraged by my mother, Renee H. Nash, who had been an English musical comedy star and by Frederick Jagel, a leading tenor at the Metropolitan Opera for twenty-four years. The Jagels were our neighbors in Pelham, New York. I always enjoyed listening to them talk about the opera world, but I was enthralled by stories of their friend Geraldine Farrar. They were guests at her birthday and New Year's Eve parties and Mr. Jagel had witnessed her performances as Thäis, Madama Butterfly, Carmen, Marguerite, Tosca and her spectacular farewell performance as Zazà.

Eventually I was to have a ten year career as a dramatic coloratura soprano in European opera houses and then decided to become a teacher. When it came time for me to write my dissertation as a candidate for the degree of Ph.D. in theatre arts at Indiana University, my adviser, the noted theatre historian Dr. Oscar G. Brockett, suggested I write on the life and career of an operatic singing actress. It seemed obvious that Miss Farrar should be the ideal subject for my dissertation. Since no one had ever written about her, I began my research.

Having learned that Miss Farrar had donated her seventy years of memorabilia to the Music Division of the Library of Congress, I arranged for a visit to see the Farrar Collection. Our family friend Mr. Francis Robinson of the Metropolitan Opera wrote a letter of introduction for me to Mr. Edward N. Waters, chief of the Music Division, whose staff treated me royally during my week's stay in Washington. Miss Farrar and her mother had preserved in scrapbooks probably everything ever written about or to the diva from her debut in Berlin until her memorabilia was presented to the Library of Congress in 1954. Professor Walter J. Meserve had advised me to quickly overview the entire collection taking note of important items. "Don't waste time attempting to read them in detail. Go back later and photocopy them. Then you will have your own reference library to take home." I followed his advice and rarely needed to refer to other sources while writing my dissertation. On my final day in Washington, Mr. Waters and I had a lengthy visit and he informed me that Mr. Robinson had been one of the first people to see the collection. He and Miss Farrar had been friends for many years. When he began to look at one of the scrapbooks, he noted the fragile condition of the articles. He closed the book and said to Mr. Waters: "Some day a scholar will come to study this collection and I do not want to deprive them of seeing these items in perfect condition." I was the scholar!

Soon after, Miss Sylvia Blein, who had served as Geraldine Farrar's housekeeper and companion for more than fifty years, graciously granted me an interview. Over little cakes and cups of tea, she shared her memories of the distinguished diva and answered many questions for me. "Whether it was fur, lace or Bird of Paradise plumes, Miss Farrar insisted on the real thing for her costumes. She was always first class." These words epitomized Geraldine Farrar's career.

After graduating, I joined the theatre arts faculty at the University of Minnesota. Since publication is obligatory for university faculty, I decided to edit my dissertation, which was published in 1981. Other books and articles followed.

In 1995 my late colleague Professor Emerita Patricia Turner and I wished to interview the African American opera diva Miss Camilla Williams. "What have you and Dr. Nash published?" she asked. When Patricia mentioned that I had written a biography on Geraldine Farrar, Miss Williams exclaimed: "Did you say Geraldine Farrar? She was my mentor and friend who opened the door to my career in opera. You can interview me this afternoon if you wish!" The interview eventually led to an article and highly informative discussions on Geraldine Farrar, who shared her wealth of professional experience with Miss Williams from 1945 to 1967.

Miss Farrar wrote two entertaining autobiographies—*Geraldine Farrar: The Story of an American Singer by Herself* and *Such Sweet Compulsion*— but no book-length study had been made of her life and career. Edward Wagenknecht's *Geraldine Farrar: An Authorized Record of Her Career* contains a personal "Appreciation," a list of her operatic roles, motion pictures, recordings, six concert programs and a selected bibliography. My biography met the need for a detailed account documenting this stellar performer's major contributions to the history of opera and films but went out of print in 1983. I have received numerous requests for information on the book's availability, but it was completely sold out.

Since my interview and conversations with Miss Williams from 1995 to

2011 revealed an entirely unknown aspect of Miss Farrar's life as an advocate for a pioneering young African American classical singer as well as her messages to Marian Anderson via Miss Williams, I realized that my biography needed to be revised and re-issued.

Two incidents also motivated my desire for a new edition. Soon after the original publication of this work in 1981, I visited a ninety-five-year-old lady in a Vermont nursing home. A staff member warned me that she never spoke or responded to the comments of others. I had been told by her daughter that she had seen Miss Farrar as Puccini's Madama Butterfly in the early 1900s and mentioned the singer's name to her. For a fleeting moment, the impassive face lit up, and she said: "Oh, she was so very beautiful!"

Then in the fall of 2011 I discovered a University of Minnesota theatre colleague's love of opera and knowledge of Geraldine Farrar. "How do you know of Geraldine Farrar?" I asked her. "Everyone who enjoys opera knows about Geraldine Farrar," Christine Swartwout replied. "She broke the glass ceiling before there was one."

David Belasco was right. Miss Farrar still "remain[s] in the heart of the world."

Introduction

"In my humble way I am an actress who happens to be appearing in opera,"[1] claimed Geraldine Farrar, who throughout her operatic career was always willing to sacrifice tonal beauty to dramatic effect. She believed that singing, even in an operatic performance, was of secondary importance. Certainly she realized her approach was not without its critics. And she did not deny that ideally opera unites the arts of music and drama. But Miss Farrar staunchly advocated the recent trend toward the subservience of singing to acting. According to this dramatic, highly emotional artist, music must always serve the drama.

It seemed absurd to many that anyone with such a beautiful voice should have chosen to emphasize her histrionic rather than her vocal gifts. However, Miss Farrar persisted in her defiance of tradition, convinced that "this generation has developed a new and most interesting type, the singer-actor, 50 per cent dramatic talent; perhaps even 80 per cent dramatic talent. That is what the audiences of today want. In the opera of other days one person came to the front of the stage and warbled, then stood aside while another person warbled, and then two warbled together. Today people want something more than a voice."[2] For nearly twenty years, she was to bring "dramatic insight and real acting ability to her roles."[3]

As a young student in Boston, New York, and Paris, Miss Farrar constantly attended the opera. Although she admired the superb vocal techniques of such great stars as Nellie Melba, Jean de Reszke, or Adelina Patti, she was disturbed by the lack of theatrical illusion in the settings, in the costumes, and in the staging of the various productions. After her retirement in 1922, she criticized the Metropolitan Opera's "sketchy" sets which she declared "called for some credulity on the part of the spectators. Their shabbiness was doubtless accounted for by their versatility, for the same sets, frankly undisguised, had an enormous repertoire. The Prison Scene in *Faust* would obligingly become the dungeon of *Trovatore*, and even the judgment hall in *Aida* bore it a strange family resemblance."[4]

Traditionally, opera stars supplied their own historically inaccurate costumes, and according to Miss Farrar, "as splendor and finery were the recognizable mark of rank and big cachets, most of these costumes were entrusted to the experts of the Rue de la Paix [Paris's street of fashion designers]. The results often bore a curious analogy to the contemporary and fashionable silhouette, even though the characters they clothed were supposedly denizens of prehistoric forests or palaces of the moyen age."[5]

Miss Farrar was also irritated by the blocking of movement and positions, which she stated were almost nonexistent. Most of the singers refused to follow the suggestions of a director and their only concessions to the drama consisted of a few conventional gestures which would not interfere with their singing. Tonal perfection was the vocalist's chief concern, and Miss Farrar knew this when she entered her career. It was reported of the renowned nineteenth-century soprano, Adelina Patti, that "she never acted; and she never, never felt."[6] Every singer knew, according to Clara Louise Kellogg, one of America's first opera stars, that "emotions are what exhaust and injure the voice."[7] Clearly, Charlotte Cushman, the prominent nineteenth-century actress, was right when she said of Miss Kellogg's acting: "the girl doesn't seem to know that she has any arms."[8] According to David Belasco, Miss Kellogg was one of those superb vocal technicians who "would step to the front of the stage and sing the music allotted to them with very little effort to impersonate character."[9] Or, as George Bernard Shaw noted: "Half the attention to the singers is given to the prompter, half to the conductor, and the rest to the character impersonated."[10] But Miss Farrar was different.

In the late nineteenth century, stars tended to ignore the suggestions of the stage manager, who then fulfilled the duties of operatic stage director. In fact, in 1900, W.J. Henderson of the *New York Times* wrote:

> The stage management at the Metropolitan continues to be bad, or perhaps it would be nearer the truth to say that there is no stage management at all as it is understood in the theatre. One reason for this is the prevalence of the star system. To present a play with effective stage management it must be possible for the stage manager to work out a scheme or action and grouping. He cannot do this in the Metropolitan Opera House because the stars will not obey him. If the stage manager attempts to tell one of Mr. Grau's high priced singers what to do he is snubbed. So he confines his attention to an indifferent chorus and the scene shifters.[11]

The principal singers objected to reforms, remarked Henderson, "because they [would have to] change their traditional or routine stage business to meet the requirements of the new arrangements. And as the star singers are not under the command of anyone, not even the manager, they cannot be compelled to fall in with the new ideas, and so good-bye to the ideas."[12] In her forty years of singing Wagner's Isolde, the famous German soprano, Lilli Lehmann, claimed she had never deviated in the slightest degree from her original conception of the role. "She knew and could describe," Geraldine Farrar once stated, "just where and how, throughout the long score she lifted an arm or turned her head, sat down, took so many steps to left or right, and so on."[13] This, however, was not the style of acting Miss Farrar would tolerate for her own performances.

Several of the singers specifically stipulated that they should not be obliged to attend any rehearsals when stage movement might be discussed. Adelina Patti had this article written into her contract at Covent Garden: "Madame Patti shall be free to attend Rehearsals, but shall not be required or bound to attend them."[14] And "Madame" often chose not to attend but instead sent her maid to inform the cast of her probable actions in the performance. Frequently, she had not even met her colleagues before singing with them on stage. James Henry Mapleson, a nineteenth-century manager of Drury Lane and Covent Garden, recalled that on one occasion, the baritone was formally introduced to Patti during the performance by the tenor who incorporated the words into his vocal part.[15] Nellie Melba, on the other hand, did condescend to attend rehearsals, but Henderson recorded that "she had no need to rehearse what she does on the stage. That she can do without ten minutes of thought. All she has to do, and all she seems to try to do is to stand behind the footlights and pour out her silvery voice."[16] This magnificent singer, like many of her associates, could not or simply would not act.

"Operatic performances of early days," summed up Henderson in 1900, "were conducted on the same plane, with a few stars and bad scenery, bad stage management and poor orchestras."[17] He even facetiously suggested that operatic staging was a lost art, claiming he had searched in vain for some evidence that "one thoughtful mind had arranged the action and the groupings in operatic performances."[18] Instead, he stated, "the stage management at the Metropolitan displays the most astonishing lack of intelligence. No attempt whatever is made to create even the simplest theatrical illusions, and anachronisms, impossibilities, and at times even idiocies crowd the stage." The chorus in their "wretched" costumes looked like "a regiment of scarecrows,"[19] the scenery looked "old, worn, and cheap," the lighting looked "painfully thin," and the stage effects were "slovenly,"[20] he added. Others who attended Metropolitan Opera performances during the fin de siècle also were appalled at the lack of dramatic verisimilitude and recalled that breezes caused the mighty tree trunk in Wagner's *Die Walküre* to flutter,[21] and that the house gas lights were kept turned up during the entire performance.[22]

Apparently production standards at Covent Garden were no better, because George Bernard Shaw noted "how far the Opera House is behind the theatre in England" and went on to state: "For want of a stage manager, *Tannhäuser* was made a laughing-stock.... One gets at last to quite look forward to Valentine [in Gounod's *Faust*] attempting a dashing exit through an impracticable door into his house opposite the cathedral, and recoiling, flattened and taken aback, to disappear ignominiously through the solid wall at the next entrance."[23]

Since there was generally little or no attempt outside of Wagner's Bayreuth to create a consistent sense of dramatic illusion, even there the singers are said to have moved like soldiers under orders.[24] Superb singing was the operatic artist's primary concern at the turn of the century.

During the late nineteenth century, however, several singers began to rebel against this practice, and gradually they helped establish a new operatic species—the singing actor. From 1871 until 1892, when he retired from the lyric stage to teach operatic singing at the National Conservatory in New York, Victor Capoul was referred to as "the most ardent and fascinating lover known to opera in America"[25] and always bore himself with "habitual ease and grace"[26] on stage. This same elegance of bearing was noted in his pupil, Geraldine Farrar, who studied with him for several months in 1897 before he became stage manager of the Paris Opéra.

Another operatic idol of that era was Capoul's countryman, Victor Maurel, who believed: "through pose and action, through expression of face, gesture, voice, everything—[he] must make [the] character real to the audience."[27] One of his colleagues, Emilio de Gogorza, claimed that Maurel literally "lived"[28] the role of Rigoletto; while the famous Wagnerian soprano, Lilli Lehmann, recalled that she was so deeply moved by his impersonation of the dying Valentine in Gounod's *Faust* that she was unable to speak for several hours after the performance.[29] Iago in Verdi's *Otello* was one of his finest roles, which he often performed to the Otello of the famous Italian tenor, Francesco Tamagno, of whom Constantin Stanislavski wrote:

> He was a bad actor, but he was not talentless. That is why it was possible for him to create wonders. His Otello was a wonder. It was ideal, both musically and dramatically. He studied this part for many years ... with such masters as Verdi himself (musically) and Tommaso Salvini (dramatically). Tamagno was great in this part not only because of the labor of the two masters, but also because of the temperament, the sincerity and the feeling for truth given him by God. The masters of technique, his teachers, were able to uncover his talented spiritual being. He could do nothing for himself. He was taught to play the part, but the means used to make him do so remained mysteries to him. They were art and technique. Like the majority of actors, he worked on his part, but he was not an artist.[30]

Regarding Tamagno's performance of the Venetian Moor on March 3, 1890, at the Metropolitan Opera House, the *New York Times* reported, "He is what few singers are—a thoughtful person who aims at an eloquent expression of the meaning of the poet as well as of the musician. He is an actor of uncommon power for the operatic stage. His impersonation of the Moor is, of course, based on Salvini's, and is physical in its force rather than intellectual; but it is a piece of acting which would be creditable to the theatre as well as to the opera house."[31]

Three years later, the fascinating French soprano, Emma Calvé, whose performances united the arts of singing and acting on the operatic stage, performed the role of Carmen at the Metropolitan Opera. She scored the most sensational triumph of any singer in the United States during the nineteenth century. "Even now," wrote the New York music critic, Henry Krehbiel, in 1908,

> I cannot recall anything as fine in the region of combined action and song.... There was as little convention in her singing as in her acting ... she saturated the music with emotion. Much of it she seemed to sing to herself, declaiming like dramatic speech whose emotional contents had been raised to a higher power by the melody. In moments of extreme excitement one scarcely realized that she was singing at all. Carried along by the torrent of her feelings, her listeners accepted her song as the only proper and efficient expression for her emotional state. The two expressions, song and action were one; they were mutually complemental.[32]

This unfamiliar style immediately appealed to the American audiences as it had done to the European, and gradually the public began to desire dramatic as well as vocal interpretations by their operatic artists.

Soon to follow in Calvé's path were three stars of the same magnitude—Mary Garden, Feodor Chaliapin, and Geraldine Farrar. Personality and magnetic dramatic talent were the keys to Mary Garden's immense success in opera. It is reported that "her gestures for every part were studied to the last degree."[33] While studying in Paris at the turn of the century, she stepped in for the ailing soprano, Marthe Rioton, during a performance of Charpentier's *Louise* at the Opéra Comique on April 13, 1900, and overnight became one of the most popular singers in France. Due to her scintillating personality, she was chosen to sing Massenet's *Manon* with Enrico Caruso, who, she claimed, "was very afraid of me, because he was a gorgeous singer and I was an actress."[34] In 1902 Claude Debussy created the role of Mélisande for her, and during the next thirty years, she was the leading interpreter of the modern lyric heroines of Charpentier and Massenet. It seems that with their realistic portrayals of degenerate operatic heroines, both she and her contemporary, Geraldine Farrar, shared the ability to raise the ire of the American clergy. Miss Garden's daring impersonation of Strauss' *Salome* was denounced by the evangelist, Billy Sunday, and was even banned in Boston and Milwaukee.

Like Mary Garden, Feodor Chaliapin, the famous Russian basso, possessed a dynamic personality as well as superb dramatic technique. Stanislavski maintained that this magnificent singing actor was the greatest "natural" exponent of his acting method. Even without his exciting voice, claimed Stanislavski, Chaliapin would have been famous for his acting, because, as with Duse and Salvini his body was in complete subjection to his will.[35] Others agreed with the great Russian director. In his book *Opera: Front and Back* Howard Taubman wrote: "Chaliapin was one of those artists who would not listen to conductor or stage director. He was a law unto himself both in rehearsal and in performance. He got away with it because some of his impersonations were creations of indisputable genius.... Chaliapin had a way of taking command of the proceedings. He undertook to advise his fellow artists on their stage deportment, their acting and even their singing."[36]

According to Miss Farrar, who sang with him on many occasions, he could be an excellent partner if one were always on guard against his blatant attempts to upstage others in the cast. "He would envelop one, as it were," she explained, "and sing over one, so that one just disappeared. And so one had to restage the scene a little. But not at the dress rehearsal, of course, or he would have thought of a way round it. Just on the night."[37] In Miss Farrar, Chaliapin had found his histrionic match. This anecdote also reveals what little attention even fine singing actors and actresses paid to stage directions and how each artist felt free to change his performance at will.

Chaliapin and Farrar, like Calvé, Maurel, Capoul, and Garden, placed special emphasis upon acting, thereby defying the operatic tradition of denigrating drama in favor of song. For nearly three hundred years, performances of opera had been noted for virtuosic vocalism and conventionalized acting. It was in such an operatic world, presided over by Melba and Patti, that Geraldine Farrar appeared in 1901. She refused to conform, seeking rather to realize her own vision of what opera should be—a musical drama. Dramatic interpretation was of primary importance to this operatic rebel, who would spend more than twenty years of her life and talent striving to attain her ideal.

✦ ONE ✦

The Early Years, 1882–1906

Geraldine Farrar's New England family heritage was a musical one. Her maternal grandfather, Dennis Barnes, was a teacher of violin in Melrose, Massachusetts, near Boston and his daughter, Henrietta, shared his passionate love for music. At the age of seventeen, Henrietta Barnes married a handsome and charming young Melrose haberdashery store-owner, Sidney D. Farrar, with whom she sang in the choir of the First Universalist Church. Both possessed excellent "natural" singing voices. One year after their marriage, Mrs. Farrar gave birth on February 28, 1882, to a daughter, who, according to family legend, hummed in her cradle and, at the age of three, sang a solo in a church concert. The young mother eagerly encouraged the vocal precocity of her daughter, Geraldine.

In her first autobiography, *Geraldine Farrar: The Story of an American Singer by Herself*, Miss Farrar wrote that she "could not remember when [she] did not intend to sing and act."[1] Even as a child, she possessed that vivid imagination which identifies the creative actor. She recalled that she spent hours staring at the flames in the fireplace to create mysterious images of thought. An avid reader who dramatized the stories of her literary heroines and acted them out to musical accompaniment, she was convinced that some day she would become a famous opera singer. In addition to her mother, Miss Farrar used her dog and cat in these dramatizations, and Mrs. Farrar also made costumes for the entire cast of characters. In these events, Miss Farrar was always the star. Her father, who by 1884 was not only a haberdasher but also first baseman for the Philadelphia Phillies National League Baseball Club, comprised the enthusiastic audience. Later, Miss Farrar wrote that she "dreamed of the times when, [she] would appear before immense audiences as the beautiful heroine of [her] dreams and hold them fascinated by [her] song and personality."[2] From early girlhood, she was conscious of her own personal magnetism and often experimented to observe its effects upon others. Her enthusiasm and boundless energy inspired the

Sidney D. Farrar, Geraldine's father, 1916, and Henrietta Barnes Farrar, Geraldine's mother, also 1916.

children around her in the theatrical productions of her school, church and community.

Convinced that a thorough knowledge of music, history, languages and literature were indispensable to a singer, Mrs. Farrar gained permission from the School Board of Melrose High School for her daughter to specialize in these studies. In addition to her academic work, she learned to play the piano and began singing lessons in 1894 at the age of twelve with Mrs. J. H. Long, a well-known vocal teacher in Boston. During her adolescence, she attended performances of Henry W. Savage's Castle Square Opera Company and of Maurice Grau's Company. Miss Farrar became familiar with much of the grand opera repertory. In 1896, she first heard the famous singing actress, Emma Calvé, as Carmen. Of this experience she wrote: "I completely lost my head over this remarkable performance. This, then, was the visualization of all my dreams of years. This triumph I had witnessed was that toward which all my hopes, fears, and prayers had been directed. This wonderful creature was what I hoped—nay, intended—to become."[3] In this production, the tenor was Jean de Reszke, who granted Miss Farrar an audition and advised her to consult Louisa Cappiani, a prominent New York voice teacher of light-opera singers. After a discussion with her parents, it was decided that she should go to New York to develop her talents. Leaving her father in Melrose,

Miss Farrar and her mother moved to Manhattan. She sang for Madame Cappiani, who was so impressed by her voice that she asked the young singer to sign a three-year contract with her. Miss Farrar's mother felt that her daughter was too young to have her "future controlled in any way"[4] and refused the teacher's offer.

Soon after, while on vacation in Maine, Miss Farrar met another well-known New York teacher of singing, Miss Emma Thursby, with whom she began to study in the fall of 1897. Miss Thursby had studied with the dramatic soprano Erminia Rudersdorff a student of Manuel García II and the first exponent of the García vocal method in America. Madame Rudersdorff was the mother of the distinguished actor Richard Mansfield.

A youthful Geraldine Farrar, 1916.

Miss Farrar also studied acting with a teacher of the Delsarte system, which had been brought to the United States in the 1870s by the American dramatist, actor and theatre technologist, Steele Mackaye, a student of François Delsarte. This popular method of acting was devised by Delsarte, the nineteenth-century French actor and teacher, who attempted to analyze how thoughts and feelings are externally expressed. Coming to the conclusion that the theatrical performer could communicate his internal motivations to an audience through physical movements, he gradually developed an intricate system which attempted to pinpoint the ways in which various parts of the body could be used to convey specific ideas or emotions. As Delsarte's adherents promulgated and popularized his theories throughout Europe and America, the system degenerated into a series of mechanical gestures and poses, without exploring the internal motivations underlying the external signs. It was this corrupted version of Delsarte's method to which Miss Farrar was subjected in the 1890s. She soon learned to deplore such an artificial style of acting, and in later years, described her lessons thus: "Herded into a class of a dozen, no more ungainly duckling than myself could have been imagined. In this company, on the stroke of a beat, hands, bodies, and faces would try to respond to conventionalized attitudes and expressions as prescribed. Needless to say, I defaulted in every particular, first in silence, then in expostulation."[5]

Completely frustrated, she withdrew from the class and studied deportment at the National Conservatory with the famous singing actor, Victor Capoul, who, according to a French magazine article, was "taken by the exceptional musical gifts which the petite candidate possessed ... he wished to occupy himself with the progress of the young girl in whom he discerned a future lyric tragedienne."[6] For several months, he instructed her "in every detail"[7] of roles such as Thomas' Mignon (*Mignon*) and Gounod's Juliette (*Roméo et Juliette*), operas in which he had established himself as one of the nineteenth century's leading operatic stars. His emotional fervor and graceful bearing had enabled him to succeed on the lyric stage even after his voice had deteriorated in the 1880s. Like her teacher, Miss Farrar later exhibited dramatic intensity and elegance of movement, which aided her in becoming the leading prima donna of the Metropolitan opera from 1906 until 1922. These talents also assisted her in remaining a popular star during a four-year period of vocal crisis.

During her year of study in New York, Miss Farrar attended the opera and theatre. Her scrapbook for 1898 is filled with programs, theatrical photographs, reviews, and fascinating marginal comments written in her own bold handwriting. "She looked a queen and goddess—and I love her—for her mortality," she wrote of Lillian Nordica, the New England Wagnerian soprano, who was later to play a major role in her youthful admirer's career; and of Emma Calvé she recorded: "She wore an embroidered gown—two scarlet poppies in her hair—she was so beautiful."[8] There are programs of Nellie Melba in *Faust, Roméo et Juliette, Lucia, The Barber of Seville* and *La traviata*; *The Sign of the Cross* as presented by Ben Greet's London Company; of *The School for Scandal* and *The Country Girl* starring Ada Rehan at Daly's Theatre; of Mrs. Minnie Maddern Fiske in *Tess of the d'Urbervilles*; of James K. Hackett in *Rupert of Hentzau*; Mrs. Lesley Carter in *Zazà*; Richard Mansfield in *The Devil's Disciple* and *Cyrano de Bergerac*; Olga Nethersole in *The Termagant*; and of Julia Marlowe in *The Countess Valeska*. During this year, she was introduced to the legitimate stage and for the rest of her life remained an avid theatergoer, asserting that every young singer should make an earnest study of the drama.

In that same year, Emma Thursby arranged for her pupil to sing for Lillian Nordica and Nellie Melba. Melba wished to place the young artist under her exclusive tutelage. As with the offer from Louisa Cappiani, Mrs. Farrar refused, convinced that her daughter's future should remain unrestricted. Also arranged was an audition with Maurice Grau, director of the Metropolitan Opera Company. He predicted a brilliant future for Miss Farrar and agreed with her mother that the young singer now needed study and performance experience in Europe. So great was the faith of Miss

Farrar's parents in her talent that they were willing to sacrifice everything for it.

In September 1899, after having sold the family store and obtained a loan of thirty thousand dollars[9] from the Boston philanthropist, Mrs. Bertram Webb, the Farrar family sailed for France. Following interviews with various Parisian teachers of singing, Miss Farrar selected Antonio Trabadello with whom she studied from October 1899, until September 1900. This noted Spanish vocal pedagogue numbered among his students the popular American soprano, Sybil Sanderson, and the later distinguished Scottish singing actress, Mary Garden. He taught his pupils to sing naturally and to practice by using Italian vowels and compositions even if they were to perform in another language. Perhaps Miss Farrar's choice of a foreign teacher was deliberate, because she did not approve of the French vocal school which sacrificed dramatic expression for beauty of tone.

The programs in Miss Farrar's scrapbook of 1899 attest to her attendance of Augier's *Les fourchambault*, Sardou's *Madame Sans-Gêne* starring Réjane as Catherine and Duquesne as Napoleon, as well as *Hamlet*, *L'aiglon*, *La Dame aux camélias*, and *Tosca*, all with Madame Sarah Bernhardt. Miss Farrar became a lifelong admirer of "La Divine Sarah" and following the performance of *Hamlet* wrote in her scrapbook:

> My first hearing of "La Divine Sarah" and I have rarely enjoyed anything so much in all my life. I understood nearly every thing she said. Her art is magnificent and her lack of gestures noticeable. There is nothing to be desired when she stands before you! Perhaps she "poses," but it is as no one else could, and I would only like the opportunity to compare her with Duse. It was my first experience with Shakespeare and her Hamlet was a most charming and irrestible [sic] presentation of interest. She is indeed a marvelous woman and vibrant eyes—and whole expression. The range and variety of her voice all that could be desired.[10]

In later years, Miss Farrar would be noted for her superb facial pantomime, as well as for the wide range of her vocal coloration, and she claimed that she had learned much of this art by observing Madame Bernhardt.[11]

In addition to her singing lessons, she studied stage deportment with Madame Martini, another advocate of the Delsartian system. Once again, the young singer rebelled against what had become by then a mechanical school of acting. She was forced to study facial expressions in a mirror, to walk along chalk lines, and to repeat gestures time after time at specific phrases. "Madame would say," related Miss Farrar, "after ten bars, lift the right hand; two more, then point it at the villain; walk slowly toward the hero; raise your eyes at the twentieth bar toward heaven; and conclude your aria with a sweeping denial, sinking gently to the floor."[12] Miss Farrar frequently argued with her teacher because she never was told the motivation for these movements and consequently felt that "it seemed to be all artificial, all outside, and there was no sincerity in any of it." She went on to say, "There were things in me that were not having any expression at all, and I couldn't express them with the conventional gestures that that class of girls were being taught. I looked at them and they were graceful enough, but perfectly meaningless."[13] After two months, Miss Farrar abandoned her acting lessons. Having decided to teach herself, she "devoted the time to reading, observing actors and actresses, and visiting galleries to study poses from painting and statuary."[14] As with Giuseppi Verdi, Miss Farrar believed that singers should study the drama, poetry, painting and other arts. She believed that "education along all lines but adds to the richness of one's background."[15]

Miss Farrar's stay in Paris was cut short by a fortunate accident. For many years, she had worn a silver locket containing a picture of Lillian Nordica. Early in 1900, seeing the diva drive by in an open carriage, she threw her talisman into Madame Nordica's lap. Recognizing her own picture, the American prima donna stopped to talk with her audacious young admirer, who reminded her of their first meeting in New York. Madame Nordica invited Miss Farrar to sing for her and her husband, Zoldan Dome, a Hungarian tenor, on the following day. After listening to her, the Domes became intensely interested in this talented young singer. They recommended that she study in Berlin with a Russian-Italian tenor and teacher, Francesco Graziani, whose book on vocal pedagogy had impressed Mr. Dome.

In the autumn of that year, having made little progress in her studies with Trabadello, Miss Farrar followed their advice. Armed with letters of introduction to German friends of Madame Nordica, the Farrar family moved to the German capital. Miss Farrar commenced singing lessons with Signor Graziani who, unlike Trabadello, had a thorough knowledge of tonal color and breath support—areas which the young singer needed to perfect.

Among the friends to whom Madame Nordica had written was the wealthy and socially prominent Frau Adolph von Rath, wife of Berlin's leading banker. Miss Farrar was invited to attend her receptions, at which the elite of Berlin society were present. The von Raths took a keen interest in Madame Nordica's young acquaintance, who also happened to be a student of Frau von Rath's protégé, Graziani.

In the spring of 1901, Frau von Rath invited a distinguished audience, including Count von Hochberg, Intendant of the Berlin Royal Opera, to hear Miss Farrar sing at an afternoon musicale in the elegant ballroom of her magnificent town house. Miss Farrar realized the importance of creating the correct atmosphere to enhance her vocal performance. She requested that the velvet curtains be drawn and that the lights be turned on, as if it were an evening soirée, so that she could create an "appearance." She also was intensely aware of the importance of costuming and chose for the occasion an elegant, pale-blue, silver-embroidered, crepe-de-Chine evening gown with diamonds and pearls as accessories. "I can remember now the suppressed murmurs of 'The crazy American!' when I appeared," she later wrote of that occasion; "but I obtained the compliment of immediate attention and created the effect I wished."[16] Her fondness for elaborate display was already evident.

She had selected three arias—"Je veux vivre" from Gounod's *Roméo et Juliette*, "Stridano la su" from Leoncavallo's *I pagliacci* and "Sempre libera" from Verdi's *La traviata*—each of which perfectly suited her vibrant, well-focused, flexible lyric soprano voice. Her unusually rich middle register was beautifully blended into the upper and lower registers, resulting in an even vocal quality from F below Middle C to D above High C. After having heard her three French and Italian selections, Count von Hochberg asked her to learn, in German, "Elsa's Dream" from Wagner's *Lohengrin* for an audition with orchestra at the Royal Opera House. Ten days later, she sang again for the Count and was offered a three-year contract at the Royal Opera to perform roles appropriate to her youth and lyrical voice. So anxious was von Hochberg to secure the services of this fascinating young American, that he granted her permission to sing in Italian until she had mastered the German language.

She immediately began to study with Frau Eva Wilcke, a well-known Berlin teacher of German, French, and Italian diction with whom she was to prepare all her roles. Von Hochberg thought that this beautiful young woman and singer would prove "a novelty, quite different from the stout ladies who waddle about protesting their operatic fate to spectators who find it difficult to believe in their cruel lot and youthful innocence."[17] In Geraldine Farrar, the Count recognized a rare combination of youth, vocal and dramatic talent, personality, and physical beauty. Even at the age of eighteen, Miss Farrar possessed that elusive quality—glamour which was to be associated with her for the next twenty years.

With her debut arranged for October 15, 1901, as Marguerite in Gounod's opera, *Faust,* Miss Farrar spent the summer at Switzerland's Lake Constance. There she evolved her own conception of Goethe's heroine, whom she believed to represent "universal maidenhood, instinctive with warm and womanly desires." She wished to portray a youthful, timid Marguerite who girlishly and half in fright abandons herself "to the impetuous and ardent wooing of so unusual a lover as the handsome young Faust."[18] Miss Farrar rejected the traditional stage business passed down for nearly half a century to all Marguerites since the time of Madame Caroline Carvalho, who had originated the role in 1859 in Paris. "In such an out-of-date, old opera I sometimes begin to wonder if the audience is not being bored by the whole thing," she later wrote, "and it is hard to make Marguerite dramatically vivid when in such a psychological condition.... I am simply trying to make Marguerite a human being.... She was supposed to be such in the old German drama, but in the opera a singer is criticized if she makes Marguerite anything but a milk-and-water pulverized-sugar dilution of the original."[19]

Rather than imitate the actions of others, Miss Farrar wanted to interpret the role in her own way. During the meticulous rehearsals, the stage manager permitted her to add entirely new pieces of stage business to the Berlin production. Unlike many prima donnas of the past who swept grandly onto the stage in the Kermesse Scene, Miss Farrar's entrance was shy and unobtrusive, as was her glance of inquiry to the handsome young gentleman who offered her his arm.[20] She moved, acted, and actually looked like a beautiful sixteen-year-old-girl.[21] There was a childlike delight in her actions as she viewed the jewels at the beginning of the Garden Scene, and her timid confidences to the ardent young Faust gradually changed to passionate avowals of undying love.[22] Miss Farrar began the Garden Scene as an innocent young girl and ended it as a newly awakened woman consumed by her passion for Faust. Other Marguerites had remained seated at their spinning wheels throughout the entire "Roi de Thule" aria, but Miss Farrar arose after the first verse and wandered dreamily about the garden, observing and picking the flowers, as she wondered about her ardent admirer.[23] She even defied tradition by singing the "Jewel Song" with a mirror in her hand as she admired her elegant appearance,[24] rather than stepping to the front of the stage to perform a series of exciting but emotionally colorless runs and trills. Also she inserted effective laughter into the vocal line. Miss Farrar remained in character and incorporated the aria into her portrayal instead of turning it into the usual abstract display of vocal pyrotechniques as witnessed in the performances of Adelina Patti and Nellie Melba.[25]

Unlike her German colleagues, whose wigs and costumes were furnished by the opera house, she gained permission to adopt the American system of providing her own. These were designed and made in Paris by Marie Muele. "As Marguerite I wore a blond wig," wrote Miss Farrar, "but instead of parting it in the middle, I combed it straight back, as children wear it, and instead of letting the pigtails hang, as all the Marguerites have done, I drew them around my head and pinned them. For one so slight as I am a cloth skirt would not be becoming, and crepe de Chene [sic], two rows away looks like silk. I had my blue crepe skirt accordion pleated to emphasize the lines and give me a figure. Every woman wants a figure if she can have it."[26] To the blond wig and crepe-de-Chine dress she added a lace bonnet and a pair of high-heeled shoes with jeweled buckles. This tendency toward exaggeration in costuming, which emanated from her theory that beauty was more essential than historical accuracy or appropriateness,[27] was to be evident in many of her later roles.

Despite several critics' disapproval of her singing in Italian, Miss Farrar's debut was "a complete success"[28] with both press and public fascinated by this young American singer who possessed individuality and exceptional histrionic gifts. The *Norddeutsche Zeitung* wrote of Miss Farrar's debut:

Geraldine Farrar as Marguerite, 1901 (Library of Congress, Music Division).

> Tall [Miss Farrar was only 5' 3"], extraordinarily dainty of stature, graceful of movement, with expressive childlike features— she thus immediately appeared before us as something special, as a personality. At last once again a figure and not just a stereotype, at last once again an individual.... America already has sent us many excellent singers, such as Emma Albann and Lillian Nordica, who possessed sweet voices and great skill more than Farrar at the moment. They, however, did not understand how to capture our hearts as did the new opera guest with her very first role. They were only singers, this one is a dramatic artist, even though she undoubtedly has several things to learn. She continually remains with the role and the situation. She does not sing and play a role but rather experiences an action.[29]

Another Berlin critic recorded:

> It is reported that the lady is a novice at the very beginning of her theatrical career. If this is truly the case, then we are dealing with a significant, genuine dramatic talent, since there is nothing unfinished or immature in this vocally and dramatically secure performance of Margarethe. There actually were even several moments of fascinating beauty. The guest reached her highpoint at the conclusion of the third act where the window opens, and Gretchen, believing herself alone, sings out into the moonlight her longing for her beloved. Thoroughly charming and beautifully animated was the scene with

the casket of jewels in which a lovely symmetry was expressed between the musical presentation and the dramatic figure. Geraldine Farrar left behind the impression of an artistically individual nature.[30]

In her second autobiography, *Such Sweet Compulsion,* Miss Farrar referred to her distinctive beginning, using a quotation from a review in the *German Times*: "Opinions as to her voice might differ, but on the subject of her acting there can be but one verdict. She has dramatic talent of the highest order. She did not walk through her part with the accustomed somnambulism of singers who tread operatic boards for the first time. She was a living, loving, suffering Margarethe, not merely a singing automaton."[31] That she was more than just the ordinary beginner also was noted by the critic "H.N.": "Fraulein Farrar is not as yet a master, but she most certainly also is no ordinary appearance; she is vocally, musically, and dramatically exceptionally talented and possesses individuality."[32]

This very individuality had motivated her innovations, such as the picking of flowers during the conclusion of the "Roi de Thule" aria, of which "H.N." commented: "She interests because she remains free from the stereotype and follows her own inspiration. One does not always have to be in agreement with what she does and yet will be able to admit that an artistic purpose leads her.... Alone, it delights one that the artist surrenders herself to the role and that she also acts when singing."[33] Another critic wrote: "That was entirely new to me, nevertheless—so far as I'm concerned, why not!"[34] From the very beginning of her career, Geraldine Farrar's remarkable dramatic instincts were evident.

Her singing was praised for beauty of tone as well as for variety and intensity of emotional coloration, but an occasional shrillness in the top tones was observed whenever she forced the voice beyond its normal volume. This tendency "to unleash temperament to the detriment of vocal discretion"[35] was to be noted in her singing for the next twenty years. She was convinced that tonal beauty should be sacrificed "whenever it seemed to interfere with dramatic effect."[36]

Miss Farrar's next role was Violetta Valery in a revival on November 29, 1901, of Verdi's opera, *La traviata,* with new scenery and sumptuous costumes. "Afire with memories of the great Sarah as Marguerite Gauthier,"[37] she created this role. Unfortunately, there are no records indicating whether she actually incorporated any of the famous French actress' staging into her operatic portrayal of the Parisian courtesan. It is doubtful that she did, however, because Miss Farrar claimed in a 1901 newspaper interview that although she had seen the performances of many great actresses, she never had adopted anything from them, preferring to create from within herself.[38] Once again, she defied tradition by adding entirely new costuming and pieces of stage

Farrar as Violetta, 1919.

business to a well-known operatic role. When her mother objected to her daring décolletages, she replied: "But mother, can't you understand I am *not* your daughter on the stage, but am an *artist* who is playing Violetta. She has nothing to do with me as Geraldine. I must act as I think she, not I, would act!"[39]

From the opening of the first act, she introduced novelty into the role. Instead of making the usual operatic grand entrance strolling in on the arm of a gentleman as the curtain rose, she sat with her back to the audience eventually rising to mingle with her guests. At the end of the "libiamo" duet, Miss Farrar drank from her future lover's glass rather than from her own. Then she tossed it away instead of replacing it on the table as had been done by nearly all Violettas since the opera's premiere in 1853. She sang the famous aria "Ah, forse è lui" in an elegantly pensive mood seated on a chair with her head resting on her right hand, instead of standing directly behind the footlights in the center of the stage. During the second act scene with Alfredo's father when she promised to renounce his son's love, there was an expression of forlorn despair on her face while seated on the sofa with her hands clasped tightly in her lap. Throughout the opera, even when Violetta was not the center of attention, Miss Farrar remained in character. She added subtle realistic details such as hiding her face behind a fan to conceal her coughing seizures while the two rivals for her love played cards during the third act. At the beginning of the last act, she lay on a couch, her face suffused with a rosy hue from the firelight and the lamp near her head. As interesting touches, she substituted parlando for the usual singing in the reading of Germont's letter and quickly concealed Alfredo's picture when he entered. Unlike previous interpreters, she subordinated the pathological aspects of the death scene by eliminating the traditional coughing seizures. One Berlin critic wrote: "She wilted away like a flower broken by the storm of life."[40]

Aside from the stage business and costuming, Miss Farrar was particularly interested in the make-up for this role. Violetta had to be ravishingly beautiful since she was a popular courtesan, but her complexion had to be pale because she was consumptive. In the third act, Miss Farrar attained a particularly dramatic effect with her costume and make-up. The deathly white she painted her face was emphasized by her crimson lips and black hair, as well as by her pale yellow gown and enormous black ostrich feather fan. This effective and innovative make-up in the third act led a Berlin critic to write that "by means of make-up she appeared so ill that even without coughing seizures and other signs of a severe illness her early death was foreseen;"[41] additionally her costumes were "works of art in the sense of a noble accord with the performance and the surroundings."[42] One critic, however, did object to the "gigantic Rembrandt hat"[43] which she wore for the entire second act. Inordinately fond of spectacular headgear, Miss Farrar was often to wear bonnets, diadems, hats, feathers, mantillas, and ornamental combs in her various portrayals.

Although the public enthusiastically voiced its approval of this young singing actress's original interpretation of a tradition-bound operatic role, the critics were more reserved in their judgments. It was noted that while she had been completely credible as the young and innocent Marguerite in *Faust*, Miss Farrar was not so believable in the role of an experienced courtesan during the first act of Verdi's opera. "Too youthful in figure, as in her entire appearance," commented one critic, "she also did not quite know how to invest her portrayal with the free and nimble tone of the finer demimondaine."[44] Another critic, however, wrote that once the heroine had renounced her former life, the young singer was able to portray convincingly the woman who willingly sacrificed her life for her beloved.[45] Her consistency of motivation was praised by one critic: "She possesses much that Violetta requires: a slender, supple, winning appearance; lively, extraordinarily carefully thought out acting, which in the first act already foreshadowed the tragic end."[46] Another expressed an opinion which was to be echoed time and again in the future about Geraldine Farrar: "She acted very naturally, remaining always conscious of the action in which she found herself, and understood how to interest, indeed how to captivate thereby, almost more than by her singing."[47] The beauty of her voice, especially in the middle register, was praised, but a tendency toward forcing some of her top tones and labored coloratura was noted.[48]

Members of the Berlin Opera were often invited to perform as guest artists with the ducal Royal Opera in Magdeburg, a small town near Berlin. During a performance in 1904 of *La traviata* as Miss Farrar threw away Alfredo's glass at the end of the first act "libiamo" duet, and "the glass shattered to the floor, an uniformed attendant dashed from the wings, dustpan and broom in hand and took his time in carefully removing all traces of this radical departure from tradition." Losing her usual composure, Miss Farrar began to laugh, and it was some moments before she could resume the character of Violetta for the concluding aria. At the close of the act, she was handed a bill for "glass breakage, value 15 pfennig"[49] causing the young prima donna to burst into laughter again. At her next appearance in that opera at Magdeburg, she eliminated this piece of stage business from her portrayal.

In 1902 Miss Farrar added three new roles to her Berlin repertory — Nedda (Leoncavallo's *I pagliacci*), Zerlina (Mozart's *Don Giovanni*) and Juliette (Gounod's *Roméo et Juliette*). On the evening of March 7, a guest star fell ill, and Miss Farrar assumed the role of Nedda without a stage rehearsal. The public remained faithful to their young favorite, but the critics were not so enthusiastic, feeling that this role was not suited to her particular talents. Convinced that her elegance of appearance and movement hindered her from portraying a woman of the streets realistically, they regarded her performance as overly refined, lacking the necessary coarseness. One reviewer even stated that "one does not believe that she would be capable of keeping her troublesome admirer away from her with a whip,"[50] and another reported that "her portrayal was quite spiritless despite all external precipitation and activity."[51] "Nedda was a little animal, a horrid barbarian,"[52] Miss Farrar said in 1910, and later stated that "at best [she is] no very grateful part."[53]

It is not surprising that Nedda never became one of her more popular roles. But she did add two interesting touches to the traditional stage business. Instead of making her entrance standing in the comedian's donkey wagon, she rode on stage seated on the animal's back; and at the close of the first act, when Canio hurled her from him, she rolled over on the stage floor three times instead of merely lying inert.[54] Vocally, the critics felt that Nedda was too dramatic for the young singer, causing her to force the middle and the top registers of her voice. They also suggested that it was time she performed her roles in German like all the other members of the Berlin Opera.

On November 23, Miss Farrar sang her next part, Zerlina, in German. This time, her impersonation was praised by both press and public alike as delightful, warm-blooded, and light hearted. The young singer imbued the character with sly artfulness and coquetry. She was shy and yet arch with the jaded Don, while affectionate, contrite and cajoling with her good-natured, jealous, and not-too-bright young country fiancé, Masetto. Neither aristocrat nor rustic was immune to the enchanting wiles of Miss Farrar's beautiful and charming young peasant girl.

Her Zerlina was followed on December 2 by her portrayal of Gounod's Juliette. The prima donna caused a sensation by singing much of the bedchamber scene languorously reclining on a couch, locked in her beloved's arms. Miss Farrar's portrayal of Juliette as a beautiful, young, dark-haired Veronese girl, expressing genuine childish joy upon entering the palace hall led by the hand of her father, was a refreshing contrast to the statuesque prima donnas of past generations. Her love scenes with Roméo were marked by an exciting impulsiveness. Realizing that she could not compete with the thrilling "coloratura effects"[55] of a Marcella Sembrich or a Nellie Melba, she slowed down the tempo of the famous first act "Waltz Song" in order to create a dreamy pensive mood, as though thinking aloud. In the following acts, her girlish demeanor gradually matured to womanhood as her love for Roméo increased, and her cries of agony in the tomb amongst the family dead were heartrendingly realistic. The public was again enthusiastic in its endorsement of Miss Farrar's Juliette, but the critics were divided in their opinion of her performance. Some approved of her portrayal, while others complained that her movements were exaggerated and without internal motivation. "Her acting was in part unintelligible to me; it seemed to me to be planned more along the lines of pointed grace and sweeping gestures than to be the manifestation of inner motivations,"[56] wrote one critic. Another commented: "Is the public right or the critics? In this case, we wish to judge in favor of the former."[57]

Later that season, after one disastrous attempt on February 2, 1903, to sing the dramatic role of Leonora in Verdi's *Il trovatore*, Miss Farrar confessed she was "vocally ... as adequate as a cricket"[58] and felt "the need of the careful instruction of a master."[59] She began voice lessons with the famous German operatic soprano and vocal pedagogue, Lilli Lehmann. Madame Lehmann had recently returned to her home in Berlin after an extensive period of singing abroad. She not only was an impeccable vocal technician but was also a superior actress whose operatic repertoire encompassed 170 roles in French, German, and Italian, ranging from the dramatic works of

Wagner to the light operas of Offenbach. Aside from her performances at Bayreuth, the Berlin State Opera, the Metropolitan Opera, the Paris Opéra, Covent Garden, and the Vienna State Opera, she was for many years a principal artist and director of the Salzburg Festivals, to which she brought Miss Farrar as Zerlina in 1906. For nearly forty years, she also was one of Europe's most prominent teachers of singing and in 1902 wrote a book on vocal pedagogy entitled *Meine Gesangskunst*.

From 1903 to 1906, Miss Farrar had a daily lesson with Madame Lehmann. In later years, when singing at the Metropolitan, she returned each summer until 1914 for further study with her teacher. Lilli Lehmann was "a rigorous taskmaster"[60] whose pupil later wrote of her lessons:

Lilli Lehmann, Geraldine's teacher and friend, 1916.

> No meager lesson of twenty or thirty minutes, ... a lesson lasted according to the endurance of the pupil. Mine were from two to three hours a forenoon. Singing, discussion, inquiry on my part, illustration on hers. Did I beg the exposition of a phrase, it was nothing for Lilli to prepare herself quietly and attack the most grandiose aria, such as Norma's Casta Diva, the Liebestod or a simple Lied.... Her conception of bel canto would shame many a professed native Italian pedagogue, and she believed in beautiful singing at every and all times. Of course we had arguments, but I know she respected me for my ceaseless whys and constant demands for enlightenment and free thinking.[61]

Although Madame Lehmann jestingly referred to Miss Farrar as "an obstinate and willful little wretch,"[62] she admired her intelligence and allowed her to maintain her own individual approach toward dramatic interpretation. Once, when Madame Lehmann disagreed with Miss Farrar's interpretation of a certain musical phrase and illustrated it for her pupil in the way she felt it should be performed, Miss Farrar told her that "I don't feel the sense of the text and the phrase that way.... That manner is you, and the other is me, and unless I feel my way, I cannot sing or give of myself."[63] However, Madame

Lehmann did strive to subordinate her favorite pupil's fiery temperament to artistic taste. "Impulsive, restless from nervous energy, quick to change, seldom to be relied on to repeat the same 'business,'" commented Miss Farrar, "I found under her guidance, repose, economy of gesture, eloquence of attitude, and clean singing.... My hands—large, nervous, and of almost Southern flexibility—have always given me trouble. Lilli Lehmann warned me that I used them and my arms too much to express what I should have put into my face. She tied them together behind my back for many a weary lesson till I conquered the feeling of trying to employ 110 digits instead of the normal number, and learned to use my face."[64] Madame Lehmann constantly reproached her student for acting during her lessons, but Miss Farrar could no more prevent this than she could breathing.

She also was instructed in the vocal arts of forward tonal placement, equalization of vowels, even registration, and clear diction. According to Madame Lehmann, the vowel "e" was the perfect headtone which placed all vocal sounds from the lowest to the highest registers into their natural position in the head cavity. The point of concentration was between the eyes. Once this vowel had been mastered, she demanded that all the others should sit in exactly the same forward position. This uniformity of sound had to pass from the lowest to the highest registers without any apparent break. She accomplished this by teaching her students the famous Lehmann great scale which consisted of an octave series of ascending and descending whole and half tones. "It was sung upon all the principal vowels," recorded Miss Farrar, "and it was extended stepwise through different keys over the entire range of the two octaves of the voice. It was not her advice to practice it too softly, but it was done with all the resonating organs well supported by the diaphragm, the tone in a very supple and elastic watery state. She would think nothing of devoting from forty minutes to sixty minutes a day to the slow practice of this exercise."[65] Equalization of the three registers had always been paramount to Miss Farrar. In 1897, she had dared to tell Nellie Melba that "those are not pretty sounds,"[66] when the famous diva had demonstrated the Italian method of chest tones which causes a break between the middle and lower registers. Later, Miss Farrar often augmented the Lehmann scale "with various florid legato phrases of arias selected from the older Italians or Mozart, whereby [she could] more easily achieve the vocal facility demanded by the tessitura of *Manon* or *Faust*, and change to the dark-hued phrases demanded in *Carmen* and *Butterfly*."[67] Madame Lehmann insisted that vocal texts be pronounced naturally, as in speech, and she forbade exaggerated use of lips or mouthing of words. The face remained undistorted, relaxed, and the singer was enabled to use it for dramatic interpretation. It was in large part due to the superb training given her by Lilli Lehmann that Geraldine Farrar was to be noted for the evenness of her voice, for its vibrant forward production, for her impeccable diction, and for her superb facial pantomime.

In addition to her vocal studies with Madame Lehmann, in May 1903 Miss Farrar studied the role of Manon with its composer, Jules Massenet, in Paris. The opera was based on a popular novel by the Abbé Prévost and Massenet allowed the young prima donna much freedom to develop her own conception of the heroine. The production was a resounding success when it opened on December 1, 1903, mainly because of Miss Farrar's exquisite interpretation of this wayward but charming romantic figure, of whom she wrote: "Here in a single character breathes all women in one—charm, allure, and fascination in song and drama."[68] She imbued the character with such charm and grace that she retained the sympathy of the audience, despite the shallow heartlessness of the beautiful but irresponsible young woman, who selfishly demanded the love of all, but remained passionless herself.

One critic wrote that "the appearance of the artist was so interesting that one did not want to take one's eyes off her, and, when she was not there, her next appearance was awaited with impatient suspense."[69] In the first act, she presented a charming picture as she sat beside her band-box under the linden tree. Of her entrance in the third act Cours la Reine scene, a reviewer wrote that "as she descended from the sedan chair, in the festive attire of the Queen of Beauty, the audience was enraptured."[70] Her Parisian made costumes for the luxury-loving Manon were of the finest brocades and laces. During one of Miss Farrar's many visits with the German Royal Family, Crown Prince Wilhelm and Crown Princess Cecilie admitted that they enjoyed the opera not only for its lovely music but also for her magnificent gowns.[71] But it was the intensity of Miss Farrar's acting in the Saint Sulpice scene which caused the greatest excitement when she dragged herself on her knees to the feet of her lover and entreated him to renounce his intended ecclesiastical vows. The thrilling look of triumph on her face as she realized her lover had finally succumbed to her pleadings resulted in a furor in the audience, as did the touching simplicity of her death in the last act. The critics were unanimous in their praise of Miss Farrar's glamorous appearance and sensitive acting. A French reviewer stated: "Miss Farrar, exquisite as Manon,"[72] and one of his German colleagues added. "Miss Farrar looked ravishing as Manon and gave herself completely to the role."[73] These opinions were echoed by an American critic: "Miss Farrar as Manon was ideal. She embodied the part to perfection, and left nothing to be desired either in her singing or acting."[74]

Aside from Miss Farrar's dramatic portrayal, the press praised her vocal progress since studying with Madame Lehmann. "Under the guidance of the vocal master, Lilli Lehmann," commented one critic, "her vocal technique has matured and gained security,"[75] while a colleague added:

Fraulein Farrar, under the guidance of Lilli Lehmann with whom she recently started to study, has done away with all that which still prevented her from being one of the best, we could confidently say, the best coloratura of our Royal Theatre [Miss Farrar did not possess a coloratura voice but rather a very flexible lyric voice]. The voice has so strengthened that she mastered the strenuous demands of this role to the very last tone; her rarely beautiful sound always services the artistic conception; intonation and coloratura are infallible and also the top tones are not defective; top C and D possess power and splendor.[76]

For the next twelve years, Miss Farrar was to study with Madame Lehmann, to whose influence she attributed much of her success.[77]

By the end of 1903, she had established herself as one of the most popular stars of the Berlin State Opera. Her contract was readily renewed for another three-years. In addition to her growing fame in Germany, she was also becoming well-known in European operatic circles. Raoul Gunsbourg, director of the Monte Carlo Opera, offered her a guest contract to sing *La bohème* with a young Italian tenor named Enrico Caruso. Monsieur Gunsbourg was always on the lookout for interesting new talent, and a French periodical reported that "he had been impressed by the velvet quality of [Miss Farrar's] voice in the upper register, by the theatrical intelligence of the singer and by the personality which she succeeded in giving to that conventionalized role of Gretchen."[78] Miss Farrar accepted the offer with alacrity, realizing that a successful debut at the showplace of Europe could lead to contracts with the leading opera houses of the Continent and ultimately with the Metropolitan Opera in New York.

During the rehearsals, Caruso sang with only half of his normal volume in order to save his voice for the performance on March 10, 1904. On the night of the performance, Miss Farrar was dumbfounded by the glorious

Farrar as Manon, 1919.

singing of her colleague and nearly forgot her own cue until the conductor rapped his baton. Both artists were enthusiastically received by a distinguished international audience. This was the beginning of an operatic partnership which Harold Schonberg of the *New York Times* has referred to as "the most popular singing team the Metropolitan ever had."[79]

After another successful Berlin season, in which she had added on November 17, 1904, the mezzo-soprano role of Thomas' Mignon to her list of portrayals, Miss Farrar returned in the spring of 1905 to Monte Carlo. She sang the roles of Marguerite in Berlioz's *La Damnation de Faust* on March 1 and Gounod's version of Goethe's classic on March 5. The press were liberal in their praise of her portrayals of the two Marguerites, in which she displayed "a remarkable sense of dramatic expression."[80]

While performing these two roles, she was suddenly requested by the management to assume the lyric soprano lead in the world premiere of Mascagni's *Amica* on March 8, from which Emma Calvé had mysteriously withdrawn. Within five days she learned the role of the beautiful and passionate young Piedmontese peasant girl, Amica, who is torn between her duty to her fiancé, for whom she does not care, and her love for his elder brother.

Impressed by her five-day feat, Count Isaac de Camondo, a wealthy patron of the arts, asked Miss Farrar if she would sing the lyric soprano role of Zephirine in his opera, *Le clown*, composed to a libretto by Victor Capoul. Capoul was stage manager of the Paris Opéra and Miss Farrar's former New York teacher of acting.

Before performing in this opera, however, she returned to Berlin, and in addition to her previous roles, sang Auber's Angela in *Le Domino noir* on November 28 and Wagner's Elisabeth in *Tannhäuser* on December 20. By this time, her voice had developed from a light to a full, but flexible, lyric soprano, referred to by the Italians as a spinto. This added power and richness enabled her to perform both the ingénue roles of Auber and the light dramatic parts of Wagner.

The libretto for Auber's comic opera, *Le Domino noir*, is by the playwright, Eugène Scribe, and abounds in disguises, accidental meetings, and a last minute reprieve for the heroine by the convenient arrival of a letter from the Queen. Miss Farrar was very popular as the young novice who is released from her religious vows in time to marry the handsome Count with whom she had fallen in love at a masked ball. The young diva thoroughly enjoyed the opportunity to perform spoken dialogue on the operatic stage for the first time.

The saintly Elisabeth in Wagner's opera was a decided contrast to Scribe's capricious heroine, and Miss Farrar spent many months preparing the role with Madame Lehmann, who had insisted upon economy of gesture, as well as richness of facial expression. In a 1908 interview with the *New York Sun*, Miss Farrar described the evolution of her only Wagnerian portrayal:

> In that role I had a very difficult proposition. As you know, the saintly woman is always more or less stupid and uninteresting. She comes on the stage handicapped by that feeling we all have toward her, partly from our own experience, partly because literary tradition has made her so.... She is pitted in the struggle against Venus, the luscious, fascinating, subtle, suggestive one, the type that from the beginning of things has an easy time overcoming man's resistance. What is there for her to have? Only the force of her own personality. She has to make men feel that the spiritual is better worth while than the mere animal allurement, make them feel it intensely. You have got to go through the spiritual struggle yourself before you can convince others of its conquering power, and that is not always an easy task for a young woman who is not herself over-spiritualized, who has a healthy, normal appetite, and who has an overabundance of youthful vitality. I studied ten solid months on that role, and finally reduced it to the belief that it was a matter of the light in the eyes.
>
> I looked at hundreds of old masters ... succumbed to that uncanny power in the eyes, where the art of the painters had been concentrated. The eyes of those old masters have a light in them so effulgent that you are bound to recognize it and its right to immortality. They knew!
>
> To make Elisabeth great she must have that effulgent light. It was by that she conquered, saving the man she loved from every evil and from the swords of his enemies.
>
> I raise the arm it must be something more than the gesture commanded by the score, and that something more must grip the audience so that with the uplift of the arm they get the spiritual uplift as well from the face.[81]

It seems rather doubtful that an "effulgent light" in Miss Farrar's eyes would have been visible to someone in the audience one hundred feet away.[82] But the radiance and sweetness of her personality, combined with the expressiveness of her features and gestures did succeed in creating an eloquent portrayal of the beautiful and saintly young woman whom Wagner referred to as "the woman who like a star of heaven points the way upwards to Tannhäuser out of the cave of sensuality of the Venusberg."[83]

The elegant diva's impersonation expressed the grace, serenity, and natural dignity of the Landgrave's daughter, who renounced the world to pray for the soul of her beloved. Her opening scene was novel since she entered the Singers' Hall in a state of demure and sentimental reverie, instead of with the usual "joyous"[84] entrance specified in the score by Wagner. Perhaps the young singer was attempting to avoid the "usual boisterous greeting"[85] made to the hall by other sopranos. Later, she glanced understandingly at Tannhäuser in the tournament scene rather than leering or simpering.[86] During the young knight's boasts of his stay in the Venusberg, Miss Farrar did not resort to horrified grimaces and staggers. Instead, she showed only genuine concern for Tannhäuser's fate. Not until she had saved him from immediate death at the hands of the other contestants did she cover her face and sadly weep for herself.[87]

The members of the press were lavish in their praise of Miss Farrar's portrayal, and Madame Lehmann added her own feelings in a personal letter: "The criticism is splendid and quite in accordance with my own sentiments and conviction. I must tell you once more that it was an *extremely* beautiful and good thing, and that you will not, perhaps, succeed again in making it so infantine, demure, and saintly, even with this slight impulse to live and love. It was very beautiful, and just as I always wanted to see this role done."[88] Miss Farrar had succeeded in creating a chaste, yet loving heroine, and it is interesting to note that Richard Wagner had written of this character "the difficulty for Elisabeth lies in the fact that the portrayer has to give the impression of a very youthful and virginal simplicity without betraying that in reality she possesses experienced, fine womanly feelings which enable her to fulfill her task."[89] A solution had been found by the young singer. Elisabeth remained her favorite portrayal, and she never attempted to alter it.

During a performance of *Tannhäuser*, the Venus was sung by a good-natured but corpulent mezzo, who was rather casual about her duties as the seductive Goddess of Love. As Miss Farrar was standing in the wings "quivering with excitement and intensity" before her entrance in the second act, she was greeted by the Venus of the evening. The singer's wreath was askew on her blond wig, while in one hand she held a ham sandwich, and in the other a seidel of beer. Smiling at Miss Farrar, she jovially called out: "Yes, child, go sing; meanwhile I'll eat something."[90] Geraldine Farrar rebelled against this indifference to the dramatic import of a role and to the intense concentration required for its portrayal. A new operatic era was dawning, and as a German reporter wrote: "It is no longer sufficient merely to stand on the stage and sing skillfully; the new opera demands commanding mime and play of features. The opera singer should be armed with the entire apparatus of the actor, his voice there may be only a part, even if it constitutes the most important part. The demands of the new time were met to a high degree by Geraldine Farrar."[91]

After the 1905 Berlin season, Miss Farrar traveled to Monte Carlo. On February 13, 1906, she sang the role of Sita, the lovely young Indian maiden, in Massenet's opera, *Le Roi de Lahore*, which has a ballet in the third act. The solo dancer in this performance was a young ballerina by the name of Mata Hari who eventually gained notoriety as a German spy in the First World War. Eleven days after Miss Farrar's performance of Sita, she created the role of Margarita in the world premiere of Saint-Saëns' *L'ancêtre*, and on March 15 she sang Queen Elisabeth in Verdi's *Don Carlo* with Feodor Chaliapin as King Philip. In April, she went to Paris and performed the lead in Count Camondo's opera *Le clown*. The Count had hired the entire Monte Carlo Opera Company to sing three performances of this work at Paris' Nouveau Theatre. In this opera, which opened on April 26, Miss Farrar played the part of a fascinating young circus performer who is torn between her desire for a life of glitter and ease and her fondness for a poor clown. "Miss Farrar," reported *Le Figaro*, "made a marvelous creation of Zephirine. She played the character with a versatility and a really extraordinary variety of talent; she furnished it with febrility, tenderness, and a superbly intense passion."[92]

At the beginning of October, Miss Farrar fulfilled a special engagement in Warsaw, singing for the first and last time in her career the dramatic soprano role of Maddalena in Giordano's *Andrea Chénier*. Soon after, as a special favor to the Berlin management, she performed the role of Gilda in Verdi's *Rigoletto*, enabling Caruso to include the Duke of Mantua among his guest appearances that season. Realizing that the difficult coloratura role of Gilda with its high E flat was not her "real vocal meat,"[93] she never sang that part again.

It was also at this time that Richard Strauss, the prominent German composer and conductor, asked Miss Farrar to perform the lead in his opera *Salome* at the Berlin Royal Opera. At his request, she had attended the premiere on December 9, 1905, in Dresden. Although "the dramatic and pictorial probabilities of the role" fascinated her, she refused his request. The young prima donna realized that the highly dramatic vocal demands of the score would sorely overtax her basically lyric voice. "You, Farrar, have such dramatic possibilities," argued Dr. Strauss, "[you] can act and dance half-naked, so no one will care if you sing or not."[94] Strauss even offered to rewrite various musical passages for her, but she remained adamant in her decision, wisely rejecting a role which might have done her voice immeasurable harm.

By 1906, Miss Farrar had made rapid progress, both vocally and dramatically, since her 1901 debut at the Berlin Royal Opera. As an actress, she excelled in the youthfully romantic roles of Gounod's Marguerite and Juliette, Massenet's Manon, Thomas' Mignon, and Wagner's Elisabeth. She also was well suited to the ingénue parts of Mozart's Zerlina and Auber's Angela. Her portrayal of the self-sacrificing Violetta in the latter acts of Verdi's *La traviata* was deeply moving, but she was still unsuccessful in her attempt to impersonate the first act's demimondaine figure. Roles of a degenerate nature were not yet within the scope of this young singing actress. Her representation of the dissolute Nedda lacked conviction. Romantic roles of early youth were to remain her finest impersonations. Although her acting was often marred by excessive movement, she was learning economy of gesture, so that by 1906, she was described as the most finished actress on the German operatic stage: "No one on the stage is more natural and unaffected as she, no one understands better how to support and to supplement the voice through the means of mime. We gradually have become so accustomed to the acting importance of Farrar, that we accept it as somewhat self evident.... Thereby we do an injustice to this artist, who for the first time knows how to present with indefatigable thoroughness the individual characteristics of a figure, such as we until now jealously admired in the French theatre."[95]

Vocally, her rich and flexible voice was ideally suited to the lyric repertoire. Slowly, however, it was increasing in size and she began to perform light dramatic roles. Her singing was still blemished by occasional forcing, but under the guidance of Lilli Lehmann, she was striving to overcome this tendency.

Miss Farrar was now recognized as one of the most talented singing actresses in Europe, and during the summer of 1906, signed a contract with the Metropolitan Opera Company. On November 26, 1906, at the age of twenty-four, she made her debut as Juliette at the opera house over which she was to reign as queen for the next sixteen years.

✦ Two ✦

At the Metropolitan Opera, 1906–1908

"Someday I will, I must, sing there,"[1] Geraldine Farrar had declared at the age of seventeen when she saw the Metropolitan Opera House for the first time. Since its inception in 1883, that famous institution had become one of the world's leading opera companies. Emma Calvé, the de Reszkes, Nellie Melba, Victor Maurel, Francesco Tamagno, Lillian Nordica, Lilli Lehmann, and many other famous opera stars of the fin de siècle had performed there. Now Miss Farrar's name was added to this distinguished roster.

The Metropolitan Opera had always been Miss Farrar's "ultimate goal,"[2] and she negotiated an "ironclad"[3] contract, "determined to enter en dignité"[4] and to "have the proper opportunity to appear before the public."[5] Aside from her guaranteed operatic repertoire and performances, she "was to sing in no private houses unless agreeable to her and only for special compensation; and she incorporated every possible clause imaginable about dressing-rooms, drawing-rooms on trains, carriages, railroad fares for [her] mother and [her] maids on tour, and in fact every conceivable concession which the most arrogant prima donna might demand."[6] Also included in her contract was the stipulation that if her services were required in Berlin, the Metropolitan would immediately release her for that period of time. Heinrich Conried, the Metropolitan's general manager, claimed that not since Adelina Patti had any artist known as much about protective clauses as Geraldine Farrar. Henrietta Farrar had familiarized herself with legal procedures for theatrical contracts, so that her daughter would have sufficient opportunity to display her talent and establish her position at the Metropolitan, free from the political machinations of rival sopranos already entrenched in the public's favor.

When Miss Farrar joined the Metropolitan Opera Company in the autumn of 1906, she was practically unknown to the average American. Nor did her reputation as an accomplished singing actress in the opera houses of Europe guarantee her a comparable reputation in the United States. She had to make her own way, and wishing to do her best she was irritated by many of her colleagues' indifference to stage rehearsals, which they treated "as if the occasion was a social tea, and the time for rehearsal begrudged."[7] Accustomed to the strict discipline of the German theatres in which the stage business was meticulously worked out in long arduous rehearsals, Miss Farrar was appalled at the Metropolitan artists who "hardly bothered to sing in half-voice, and hatted and gloved, paraded to and fro."[8] Beauty of tone rather than dramatic characterization was their chief concern, and Heinrich Conried, like his predecessors, Henry Abbey and Maurice Grau, favored the star system. "The star," recorded the music critic Howard Taubman, "was omnipotent. The secondary singers were, in the terms of the day, 'cats and dogs.' The chorus and ballet were small and the sets were rudimentary."[9] Theatrical illusion was conspicuously absent, according to W. J. Henderson.[10] Puccini complained in 1907 concerning the premiere of his opera *Madama Butterfly* at the Metropolitan that he "had to struggle to obtain two full-dress rehearsals, including the general. Nobody knew anything. Dufrisch [the stage manager] had not taken the trouble to study the mise en scène, because the composer was there."[11] The star system reigned triumphant at the Metropolitan.

On November 26, 1906, Miss Farrar and the French tenor Charles Rousselière opened the opera season in a revival of Gounod's opera, *Roméo et Juliette,* which formerly had featured Nellie Melba and Jean de Reszke as the ill-starred lovers. Miss Farrar had often performed with Monsieur Rousselière in Monte Carlo, and "they were agreed upon the stage pictures with little difficulty."[12] In the first act ballroom scene, Miss Farrar was a "beautiful vision"[13] in her rose-colored, diamond-studded, sheath-like gown that had been modeled by her Parisian dressmaker after Botticelli's painting, "la bella Simonetta." All eyes were fastened upon her, and there was a prolonged outburst of applause following her half-whispered day-dreaming rendition of the famous "Waltz Song," in which she slowly swayed from side to side while fluttering a large feather fan. The critic of the *New York Herald* commented that "her singing of the famous waltz song was far slower than is customary, but interpreted thus it proved novel and was robbed of its original commonplaceness."[14] At the conclusion of each act, the young American soprano was recalled many times by the New York public who had discovered an exciting new star.

With this opera, as in Miss Farrar's subsequent musical career, one aspect was singled out for particular comment. The critics took special note of her acting, which they considered both appropriate to the music and the believable, life-like character of Shakespeare's ill-starred heroine. Henry Finck of the *New York Evening Post* illustrates this point:

> [Miss Farrar] was a Juliette to the eye ... suggesting the dark-haired, dark-eyed Verona girl of fourteen as she seldom has been suggested either in the opera-house or the theatre; indeed, the opinion was expressed by many that Juliet had never been impersonated here so realistically and artistically by any actress who was not also a singer but able to concentrate all of her attention on the play. Her facial expression is as fascinating, as subtle, as varied, as fitful as Calvé's; every note of the score is mirrored in those lovely features. The smile of youth was ever on her face in the early scenes of happiness; solemn and demure she knelt during the marriage ceremony;
> exquisitely girlish was her gesture as she gave the Friar her hand to be placed in Roméo's ... and in the final scene of agony, in the tomb, she was like a broken flower; it was tragic realism of the highest type.[15]

Another New York critic suggested that her acting was new and interesting:

> There is no record of an occasion so completely dominated by a single singer as Geraldine Farrar dominated the Metropolitan Opera House last night.... Her Juliet is a creation—as great in its way as Alla Nazimova's analysis of Hedda Gabler—as poetic as Browning's "Pippa Passes"—read in the seclusion of one's library.
>
> First of all, Geraldine Farrar is a delight to the eyes. When she appeared, led by the hand of Papa Capulet in among the courtiers that infested the old palace, she won us by her grace and charm. As her face came into view—a lovely, happy face, fringed with dark ringlets—it was beauty that attracted, and as the scene progressed it was her impersonation of the Veronese damsel that claimed first place. Such riotous joy is rare in these days of statuesque and impassioned prima donnas. Here is a new type—a feminine Peter Pan, if you will—all airy grace, and seemingly charged with perpetual youth. Her voice in the waltz song was charmingly immature—pure, fresh, birdlike.
>
> Little God Cupid works rapidly with warm-blooded Italian maidens: Juliet is suddenly changed to womanhood—and, presto! voice, action, looks are all as suddenly matured.... The girlish demeanor is slipped off with the first youthful gown.[16]

The University of Maryland's Professor Homer Ulrich thought her singing and acting so well blended that "the listeners forgot about Farrar and thought only about Juliet."[17] In some exuberance, the critic of the *Evening Sun* explained that "here was an actress who enters the American stage, exhibits the manners of a court, whispers a worn-out waltz song pensively, as if she were thinking aloud, and suddenly finds the coldest audience in the world taking her to its heart in a storm of applause that could not, would not end." He went on to say that "such serpentine grace" had not been seen on the New York stage since the advent of the glamorous American actress, Mrs. Lesley Carter, and the elegant French star, Madame Sarah Bernhardt; nor "such love-making" since the days of the sultry prima donna, Emma

Calvé. Fascinated by her rendition of the bed chamber scene, much of which she sang lying down, the same writer commented: "It may do queer things to the voice, but there is evidently a fearless originality in this youngest of the newest stars."[18] Miss Farrar defended her singing of this romantic scene in a prone position by stating that "the simple repose seems to me more fully to accentuate the sublime and lyric climax of the tragedy."[19]

Several critics, however, felt that Miss Farrar tended to overact. "She acted like one whose instincts for the stage were full and eager," wrote Henry Krehbiel of the *New York Tribune,* "but also like one who, not needing to learn what to do neglected to learn that it is possible to do too much. Had she been one half less consciously demonstrative whenever she slipped out of the dramatic picture, one half less sweeping in her movements and gestures when she was in the picture, she would have been twice as admirable."[20] Echoing his colleague's words, William R. Lester reported that she displayed "excessive impetuosity and distrust of the dramatic value of repose.... Juliette was almost incessantly in action."[21] Nevertheless, both critics agreed that she possessed extraordinary histrionic gifts, rare personal beauty, and a vital personality.

Also commented upon was the beauty of Miss Farrar's voice, which Richard Aldrich of the *New York Times* described as "a full and rich soprano, lyric in its nature and flexibility, yet rather darkly colored and with not a little of the dramatic quality and with a power of dramatic nuance that she uses in the main skillfully." Of her singing, he wrote that it was "generally free and spontaneous in delivery, well phrased and well enunciated."[22] Although William Lester and Henry Krehbiel agreed with Richard Aldrich that Miss Farrar was "a singer of remarkable gifts,"[23] they both made note of her tendency to force the upper register of her voice when singing full volume. This lack of vocal control, which resulted in a shrillness of tone, had already been commented upon by various Berlin critics. But, even though Krehbiel and Lester may have had some reservations about certain aspects of Miss Farrar's singing and acting, they fully concurred with their colleagues that the Metropolitan had indeed acquired an exciting new star.

Following Miss Farrar's successful debut as Juliette—a role which she sang only four more times at the Metropolitan—she performed the part of Marguerite in the American premiere of Hector Berlioz's *La Damnation de Faust* on December 7, 1906. Berlioz's heroine was not new to Miss Farrar who had already performed the role in Monte Carlo to the Faust of Monsieur Rousselière, her partner at the Metropolitan. Mephistopheles was portrayed by the superb French singing actor, Pol Plançon. Consisting of eleven unconnected episodic scenes from Goethe's poem on the Faust legend, *La Damnation de Faust* had been composed as a concert piece rather than as a unified theatrical work to be performed on the operatic stage. The role of Marguerite is brief and of little musical interest, but the seventh scene dream sequence allowed Miss Farrar to reveal her exceptional pantomimic powers. "The village maiden is seen asleep in her armchair," recorded the *Evening Post*. "She has a dream in which the audience sees her, as a sleepwalker, go out into the street toward the church. Mephistopheles stops her and draws her attention away from the cross to an image of Faust. Marguerite weeps and prays, and finally falls slowly to her knees. This extremely difficult scene was done by Miss Farrar with the consummate histrionic art and command of facial expression of which she gave such a delightful exhibition as Juliette."[24] The opera, however, was withdrawn from the repertory after only five performances due to the public's lack of interest.

Miss Farrar's portrayal of Berlioz's Marguerite may have been short-lived, but she was long to be associated with the heroine of Gounod's *Faust* which she added to her Metropolitan repertoire on December 31, 1906. She was again partnered by Rousselière and Plançon, and in later performances by Enrico Caruso and Feodor Chaliapin. Unlike Berlioz's concert work, Gounod's opera concentrates on one aspect of Goethe's poem, the sentimental love story of Faust and Marguerite. Gounod's musically beautiful and dramatically effective medieval maiden was ideally suited to Miss Farrar's lyrical gifts. The press praised her for her clear and naturally developed transition from the carefree girl of the first act to the guilt-ridden murderess of the last act. Essentially, Miss Farrar gave the same interpretation she had given in Berlin. According to the music critic Frederic Dean, awakening desire quivered in her voice at the beginning of the garden scene, and the abrupt recitative sections of the spinning song were treated as natural queries about the handsome young stranger who was disturbing her thoughts.[25] She spun and sang like a maiden in a dream rather than like a vocalist employing the spinning wheel merely because tradition or a prompt book dictated its use. And she even laughed in the succeeding "Jewel Song," dancing the latter part with a mirror in her hand as she admired herself, adorned with her admirer's dazzling gifts. During the love scene that followed, Miss Farrar portrayed a Marguerite so overcome by her own passionate response to Faust's fervent wooing that she was no longer able to stand. She groped about for support and finally sat down on a garden bench. Towards the end of this act, at the conclusion of Marguerite's love song to the night, Miss Farrar despairingly attempted to close the window against her lover. But as the curtain fell, she ran to the door and threw herself at his feet. This action was a radical departure from the conventional mild embrace at the window as the lights slowly dimmed.

In the following church scene, Miss Farrar did not begin as the traditionally crushed, half-mad sinner. She was still the beautiful and graceful Marguerite, praying to be forgiven her guilty love. Only at the end of the scene, after she had been convinced by the Devil of her eternal damnation, did she give way to complete despair because of her inability to combat the evil surrounding her. At this point in the action, she revealed an unfortunate, but not yet lost woman, who was free from all touches of insanity until after her brother's dying curse in the following act. As the curtain descended, Valentine's curse was usually hurled at his hysterical sister, who clung desperately to his dead body, despite having rejected her after having been mortally wounded in a duel with her faithless lover. A new touch was added to this scene by Miss Farrar, whose actions are described in detail by Frederic Dean:

> Marguerite lies huddled on the ground quite apart from the dead brother and the chanting villagers. Suddenly she staggers to her feet and edges up to the dead loved one. Her eyes are caught by something glittering before her. She picks it up not knowing what it is, but once realizing that it is the cross that hung about her brother's neck, she holds it out at arm's length as a thing renounced forever, and drops it on the dead man's chest. With the fall from her fingers of this emblem of goodness, hope and reason leave her and it is the mad Marguerite that literally tears her way through the crowd and disappears [screaming hysterically].[26]

To emphasize this madness, Miss Farrar went barefoot in the final prison scene.

Her Marguerite differed from that of all others who had appeared in this role. According to Dean,

> The many who played this part ... have sung this music and contented themselves with the routine of the stage business handed down to them by operatic directors with the traditions of nearly half a century. To her, Marguerite is a personality and one not lightly to be disposed of. Carefully, reverently she has studied this representative "woman of all women" of Gounod's, and has tried to present her as the composer dreamed Goethe's heroine might be in a modern, fleshly incarnation.... *Faust* was first sung on March 9, 1859 — nearly 48 years ago. It is known in every musical hamlet in Europe and America, and is a prime favorite among the operas of the world. And it has been reserved for an American girl of 24 to so vitalize its chief character by her impersonation as to give a deeper meaning to it, and to the drama in which it plays so conspicuous a part.[27]

In a similar vein, the Boston critic, Philip Hale, recorded that Miss Farrar was not "a mature, an ineffectively disguised matron, simulating laboriously the amorous enthusiasm of maidenhood," but was rather "a youthful, charming, graceful Marguerite." "Her facial expression," he added, "her gestures and her repose are all eloquent and, wonder of wonders, they are singularly suited, yet without too deliberate attention to the music."[28] Also regarding Miss Farrar's exceptional pantomimic powers, another reviewer claimed:

There is so much fascinating detail in the action and facial expression of Miss Farrar's Marguerite that ... even a deaf person, or one to whom music does not appeal, would be intensely interested to see it. And every detail is part of a general conception.... A subtle touch was her expression of disappointment on looking again into the mirror after taking off the jewels—disappointment not because of vanity, but because she felt less worthy of Faust's admiration.... In the third act youth and much of her beauty have dropped from her like a cloak, and her wan, sad face is that of a woman who suffers all that a woman can suffer; what remains is the beauty of emotion, but no longer the wild-rose beauty of the early scenes.[29]

Nevertheless, there were those critics, such as Richard Aldrich and Henry T. Parker, who maintained that Miss Farrar sometimes tended toward exaggeration—over acting the melodramatic scene within the church[30]—and toward forcing the upper register of her voice during moments of emotional intensity.[31]

In later performances of *Faust*, Miss Farrar varied her stage business from time to time, rather than subscribing to the classic method in which the performer never consciously deviated from his or her original conception of the role. Instead of singing the first stanza of the "Spinning Song" seated at her spinning wheel, she went into the house to fetch her spindle of flax and began the opening phrases from within the cottage. In the church scene, she decided to follow Calvé's example and laid the action in the square outside. Then at the opera's conclusion, she was no longer carried off into the clouds by the angels, but stood in her prison cell watching the celestial vision until she fell dead as the curtain descended.

Probably the most unexpected change in Miss Farrar's stage business occurred one evening in 1908 during the conclusion of the church scene. Suddenly leaping down from his pillar, the massive Feodor Chaliapin as Mephistopheles swept Miss Farrar up in his arms, and, carrying her from the stage, "hissed an extemporaneous 'Ha! Ha!' to the audience."[32] According to the diva, she was generally prepared to counter the wily basso's "sudden departures from the rehearsed plan" in order to add "touches of originality favorable only for the aggrandizement of Chaliapin."[33] But for once, she was completely nonplused.

Miss Farrar's growing reputation with the New York operatic public was reinforced on February 6, 1907, by her performance of Wagner's Elisabeth in *Tannhäuser*, a role in which she already had won distinction in Europe. A new note of simplicity was observed in her acting by W. J. Henderson, who wrote: "Miss Farrar disclosed an amount of artistic poise, of self-control which she had not shown in any other role. Through this her impersonation attained dignity and symmetry. Her action became well balanced and correct in meaning, ... She treated the declamation with fine intelligence and made it perform its proper function as an integral part of the drama."[34] Despite the press and public's acclaim of her portrayal, as well as her own frequent requests to perform this role, she was never again cast as the saintly Elisabeth at the Metropolitan.

On February 11, 1907, her portrayal of Cio-Cio-San in the Metropolitan's premiere of Puccini's *Madama Butterfly* launched the young American soprano on her way towards becoming "the most loved and the most respected member of the company."[35] The first American performance of this opera had taken place on October 15, 1906, at Henry A. Savage's Castle Square Opera Company. But that production was completely overshadowed by the Metropolitan's stellar presentation, which, aside from the Cio-Cio-San of Geraldine Farrar, featured the Pinkerton of Enrico Caruso, the Sharpless of Antonio Scotti, and the Suzuki of Louise Homer.

Puccini's opera was based on a recent successful play by David Belasco. It was well-known to New Yorkers and it generally followed the script's lines, except for one major difference: the stage drama's action began after the faithful Japanese wife and mother had been awaiting her fickle American naval officer for nearly three years. The operatic libretto was expanded to include the marriage ceremony and wedding night of the still naive young geisha. It was necessary for Miss Farrar to reveal Cio-Cio-San's development from innocent joy to grim despair, whereas Blanche Bates, the star of Belasco's production, never had to deal with the role's youthful aspect. Having been in Europe

Geraldine Farrar as Madama Butterfly, 1907 (Library of Congress, Music Division).

during the play's run at the Herald Square Theatre in 1900, Miss Farrar was unfamiliar with Blanche Bates' interpretation. But even if she had seen Belasco's production, it is unlikely that she would have imitated the actress's interpretation, since she always preferred to create her own conception of a role. In portraying Madama Butterfly, Miss Farrar had two advantages over Miss Bates. First, she was small of stature, and therefore visually convincing as the fragile Butterfly, while Miss Bates was tall and "scarcely the diminutive and harmless looking creature Cio-Cio-San is supposed to be."[36] Second, the operatic heroine voices her feelings in some of Puccini's most emotional, dramatic and beautiful music, while the actress expresses her thoughts in Belasco's pidgin English.

As with the play, the opera was mounted with an eye to authenticity. The first act showed a characteristically Japanese house and garden overlooking the harbor of Nagasaki in the bay below. The second act was set indoors with a view of blossoming cherry trees seen through sliding doors at the back. Perhaps the presence of the composer at rehearsals and the opening night had motivated such lavish display.

In this exciting production, Miss Farrar fully revealed her histrionic powers. "The American public embraced the soprano's Butterfly," recorded authors Charles and Mary Jane Matz "like no other single interpretation, except Caruso's Canio [Leoncavallo's *I pagliacci*]."[37]

Miss Farrar had spent many hours in research for this role and said to the authoress Mabel Wagnall that "when I was studying 'Madama Butterfly,' I read everything I could find about the Japanese. I tried to imbue myself with their spirit. I bought up old prints, and pictures, and costumes; I learned how they eat, and sleep, and walk, and talk, and think, and feel. I read on the subject in French and German, as well as in English."[38]

She designed her own costumes from the various prints she had studied and hired a Japanese maid in order to observe her personality and manners. For weeks, she worked each day with a Japanese actress, Madame Fu-ji-Ko, "whose dainty personality and grace were her model for authentic gesture and carriage." The diva "padded about [the rooms] in gay kimonos, the heavy wig elaborately dressed, her feet in little one-toed canvas shoes used by the Japanese. She shuffled, posed, danced and gesticulated under the watchful eye of the Japanese artist, herself in native costume."[39]

Miss Farrar incorporated into her portrayal of Cio-Cio-San much of her Japanese teacher's counsels—"the meekly bowed head, the modest composure, the small, shuffling steps, the serenity and grace characteristic of young Japanese women."[40] The Matzes wrote that "bow, kneel, hand gesture, fan, sleeves, head—she mastered it all and infused it with her own personality."[41]

In order to conform to the Asian brow line, she shaved her eyebrows and penciled in thin arches well above her own. She also maintained the attitude of perpetual stooping, which she found most fatiguing.

Miss Farrar describes her conception of Cio-Cio-San as follows:

> A dainty human petal, fragrant as the cherry blossoms in her garden, ... the embodiment of woman's love and unswerving devotion—such is Cio-Cio-San, ...
>
> How exquisitely girlish her meeting with the betrothed, accompanied by her laughing companions—her terror at the priest's fierce denunciations—the shy sweet surrender in the entrancing love duet that closes upon the passionate exaltation of the bridal night.
>
> Alas! Three years later there is a pale little flower, worn with watching and waiting, ... none can shake her faith—he will return—he must return!
>
> High on her proud young shoulders, the pride of her hungry heart—the living gift of love—a blond blue-eyed son, ...
>
> The roar of cannon! Quick to the terrace—yes—there come the great white warships...
>
> The little heart is nigh to break with joy...
>
> Spicy fragrance strews the floor. The wedding gown is tenderly wound around the fragile shoulders, and begins that heart breaking vigil from night till dawn! ...
>
> Voices! Like an eager, joyous child she trips down the stairs. Where is he? There stand the consul, the sobbing maid and under the trees a strange lady.
>
> Slowly the tiny creature grasps the meaning of those kind faces that would so gladly save her pain.... One kind embrace to the despairing servant—fold the little one tightly in an eternal good-bye, ... and then the relentless little hands bury the slender knife deep into that throbbing, adoring little heart, and the story of a woman's love broken on the wheel of a man's careless fancy, is over.[42]

In January of 1907, Giacomo Puccini and his publisher, Giulio Ricordi, arrived in New York to begin stage rehearsals which the composer later claimed "were too hurried."[43] According to Puccini, the stage manager was unfamiliar with the staging, the conductor could not control the orchestra, and the leading tenor, Enrico Caruso, stubbornly refused all advice. Maintaining that "nobody knew anything," Puccini took over the stage direction and remained at the conductor's elbow.[44] Puccini was rarely satisfied, and from the very start there was friction between the disgruntled, determined composer, and his strong-willed leading lady. Miss Farrar claimed that Puccini had his own ideas on the portrayal of Cio-Cio-San, but that she had no intention of changing her meticulously worked out portrayal of the Japanese heroine. Also, her practice of rehearsing in half-voice annoyed him because he was unable to judge the actual sound of her singing in the opera house. She referred to his views as being "the high irritants"[45] of the rehearsals, and

Puccini complained in a letter to his friend, Sybil Seligman, that her voice "does not carry well in the large space of the theatre."[46] Although after the premiere he grudgingly admitted that the performance "was excellent,"[47] he still argued that it "lacked the poetry he had put into it and that Miss Farrar "was not too satisfactory."[48] However, shortly afterwards at his final press interview, Puccini told the reporters that "she is delightful.... She puts something of herself into each role. I gave her very few ideas for her 'Butterfly,' the part came from her own mind."[49] Perhaps the prima donna's independence, as well as his own depressed mood, due to a severe attack of influenza which he complained to Ricordi nearly "has killed me,"[50] had temporarily colored his artistic judgment. Either Giacomo Puccini had changed his mind, or he was the perfect diplomat. Whether or not the composer approved of Miss Farrar's portrayal is really of little import compared to the fact that until her retirement from the Metropolitan in 1922, the names of Geraldine Farrar and Madama Butterfly were indissolubly linked in the minds of the American operatic public.

On the evening of February 11, 1907, in the first act of the opera, Geraldine Farrar as Madama Butterfly ascended the slope to Pinkerton's house. She carried a parasol and laughed gaily with her companions who had come to witness her marriage to the handsome young American naval lieutenant. Her face was enameled white for the wedding ceremony, and her slight girlish figure and graceful carriage readily embodied the fifteen-year-old geisha of Belasco's play. She coquetted shyly with her bridegroom and was like a joyous child as she displayed the various trinkets hidden in her voluminous sleeves. Only when an allusion was made to her father's hara-kiri knife was the fatalistic woman of the second act revealed in the light-hearted girl. Miss Farrar's Cio-Cio-San was a joyous young woman capable of complete devotion and selflessness. She was momentarily horrified when the bonze denounced her for marrying a foreigner, but she quickly recovered through her growing love for the feckless young lieutenant.

Concerning her love for Lieutenant Pinkerton, a critic wrote that "throughout this first act Miss Farrar seems to aim directly and solely at one idea—to convey to her audience a picture, at once vivid and realistic, of the little Japanese girl with thoughts for nothing but the man she loves."[51] Henry T. Parker stated:

> She idealizes Butterfly into a being of poetry and romance, transfiguring the young bride and so intensifying the humanity of the girl's emotion. She has come to be no mistress, no wife to Pinkerton, but to the flowering of all her dreams of happiness. She bows before him, but really she is bowing to her visions. She is playful with him because she is at play with her own dreams. She seems to fear him because she is tremulous with the ecstasy of her

instant happiness. She makes the glow of it suffuse all her companions. She shivers and quails when the rude blast of the uncle's interruption sweeps chilly across her paradise.... The girl sways in Pinkerton's arms; she droops upon him in utter self-surrender to the joy of devotion that enfolds her. He—and men—ask her body; she—and women—give her soul.[52]

As act two began, the curtain rose on an older Cio-Cio-San whose face and bearing bespoke the wan endurance of silent waiting. But in the ensuing dialogue with Suzuki, who had dared to doubt the inevitability of Pinkerton's return, Miss Farrar made Cio-Cio-San's expression of undying devotion and faith so convincing that Parker wrote: "Her voice, her face, her body, glow with the intensity of her expectation. Suzuki and all who hear and see wither before it."[53]

Another critic reported that "the keynote of her Butterfly in the first part of the second act is a faith so unquestioning, so impatient of any shadow of a doubt in others, so beautiful in its simplicity, its appeal goes direct to the heart of every listener."[54] When the marriage broker, Goro, offered her the opportunity of marrying again, she seized her dagger to expel him. And she dismissed her lordly suitor, Prince Yamadori, with passionate indignation because of the hope and faith smoldering within her. Her greeting of the American consul Sharpless, was almost merry, and as he began to read the letter from Pinkerton, Miss Farrar's Cio-Cio-San became a happy girl once more and reverently took it in her hands to kiss. Of this touching moment a reviewer wrote that "as the consul reads the letter, the ghost of the Butterfly of the first act returns on the wistful face, the wistful tones, the tremulous happiness of the girl's questionings. Even to Sharpless she cannot bare her faith. He speaks the brutal words: 'And if he should not come?' He has spoken the fear that has dimly lurked within her. He has made it tangible, possible. The black vista opens before her; she turns rigid as she looks; she hides her face; her tones are wan."[55] Then suddenly she left the room and returned triumphantly with Pinkerton's young son, Trouble [sometimes a child and sometimes a doll] on her shoulder. She tenderly caressed the child as she described in exaggerated baby-talk what Sharpless had hinted. The consul was unable to deliver his message to this young woman so filled with mother-love and pride in her blond, blue-eyed child—features which she pointed out to him.

When the gun sounded in the harbor announcing the return of Pinkerton's ship, the joy and triumph of Miss Farrar's Cio-Cio-San knew no bounds. She and Suzuki shook down blossoms from the cherry tree to create a flowery way in the garden behind the house. They also scattered blossoms about the room as a sign of welcome to the man Cio-Cio-San has loved so faithfully. Miss Farrar put on a gown she had worn in the first act and placed flowers in her hair. A reviewer commented that "she wastes very little time with the toiletbox, just giving the incident the necessary significance and no more. Thus she succeeds in conveying more forcibly the idea of her impatience to begin the vigil until Pinkerton shall come—a clever and most effective touch."[56] As she watched hopelessly at the shosi until the dawn came and the lights went out one by one, she was a sadly patient little figure. Henry T. Parker revealed that "the vigil by the shosi was searching as it dimmed from alert to dull expectancy, and the voice of Butterfly as she turned from the window was wan with the wistful disappointment of longing." Following her pathetic search for Pinkerton in the house, Parker continued:

> The moment of eager quest with Butterfly like some happy ghost of the self she had been in the moonlight by the little house, faded into the moment of utter disillusion. They who stood by, at least, should not know. The pride of agony stirred for an instant in Miss Farrar's tones and action. Then the instant of blank desolation, of blank despair, of blank self-abandonment in utter blackness. Across it and across Miss Farrar's face came the gleam of release in honor and in endurance to the end. As she had gone in the glowing beauty of her elation to the surrender of the first act, so now she went in the shadowed and sombre beauty of her despair to the surrender that should crown her devotion. It was less a suicide than a sacrifice. The last rapture of motherhood flamed gentle and golden across it like a pale rift in the black sunset.[57]

The tired-eyed, white-faced woman of the third act was hardly recognizable as having once been the beautiful young Butterfly of the first act. Left alone, she tore the flowers from her hair and threw them on the floor. She sadly stripped the room of its floral decorations and prepared to commit suicide by the traditional Japanese act of hara-kiri. As Miss Farrar's Cio-Cio-San was about to cut her throat with her father's knife, young Trouble ran into the room, and after embracing him passionately, she placed an American flag in his hands and bound his eyes. She then went behind a screen to stab herself, and having tied a scarf tightly around her neck, staggered out, fell prone, and struggled frantically till she reached and touched the child. "So ended," wrote Parker, "one of the most remarkable operatic impersonations, in its fusing of an idealizing beauty and a poignant humanity, in this union of the arts of the singer and the actress, that our stage now knows."[58]

The public and press acclaimed Miss Farrar's Butterfly, and her place as a star attraction in New York's operatic world was now firmly established. The press acknowledged her to be one of the leading singing actresses of her generation, and one reviewer commented:

> Modern Italian opera calls for singers who have histrionic ability, too, and Puccini's last work represents the acme of this tendency. Miss Geraldine Farrar combines the two arts with unequalled skill.... To watch this consummate actress in the first act is like looking at an enchanting series of Japanese

prints—a Japanese Juliet, in the garden scene changed from a living picture to a living woman by her love.... Her hands have the grace and eloquence of Sada Yacco's[59]; they are real Japanese hands, and she wears her kimono and obi, she walks and bows, and kneels and pleads, like one to the manner born. If she knew the language of Tokyo, she might, as Burton did in Arabia, travel through the country without being recognized as a foreigner.[60]

Another member of the press reported of her realistic acting:

Madama Butterfly is a prima donna opera, but not in the usual sense of the word. It requires an artist equally accomplished as an actress and a singer. In Miss Geraldine Farrar the Metropolitan Opera House possesses such an artist. The title role in Puccini's opera puts her power to a severe test, and she stood it last night triumphantly.... She revealed not only the universally human side of the tragedy, but imparted to it a fascinating Japanese atmosphere, in looks, curtsies, lithe movements, and diverse subtle details, as well as in dress. Her Cio-Cio-San is intensely fascinating, and it moved many to tears.[61]

One critic even felt that, although Miss Farrar was "a great singer," on this occasion she was "more wonderful as an emotional actress," adding that "the intensity of Miss Farrar's impersonation can be realized in part if one considers that she so far lifted the performance from the ordinary that the strange and disquieting absurdities of grand opera, considering it as a form of art, were utterly obliterated."[62] This sense of dramatic illusion, resulting from the emotional realism of her acting, was elaborated upon by a Montreal reviewer, who wrote: "Miss Farrar is Butterfly from the moment she appears round the bend of the path leading to the cottage on the hill above Nagasaki.... There is never the slightest suggestion of Farrar either in vocal or dramatic appeal.... All the fascination, all the pathos, all the tragedy of a great love and a great faith are epitomized in her lithe, swaying, graceful form, her pretty gestures, her extraordinary voice. Only great artists can submerge their own individualities thus."[63]

Her ability to identify with the character was also observed by a New York critic: "Miss Farrar is not only the consummate actress when playing this part, understanding every nuance and shade and color in the histrionic art, but she is more than that, for she never forgets for a moment that she is the Japanese Girl, and not only constantly maintains all the minutiae of pose and action proclaiming the characterization, but it is impossible to escape the conviction that she actually feels and lives the part as well."[64]

Despite the many paeans written in Miss Farrar's praise, there were also several dissenting voices, among whom were Puccini and W. J. Henderson. "She sings out of tune," commented Puccini, "and forces her voice"[65]; and Henderson wrote: "She sang the music with all her vocal beauty and all her familiar faults.... She was not quite certain of her climaxes and she was not altogether settled in her action."⁶⁶ There also were those who maintained that opera fundamentally is a vocal art and complained of her pronounced theatricality. Objecting to "these attempts at realism," a Chicago critic stated: "She is reported to have studied the role under a Japanese actress. In any event, she employed gestures which are so foreign to our eyes, and, for the most part, so meaningless, that we can be safe in calling them Oriental. Nature had made her tall [Miss Farrar was only 5'3"] and graceful. She sought to shorten her stature by stooping constantly. The result was an awkward distortion of naturally attractive proportions."⁶⁷

Miss Farrar's success with the public, however, was "unquestioned,"⁶⁸ conceded Henderson. In fact, so successful that in 1909, a critic claimed that "this singer has made herself so completely the ideal Japanese girl that nobody (at least no one else in the Metropolitan Opera Company) will dare to touch the heroine in the Puccini opera for many years to come."⁶⁹ Although other sopranos sang this part at the Metropolitan, for the next sixteen years, Miss Farrar was America's leading interpreter of Cio-Cio-San, performing the role ninety-five times at the Opera House and thirty-nine times on the company's tours. "Her Madama Butterfly," according to Howard Taubman in his book, *Opera Front and Back*, "was always good for a sold-out house, and it did not matter who else was in the cast."⁷⁰

Over the years, Miss Farrar made some changes in the original stage business of *Madama Butterfly*, as she had done with Gounod's *Faust* and was later to do with Bizet's *Carmen*. She was convinced that even if she had performed a role many times, there was always room for improvement.⁷¹ At the end of act one, instead of retiring into the house with Pinkerton after the love duet, she fell back into his arms and lingered there till the curtain fell "to exchange a record kiss with her stage husband."⁷² She also ceased to use white make-up because it destroyed all facial expression.

For the second act, she was constantly looking for the right child to play the part of Trouble. As she had to carry him in her arms for extended periods of time, children of eight or nine years of age had proved somewhat burdensome, and dolls were unrealistic. She also wanted one who would not cry on stage and spoil a scene—something that happened one evening in Pittsburgh while she was on tour with the Metropolitan.

In 1910 Miss Farrar introduced new stage business at the opera's conclusion which was described in detail by the music critic, Dudley Glass, following a performance of *Madama Butterfly* on May 6 of that year in Atlanta:

> The finale, the death scene, has been changed materially since Farrar made the part her own, and the new version gives her an opportunity for a tremendous climax. In the Savage production, Butterfly blindfolded the baby, placed

two little American flags in his tiny hands, stepped behind a screen and fell.[73] Miss Farrar, after clasping the baby to her breast ... leads the child to the window [gives him a doll]and sends him to play in the sunshine. Then she draws the sword of her Samurai father [stands in the panelled doorway where she had stood watching for Pinkerton], there is a shrieking sob from the orchestra, the flashing blade is buried in the soft folds of her garments—and Butterfly, writhing, twisting, rolls down the short flight of steps and lies motionless on the floor.[74]

During the same year, a New York critic also commented that the revised final scene was "thrilling as given by her, and of a degree of horror not matched by any one of less abilities than a Duse or a Bernhardt. The manner of the 'hara-kiri,' and the sensational rolling down the steps after the deed was a piece of work ... which is seldom equaled on any stage and has never been excelled in local opera."[75] On one occasion, recalled the author Carl Van Vechten, she even knocked over the rocking chair in her intensely realistic death struggles, "which often embraced the range of the Metropolitan stage."[76]

Miss Farrar said of her success as Cio-Cio-San: "I am by no means the first or the last to present a successful Butterfly. At least two singers[77] vocally my superiors have sung the part. I knew that if I was to make a mark with it, I would have to give my listeners something more than voice—for that my colleagues had already done. So I strove and worked to give them something that went beyond mere vocal expression, which is soul expression. This I feel I have been successful in doing."[78]

In an interview with a reporter from the *New York Evening Post*, Miss Farrar said that she was always amused at certain critics' dislike of her make-up in *Madama Butterfly*. She had made a study of Japanese art and life and had a celebrated Japanese actress at her first performance to criticize her make-up and acting. After the opera was over, this actress informed Miss Farrar that "a woman from the orient could not have done so well or had things more perfect." Miss Farrar thought it ridiculous that "critics do not realize that a person who is giving a performance of that kind makes a study and that things are as nearly perfect as they can be."[79]

Following Miss Farrar's portrayal of Cio-Cio-San, her growing popularity at the Metropolitan resulted in a contract with the Victor Gramaphone Company to record selections from *Madama Butterfly* and *Tannhäuser*. These recordings, which were sold all over the United States, introduced her to a large American public and provided valuable advance publicity for her future concert and Metropolitan Opera tours. For the next thirteen years, she was one of Victor's most prolific stars, recording over eighty selections from eighteen operas.

It was also due to Miss Farrar's success as Madama Butterfly in 1907 that she met two famous theatrical personalities—Clyde Fitch and David Belasco. Fitch gave a gala *Madama Butterfly* dinner party in Miss Farrar's honor after her premiere. And David Belasco, who was most enthusiastic over her portrayal of his Japanese heroine, tried to persuade her to give up opera for drama. Miss Farrar recorded in her first autobiography that "every time we meet and he says, half laughingly, half quizzically, 'Well, when are you going to forsake opera and come into the drama?' I am almost tempted to make an experiment of such interest, for the theatre has always made a strong appeal to my dramatic instincts."[80] She always rejected his offer, but they became fast friends.

One month after the premiere of *Madama Butterfly*, Miss Farrar sang her first Mimi in Puccini's *La bohème* at the Metropolitan Opera House on March 15, 1907, with Enrico Caruso as Rodolpho. She wrote of this role: "Pretty, appealing Mimi! What a quaint vision of Romance the name evokes! ... the little grisette of the Latin Quarter of nearly a century ago.... Mimi is the delicate ideal of the poet lover's enamoured heart alas, all too fragile to endure longer than the gossamer blossoms of her clever little fingers; Mimi of the paling cheek; the quivering shoulders racked with pain; the drooping head like a tired bird—pathetic and sweet in her last quiet rest in her lover's arms."[81] Although the *New York Times* claimed that Miss Farrar was "a fascinating representative of this heroine,"[82] and the *New York Tribune* reported "she ... filled the eye like none of her predecessors [Marcella Sembrich, Lina Cavalieri, and Bessie Abbott],"[83] other members of the press, such as Henry T. Parker and Sylvester Rawlings, found her acting exaggerated and her singing strident.

David Belasco, advisor and friend of Geraldine Farrar, 1916.

With a performance of Nedda to Caruso's Canio in Leoncavallo's *I pagliacci*, Miss Farrar completed her repertoire of roles for the 1906-1907 Metropolitan Opera season. Nedda had never been one of her more

Sarah Bernhardt, advisor and friend of Geraldine Farrar, 1916.

popular roles in Berlin, and the New York critics agreed with their German colleagues that her portrayal lacked the necessary coarseness. "She sings the music admirably," claimed the *New York Tribune*, "but the hot Italian blood does not course through her veins."[84] Miss Farrar did not enjoy performing Leoncavallo's faithless, animalistic strolling player and soon eliminated the role from her repertoire.

Having proved a valuable addition to the roster of the Metropolitan

Opera Company, she was reengaged by Heinrich Conried for the following fall season. At the conclusion of the opera company's spring tour, she returned to Europe for singing lessons with Lilli Lehmann and operatic performances in Germany and France. While she was singing Juliette in Paris, she met the famous French actress, Sarah Bernhardt, who invited the young American prima donna to lunch. Of this meeting Miss Farrar wrote: "She knew all about 'Juliet'—much to my surprise—even to details, such as dress, innovations in mise-en-scène, and how I had tried to infuse the modern dramatic spirit into the measures of opera.... I was to enjoy her friendship from that day on."[85] 1907 was an auspicious year for Miss Farrar. Aside from her success at the Metropolitan Opera, she had met two great theatrical personalities—David Belasco and Sarah Bernhardt—who were to play major roles in her future career.

During the 1907-1908 season at the Metropolitan Opera, Miss Farrar repeated her portrayals of Marguerite, Cio-Cio-San, and Mimi. To these roles she added Margherita (Boito's *Mefistofele*, 1907), Zerlina (Mozart's *Don Giovanni*, 1908), Violetta (Verdi's *La traviata*, 1908), and Mignon (Thomas' *Mignon*, 1908). She revealed artistic maturity in all of them.

On November 20, 1907, Miss Farrar performed her first Margherita in an elaborate new production of Boito's *Mefistofele*. As with Berlioz's *La Damnation de Faust*, Boito's opera lacks dramatic unity, being merely an assemblage of non sequential scenes from Goethe's poem. The role of Mefistofele in Boito's opera had brought European fame to Feodor Chaliapin, and it was revived especially for his debut at the Metropolitan. Miss Farrar was commended for the purity of her singing and the new simplicity of her acting in this "particularly repressed and dreamy presentation of the German maiden."[86] But Chaliapin was condemned for the crudeness of his histrionics, "seeking apparently to emphasize all the disagreeable traits ... of the Prince of the Powers of Darkness."[87] The New York operatic public and press did not understand or appreciate the Russian basso's naturalistic style of acting. But Miss Farrar recognized his genius and referred to his performance as "magnificent and compelling."[88]

As in Miss Farrar's portrayal of Boito's Margherita, so also in that of Puccini's Mimi, a restraint was evident in her singing and acting which the press claimed was now almost free from any former tendencies to force and overact. Rather than constant movement, there was an eloquence of repose in her action which led Henry T. Parker to observe: "She is beginning to learn the virtue of simplicity.... Throughout, she held her Mimi to simple lines, keeping the essential wistfulness and gentleness of the girl, and warming its flame of underlying capriciousness and tenderness, yet never heating it too high."[89] Her singing was still characterized by an exciting vitality and expressiveness, but she no longer sacrificed beauty of tone in an exaggerated attempt at emotional intensity. In the broken speech or parlando passages of the dying Mimi, Miss Farrar's tones were skillfully integrated into the score's vocal line. This also had been true of similar phrases in Verdi's *La traviata* and would again be demonstrated in portions of Puccini's *Tosca*. Her acting, which was unaffected and seemingly spontaneous, contained numerous effective and subtle pieces of stage business. "Mimi sitting with crossed legs in the midst of Rodolpho's ardent tale in the first act," reported Parker, "was a becoming touch of the grisette. Mimi, wholly absorbed in Rodolpho in all the bustle of the scene at the cafe, seeing him, hearing him, feeling him only, gave clear and just illusion of incident and character."[90] In the last act, Miss Farrar with "wistful pleasure and still contentment" tenderly took into her hands and kissed the little muff her lover had kept as a remembrance of their past happiness. And at the opera's conclusion, she "let Mimi's lifeless head slip off the pillow,"[91] using the very expression she had once seen at a death.[92] Mimi had become one of her finest portrayals, and during the next seven years, she performed the role over thirty times.

Miss Farrar added the role of Mozart's Zerlina to her Metropolitan Opera repertoire on February 12, 1908, displaying her usual originality of conception and also her talent for comedy. Instead of the velvet costume worn by most other interpreters of this role, she donned a green cloth gown, in keeping with the state of a peasant girl. "Miss Farrar is scornful of the bogie of tradition," wrote H. T. Parker, observing that "she was concerned with no classic and conventionalized figure, but with a Zerlina who is as alive and plausible and delightful in 1908 as she was in 1787 the opera's premiere." Her arias, he added, were not "set tunes but the momentary speech of this Zerlina busy with incidents and the mood of the play."[93] Charming as well as coquettish, Miss Farrar's country lass expressed "appropriately amusing little awkwardnesses,"[94] such as bashfulness upon first meeting the fascinating Don, and later wonder at the splendor of his villa. The New York, Philadelphia, and Boston press acknowledged her portrayal to be superb lyrical comedy, although Richard Aldrich and Reginald de Koven felt that she somewhat overemphasized the awkwardness. All praised her singing for its "beauty of tone"[95] and "seeming simplicity."[96]

Due to the absence of Marcella Sembrich, Miss Farrar performed the role of Violetta in Verdi's *La traviata* on February 28, 1908. For the first time at the Metropolitan Opera House, this work was presented in modern dress rather than in the traditional seventeenth century costumes.[97] Henry Krehbiel of the *New York Tribune* claimed that this innovation added "plausibility"[98] to the production. In Germany, Violetta had been one of Miss Farrar's most popular impersonations, and according to one New York critic, she "took a hand in the stage management of the Metropolitan production ... as the German Emperor allows her to do at the Imperial Opera in Berlin in recognition of her remarkable dramatic instinct." This same critic went on to say that "like no one now on the stage, Miss Farrar has the gifts of youth, personal charm, grace, and slenderness that are required to give verisimilitude to the impersonation of Violetta."[99] Miss Farrar's natural endowments were a decided asset in her impersonation of a successful Parisian demimondaine, which she now was able to portray with sufficient realism, having matured as an actress since her first performance of the role in 1901. Her portrayal, wrote Richard Aldrich of the *New York Times*, was founded upon "a clearly defined and consistently dramatic conception,"[100] and his colleague, Henry Krehbiel of the *New York Tribune*, concluded that "her Violetta was in fact a patrician and a winning figure throughout."[101] Despite her success as Violetta, Miss Farrar never again performed this role after the return of Madame Sembrich to the Metropolitan in the fall of 1908.

One week after Miss Farrar's performance of Violetta, she sang the lead on March 6, 1908, in a revival of Thomas' opera *Mignon*. It was her final premiere of the 1907-1908 season. Her portrayal of the vicissitudes of this beautiful young aristocratic Italian girl, who as a baby was abducted from her parents' castle by gypsies, led one reviewer to write: "Miss Farrar is an actress of such splendid calibre that were she not a singer she would class with the highest type of native comediennes." He claimed that Miss Farrar's "vivid personality" as well as her "individual grace and dramatic warmth"[102] were reminiscent of Julia Marlowe, America's foremost romantic actress during the first two decades of the twentieth century. So fascinating was her acting, according to Henry Finck of the *Evening Post*, that opera glasses were necessary to avoid the loss of her many subtle details. He reported that the young singing actress's facial expressions changed with the words she sang, and her portrayal was so "true to life"[103] that he forgot she was acting. The music, which lies rather low for the average soprano, was well suited to Miss Farrar's voice because of the exceptional richness of her middle register. Also, the upper register and the occasional coloratura passages were reportedly produced with apparent ease.

After Miss Farrar's last performance of Mignon on April 24, 1908, she returned to Berlin for summer and fall opera performances, in addition to singing lessons. She was to continue these activities until 1914. Both as a singer and as an actress, she made rapid progress during her first two seasons at the Metropolitan. "Miss Farrar," wrote Richard Aldrich on February 29, 1908, "has steadily grown in artistic power since she first came to the Metropolitan Opera House."[104] Her voice, which had increased in volume since her debut in 1906, was no longer forced in the upper register, and her acting was marked by a new simplicity. "Nowhere ... did she 'fuss,' accumulating and obtruding detail," reported Henry Parker of her Mimi on April 7, 1908, in Boston during the Metropolitan's spring tour. Of her singing he recorded that she "had no need to distort to gain her emotional ends. She gained them—and all the more clearly and compellingly—by singing that had beauty in itself and that kept obediently to the art of song. In a word, she was persuading her voice and not compelling it."[105] She had also developed sufficient histrionic maturity to portray the elegant demimondaine Violetta. But she was still unconvincing as the animalistic Nedda.

Starting with her debut, Geraldine Farrar was popular with the patrons of the Metropolitan Opera. They returned time and again to applaud her and spread their admiration of her artistry by word of mouth, as the press was doing in print. During Miss Farrar's first two seasons in New York, her public increased and intensified in its admiration for her. She was beginning to become immensely popular with the younger generation—particularly the women—whom the press referred to as "the sweet young things in the audience."[106] Mary F. Watkins wrote in the *Woman's Journal*:

> Her name became a household word—especially when the household contained a girl child—almost from the moment of her earliest arrival at our august Temple of Song. Every maiden in the land from subdeb to Aunt Sarah, saw herself and all her dreams and desires projected in the person of this hundred percent American prima donna. She became at once an ideal and an idol. Schoolgirls submitted to clamps upon their teeth in order to attain a feature of her beauty, schoolteachers risked pneumonia waiting outside the stage-door every time she sang.[107]

Miss Farrar was both a thrilling figure on stage and a glamorous personality off stage. This had also been true in Berlin where she was a favorite of the German Royal Family. Obligingly she lived up to the public's image of the "prima donna" covered in jewels and furs, with a Pekinese, a secretary, and two ladies' maids in tow. She even had the proverbial star's mother who accompanied her everywhere and carefully screened all who wished to meet her famous daughter. According to the authoress, Willa Cather, Miss Farrar was becoming a major box-office attraction who appealed to both the opera public and to those uninterested in classical music. Miss Cather claimed:

> She is the only artist—and she is always an artist—one can think of who might be able to hold through a performance the howling throngs that crowd the league—ball-grounds in Pittsburgh, St. Louis, Chicago, New York—and this not by singing "The Last Rose of Summer" or "The Suwanee River," as earlier prima donna used to do. She would play her own game in her own

way, but there is something in her legend, in her personality, in her beauty, and enthusiasm, that gets across to the American who is proverbially bored by the art in which she excels.[108]

Because of this ever increasing popularity with the general public, Miss Farrar attained six major concessions in her contract for the 1908-1909 season. First, she was to be granted a yearly increase in salary. Second, her guaranteed repertoire of operatic roles was to be expanded. Third, she gained prior rights to certain subscription performances in New York. Fourth, the Metropolitan Opera Company could not collect an agent's fee for her phonograph recordings or for her concert tours which commenced in 1909. Fifth, she could refuse the Metropolitan Opera's annual spring tour if it conflicted with her Berlin engagement. Sixth, she was given her own private dressing room to which she alone had the key.[109] This final right raised the hackles of her female colleagues since she was the first person in the history of the Metropolitan Opera to be so honored.[110]

With the conclusion of the 1907-1908 opera season, a new era commenced at the Metropolitan. The famous Italian impresario, Giulio Gatti Casazza, succeeded Heinrich Conried as general manager of America's leading opera company which he was to rule with the power of an autocrat for the next twenty-five years. Soon Geraldine Farrar was to become "the great Glamour Girl of her era,"[111] and "the Queen Bee of the Metropolitan."[112]

◆ THREE ◆

At the Metropolitan Opera, 1908–1915

On February 11, 1908, the ailing Heinrich Conried resigned as general manager of the Metropolitan Opera Company, and Giulio Gatti-Casazza and Andreas Dippel were appointed joint directors for the 1908-1909 season. Gatti-Casazza, the former director of Milan's famous La Scala Opera, was to have charge of the Italian works, and Dippel, a tenor with the Metropolitan since his debut in 1891 as well as an administrative assistant to Conried during the 1907-1908 season, was to have charge of the French and German. Originally, the Metropolitan's board of directors had selected Gatti-Casazza as sole executive of the company, but the boxholders had questioned the necessity of hiring a European manager when Dippel was already at hand. To pacify these wealthy patrons, the board offered Dippel the position of administrative manager and Gatti-Casazza that of general manager.

Dippel was popular with his colleagues, who trusted him, while Gatti-Casazza was "a stranger,"[1] who, it was rumored, intended to introduce "new singers" at the Metropolitan. When it was learned in November of 1908 that Gatti-Casazza's contract and not Dippel's had been extended for an additional two years, Geraldine Farrar, Emma Eames, Marcella Sembrich, Antonio Scotti, and Enrico Caruso, believing that their former associate would best protect their "artistic interests" against the wiles of Gatti-Casazza, wrote a letter to the board requesting that Dippel's contract also be renewed for a similar period of time. After due consideration, the board replied on December 2, 1908, that Gatti-Casazza was now "supreme executive head" of the Metropolitan and that Dippel was his subordinate. Dippel remained as administrative manager until his dismissal in 1910, when Gatti-Casazza was granted full managerial powers.

Sembrich and Eames retired from the Metropolitan at the end of the 1908-1909 season, and Caruso and Scotti claimed that they had signed the letter only for the sake of their colleagues. Miss Farrar "assumed all responsibility." Later, she learned to respect Gatti-Casazza and deeply regretted her part in the written challenge to his authority. Although he remained courteous and friendly to her, Miss Farrar maintained that he "never could quite forget this first sign of rebellion."[2]

At the time when Gatti-Casazza and Dippel were appointed joint directors of the Metropolitan, La Scala's leading conductor, Arturo Toscanini, consented to share the company's musical directorship with the German conductor and composer, Gustav Mahler. Mahler remained at the Metropolitan until his death in 1911, when Toscanini became the sole musical director until his resignation in 1915.

Toscanini was a demanding conductor whose authoritarian manner annoyed the equally determined Miss Farrar. During a rehearsal of *Madama Butterfly* in 1908, Toscanini stopped the young diva to correct a musical error, and she replied: "Maestro, you must conduct as I sing, for I am the star." Erupting in a fury, the famous conductor informed her that "the stars are in heaven,"[3] to which she reputedly retorted, "but the public pays to see my face, not your back." For many weeks thereafter, these two fiery personalities constantly clashed.

One evening, however, Miss Farrar consented to replace an indisposed Emmy Destinn as Butterfly, and Toscanini was to conduct the performance. Whenever Miss Farrar sang this role, the house was sold out, but since the public was unaware of the sudden change in cast, the auditorium that evening was only half-full. Toscanini smiled as he lifted his baton, reported Miss Farrar, who had proved to the Maestro that "there was also a human constellation."[4]

By the end of the spring tour in April 1909, Miss Farrar had realized she could profit from the genius of Arturo Toscanini, who, in turn, had learned to admire the high-spirited American singer's "independence of character."[5] Their relationship soon developed into a seven year romantic liaison until Miss Farrar apparently demanded that the Maestro leave his wife and children to marry her. Toscanini unexpectedly resigned in 1915 as principal conductor of the Metropolitan Opera and returned to Italy. The diva's name has also been linked with those of Germany's Crown Prince Wilhelm and Italy's Guglielmo Marconi who sent her roses for every performance.

During the 1908-1909 opera season, aside from repeating impersonations of Cio-Cio-San, Mimi, Marguerite, and Nedda, Miss Farrar added the roles of Micaela (Bizet's *Carmen*, 1908), Cherubino (Mozart's *Le nozze di Figaro*, 1909), and Manon (Massenet's *Manon*, 1909) to her Metropolitan repertoire.

On December 3, 1908, she sang her first Micaela in a revival of Bizet's *Carmen*. The production featured the Spanish gypsy of Maria Gay, whose realistic seduction scenes, throwing of orange juice at her operatic lover, Enrico Caruso, as well as her kicking, spitting, and nose-blowing, thoroughly shocked the beholders. "Vulgar and commonplace" was the general consensus of Miss Gay's interpretation. But Miss Farrar's portrayal of Micaela was praised as "something more than a lay figure."[6] Her interpretation of the innocent, sweet but rather dull village maiden, whom Don José had deserted for the fascinating gypsy, was less passive than usual. Micaela participated in the third act scuffle between José and Carmen, instead of wringing her hands on the sidelines. Although Miss Farrar's portrayal was animated, it was not exaggerated, because, according to William J. Henderson, she displayed "uncommon reserve."[7] Her singing of Bizet's lyrical music was termed "charming"[8] by the *New York Times*. Due to the press and public's disapproval of Maria Gay's interpretation, the production was withdrawn from the repertory at the end of the season. The opera was not revived at the Metropolitan until 1915, when Geraldine Farrar assumed the role of Carmen.

Miss Farrar's first performance of Cherubino on January 13, 1909, again allowed her to display her comic talent, which had been revealed the previous year in another Mozart role: Zerlina. Mozart's vivacious and amorous page, who flirted with every woman in the palace, was ideally suited to this elegant, slender, and nimble young singing actress. "Thoroughly boyish," wrote one critic, "she stood and walked like a boy, used her arms like a boy and there was an almost convincing boyishness in the slim grace of her figure."[9] When disguised in a woman's dress to escape the Count's jealous fury over his page's suspected love affair with the Countess, Miss Farrar was ludicrously awkward in the wearing of female apparel. She assumed a strident walk, in character with a country lass. Once she had discarded her disguise, however, and again appeared as a boy, she resumed her former grace and courtliness.[10] Employing "gesture sparingly,"[11] she resisted the temptation to overact. Vocally, the medium tessitura of the role enabled Miss Farrar to exhibit the rich middle register of her voice. "Every tone was perfect," claimed one critic, who added that "only the violin could match her phrasing and shading."[12] Although she rarely performed the roles of Cherubino and Zerlina during the remainder of her career, Miss Farrar was an outstanding Mozartian stylist.

Three weeks after her first performance of Cherubino, she sang the role of Manon on February 3, 1909, with Enrico Caruso as her lover, Des Grieux, in a revival of Massenet's *Manon*. Although she was not in good voice that evening, she still managed to captivate the public and critics with her histrionic ability and personal beauty. "What Signor Caruso did by his singing," wrote Henry Krehbiel in the *New York Tribune*, "Miss Farrar achieved by her appearance and acting."[13] "She is like an eighteenth century shepherdess, a figure from a Watteau picture and as fragile as a bit of Dresden china,"[14] rhapsodized another New York music critic. Her dramatic talent was gradually coming to the fore, as had already been noted by the press in 1907 for her portrayal of Cio-Cio-San. In later performances of Manon, she would also be commended for the beauty of her singing—especially after she had restudied the role with Toscanini in 1912.

As in Berlin, Miss Farrar's Manon became one of her most popular Met-

Geraldine Farrar as Tosca, 1909.

ropolitan portrayals. Over the next thirteen years, she was to perform it thirty-nine times, frequently to the Des Grieux of Enrico Caruso. Miss Farrar admired the superb vocal artistry of that famous Italian tenor, admitting that she "was torn between trying to listen to him, and yet to give [her] role its immediate attention."[15] Unlike Miss Farrar, Caruso was not histrionically endowed and, according to the American diva, "couldn't do love interest." "You sing," she often told him, "and we'll drape ourselves around you,"[16] which she did until his death terminated their successful and harmonious partnership in 1921.

At the conclusion of the Metropolitan Opera's spring tour in April 1909, Miss Farrar left for Europe. In addition to her singing lessons and Berlin performances, she studied the role of Puccini's Tosca with Sarah Bernhardt. Illica and Giacoso's libretto for Puccini's opera was based upon Victorien Sardou's *Tosca*, which the French playwright had written in 1887 for Madame Bernhardt, who soon made it one of her greatest successes. Since the opera's premiere in 1900 at the Rome Opera starring the Rumanian soprano Hariclea Darclee the vocally dramatic and theatrically emotional role of Floria Tosca had been associated with prima donna of heroic proportions and rather ponderous, statuesque movements—often referred to as the "grand manner." Miss Farrar's own slight figure and ebullient temperament were diametrically opposite to those of the dramatic sopranos, Milka Ternina and Emma Eames, who had preceded her in this role at the Metropolitan. She realized that her portrayal of the Roman diva would have to differ from their grandiloquent interpretations. She wrote of this decision:

> Knowing that my independence and determination to attack this tragic role would invite severe criticism, after these heroic portrayals had established firmly beautiful ideals, I resolved to submit my ideas to that one great and unique-authority, Sarah Bernhardt, for whom this great drama was written.
>
> I told her frankly my eagerness to essay a role which no doubt would invite discouragement among my greatest admirers, but nevertheless, I intended to make my departure from so-called previous traditions.... Then I explained what I wanted to portray.
>
> My Tosca shall be a young, slender woman, passionately in love with her painter sweetheart, a great singer, if you will, but above all, a devoted, a daring woman—no libertine (as is too often supposed), else that terrible proposal from Scarpia would not inspire her to loathing, frantic despair, and final ferocious murder—in my opinion the dramatic climax and the real awakening of Tosca.
>
> The first act, therefore, should be all sunshine, joyous abandon, gentle femininity, in contrast to the second, when Tosca must pass to a terrified, despairing, demented creature, stopping at nothing to save her lover, and her honor from the lust of the terrible Scarpia ... a wan, broken woman, in the

third act, that only intensifies her agony when her lover is really shot, and she hurls herself from the castle ramparts to death, and—who knows?

The divine Sarah did approve, and lo! in a performance in my honor, this wonderful, ageless genius enacted Tosca as I had dreamed her—eager, youthful, passionate, tragic, hopelessly despairing.[17]

After this special performance in the spring of 1909 at Paris' Théâtre Sarah Bernhardt, Miss Farrar went into the famous actress' dressing-room and "picked up innumerable hints and ideas for her own portrayal."[18] Madame Bernhardt consented to coach the young American singer in this role, and Miss Farrar recalled that "we went over the part scene by scene. She read the lines in her way, and I sang them in mine. The comparison was my lesson."[19] Miss Farrar asked Madame Bernhardt to demonstrate "how she histrionically interpreted certain phrases of the role." She did not copy the actions of the actress who had advised her to assimilate rather than to imitate.[20] Of the opening scene, Miss Farrar wrote:

> I greatly admired the composition of the first act where a huge Gothic chair, placed well down to the center of the stage, allowed a variety of plastic movements and made more of a languishing appeal in the duel of the two lovers, in their ardent embrace, as well as a picturesque frame for my slender form. In adopting this departure for my own assumption of the role, she [Bernhardt] said sadly, "Pray God you never had to do so for the same reason as I." And then I realized that her injured knee no longer permitted her to stand erect without some rest, or relief at frequent intervals.[21]

At the beginning of the 1909-1910 season, she sang the role of Charlotte on November 16, 1909, in a revival of Massenet's *Werther*. It was the first of the semi-weekly performances of opera and ballet to be presented in the New Theater on Central Park West. This theatre was created to house a dramatic repertory company, under the management of the idealistic and aristocratic young producer, Winthrop Ames. The Metropolitan had agreed to perform a series of nineteen lyric operas, three ballets and one pantomime, which were too intimate for the vast auditorium of the Opera House. At the end of the 1909-1910 opera season, the acoustics of the New Theater were declared unsuitable for serious music.[22] The Metropolitan Opera Company ceased performances there. Miss Farrar added her own criticisms by stating that this theatre "completely foiled every attempt at operatic success. One could neither hear nor see ... and when a pretty girl can't entice the tired business man, it is a poor show place indeed."[23]

Although the New Theater project was a failure, Miss Farrar was successful in her portrayal of the beautiful and placid young Charlotte, torn between duty to her husband, Albert, and love for her cousin, Werther, who shoots himself after her rejection of his amorous protestations. "She looked in the first act as if she had tripped out of a Romney," wrote one reviewer, "and the second as if she were a vivified Gainsborough.... Miss Farrar is an actress."[24] Concerning her singing, another critic reported that "her chameleonic voice was not only beautiful, it changed color with every line of the poem."[25] The darkly hued timbre of Miss Farrar's voice was well suited to Massenet's music, which lies in the middle register. With the abandonment of the New Theater by the Metropolitan Opera Company, *Werther* was dropped from the repertory after only five performances during the 1909-1910 season. Miss Farrar never again sang the role of Charlotte.

On November 22, 1909, she performed her first Tosca. Puccini's temperamental Roman diva was to become one of her most popular portrayals. During the next twelve years, she sang the role fifty-two times at the Metropolitan Opera House and nineteen times on the company's tours.

In the first act of Puccini's opera, the famous Roman diva, Floria Tosca, visits her lover, the artist and revolutionary, Mario Cavaradossi, while he is painting a portrait of the Magdalene in the Church of Sant' Andrea della Valle. Overhearing him whisper to someone as she enters, Tosca immediately suspects her lover of having a secret rendezvous with another woman—perhaps the mysterious blond model for the portrait. Finally, convinced by his protestations of love and faithfulness, she leaves the church. Cavaradossi then advises the concealed escaped political prisoner, Cesare Angelotti, with whom he had been talking as Tosca entered, to hide in his villa on the outskirts of Rome. After they leave, Baron Scarpia, the chief of police, appears in pursuit of Angelotti. When Tosca returns in search of her lover, the Baron rouses her jealousy. He shows her a fan belonging to Angelotti's blond sister, who accidentally had left it in the church while concealing clothes for her brother in a family crypt near Cavaradossi's easel.

During this opening act, Miss Farrar was exquisitely beautiful in a sable trimmed vermilion and gray gown. She also wore an elaborate bonnet with Bird of Paradise plumes. In her right hand she held an elegant gold headed walking stick, while in her left arm she carried a bouquet of red and white roses. She was not the traditionally imperious jealous Roman prima donna of past productions, but was, rather a charming, coquettish, slightly spoiled young woman, completely absorbed in her love for the handsome and ardent painter. Miss Farrar presented the first act in a new light, so far as operatic performances of the play were concerned. She made it more of a love story between Tosca and the young artist than had ever been done before. Neither did she overemphasize the diva's jealousy of the blond-haired figure in Cavaradossi's painting. Miss Farrar's Tosca was more hurt and petulant with her lover than vindictive and arrogant. She was not a practiced woman of the world, who had had many lovers, but was a young woman deeply in love with only one man. Her display of feeling was more intense when Scarpia aroused her jealousy with the fan, but even here she exhibited less wrath than dismay. Although her lover's constancy was momentarily in doubt, Miss Farrar's Tosca was more peevish than angry. The diva was a very moving figure as she left the chapel weeping.

The opera's second act takes place in the private chambers of Baron Scarpia, who condemns Mario to death for aiding Angelotti. Tosca offers the Baron money to spare her lover's life. He only laughs and demands her love instead. In desperation, she murders him.

"Miss Farrar," wrote Henry T. Parker of the *Boston Transcript* "makes the second act a long, hectic, goading frenzy."[26] Unlike the Toscas of Milka Ternina and Emma Eames, who regally avoided Scarpia's passionate advances, Miss Farrar wrenched herself from her ardent pursuer's grip after a long and violent struggle. Instead of singing the intensely emotional aria "vissi d'arte," "pathetically" and "poignantly"[27] standing down at the footlights, Miss Farrar's heroine sang the aria from the sofa, where she had just torn herself away from the Baron's attempted embraces. "Miss Farrar's Tosca," commented Parker, "so colored her tones that she seemed to be recalling some hollow and ghastly image of another self out of the surrounding blackness."[28] No longer was this aria a set piece stopping the action at a crucial moment, because the young singing actress "brought it in with so much skill that it appeared vital, necessary to her psychic unfoldment."[29] Following the aria, she crossed the floor on her knees,[30] imploring the villainous chief of police to free Mario who was being tortured in an adjoining room. Upon seeing her bleeding lover, Miss Farrar's Tosca "fondl[ed] him wildly" instead of emulating the actions of her predecessors who had been "content to bend passionately over Mario."[31] Finally, she agreed to give herself to the Baron as the price of Cavaradossi's freedom. Exhausted in mind and body, she staggered to the table and grasped a glass of wine. Slowly sipping the liquid, her eyes fell on the table knife, and a look of "murderous delight"[32] flashed across her face as she decided to stab her tormentor. Quickly she seized the weapon and menacingly brandished it at the back of Scarpia, who sat at his desk writing a letter of safe conduct to permit the diva and her lover to flee Rome forever. Enveloped in a magnificent skin-tight, white-satin gown, she waited, tightly clenching the knife to her erect and rigid body, until Scarpia had crossed the room. Then with "steel-like precision,"[33] she drove the weapon into his body. Her subsequent actions were described by a Boston critic in these words: "One of the finest pieces of acting which Miss Farrar did was her show of sudden realization of the passport. The quick search for it, and the hesitation and awe with which she drew it from his fingers."[34] She lit the candles and reverently placed two of them at the dead man's head.

After putting a crucifix on his breast, she blew out the remaining candles and made a "shuddering exit."[35]

In the last act, Tosca joyously reveals the letter of safe conduct to Mario. He is to be freed after a mock execution on the roof of the prison, Castel Sant' Angelo. After the firing squad leaves, the heroine discovers that her lover is dead. She leaps to her death from the parapet as Scarpia's assistants enter to arrest her.

"Her grief over the body of her lover was touching," reported a critic, "and most realistic was her leap to death over the ramparts."[36] Another member of the press, on the other hand, was not so enthused over the fatal leap as was his colleague and wrote: "The wall wobbled when Farrar jumped off—and one knew she was climbing down a ladder back of the scene when she ought to be floating in the moat."[37]

The public acclaimed Miss Farrar's first performance of Tosca. But although the press generally commended her emotional portrayal of the Roman diva in the melodramatic second and third acts, they tended to disapprove of her first act interpretation in which she "was inclined ... to make Tosca rather petty and petulant."[38] "She was an ingénue Tosca," commented William J. Henderson, "very young, very girlish, very naive and quite petulantly jealous.... No one could have guessed that this little Tosca was going to commit a desperate deed in the second act, for Toscas are made of sterner stuff."[39] Also, Henderson and Parker thought the plumes on her bonnet distracting and overly elaborate. "She has world conquering hats," wrote Henderson, who described her latest headdress as "a hat with feathers. They were eloquent feathers. They were prophetic feathers. They pointed north, east, west, and west-soul-west a quarter west, and neither the eye of the spectator nor Tosca could steer by them."[40]

Aside from the various criticisms of Miss Farrar's costuming and histrionic interpretation of the first act, there were those, such as Parker, Henderson, and Aldrich, who felt that the role of Floria Tosca was vocally too dramatic for the young singer. They claimed that it resulted in a reversion to her former tendency of forcing the upper register. "Tosca's music in the second act," stated Parker, "is plainly written for a voice of larger body, coarser timbre and more enduring and 'carrying' power than is Miss Farrar's ... the upper range of her voice became shrill and thin."[41] Henderson even stated that "in the upper register, in the clarion fortes called for by the score, it approached perilously near a scream."[42]

She was also criticized for her frequent use of a "hoarsely spoken"[43] parlando during moments of dramatic intensity in the second and third acts. According to Henderson, they were "uttered in sepulchre and covered tones and with nerveless manner."[44] "This is now the last device of singers in the 'advanced' modern style of opera," added Richard Aldrich, "and is supposed to add the final touch of dramatic power. It is not, however, necessary for Miss Farrar to copy the methods singers of gifts and powers inferior to her own."[45] Whether the critics fully approved of her interpretation or not, they were agreed that Geraldine Farrar was a superb singing actress. One critic wrote:

> Geraldine Farrar brought us a wonderfully vivid and fresh Floria Tosca. Miss Farrar's Tosca is all her own. She endows it with a realism, in other words a humanism that may be favorably associated with the drama, independent of its musical garb. Histrionically Miss Farrar is no novice. Her acting bespeaks an intimate study of the role, a study in which both genius and intellect are united. The ill-fated Roman singer was made to express those elemental emotions which Sardou intended for her. In the first act Miss Farrar was the capricious and willful sweetheart, in the second act, the grief-torn and, self-sacrificing heroine, and in the last act the tragic and central figure in a terrible combination of fate and circumstance. Every mood was delineated with sympathy. She rose to towering heights in the several intense scenes.[46]

Another member of the press commented: "On the dramatic side, her Tosca is the finest of a series of highly individual performances. Without a voice, she would still have the possibility of a brilliant career in the theatre."[47]

It was generally known that Geraldine Farrar had studied this role with the famous Sarah Bernhardt, and many members of the press mentioned this in their articles. The critic for *Musical America* wrote: "It was in her acting that Miss Farrar contributed something thrillingly new and noteworthy. It is said that she had modeled her impersonation after that of Bernhardt, and much of the action and 'business' which she introduced made apparent the tutelage of the French actress. It is not too much to say that at several moments of tragedy, as when the sight of the knife first suggested to her the slaying of Scarpia, her action brought her model to mind, and, further than that it would be difficult for praise to go."[48]

In a similar vein, another reviewer stated: "The expression of love and anguish, not only in her face, but in all her gestures, when the tortured man is brought in, recalled Sarah Bernhardt at her best ... while we have had some great Toscas, she is the only one who reminds one of the great Sarah in the second act; and, not by identical methods, but by the amazing power of expression, facial and vocal."[49]

Not only was Madame Bernhardt's instruction mentioned by members of the New York press, but it was also referred to by the Chicago critic Karleton Hackett, who wrote: "It is understood that the Divine Sarah herself laid bare her secrets for this act [Act II], if it were so she would have been proud had she witnessed the transcendent pantomimic powers of her artistic offspring."[50] Geraldine Farrar had proved an able pupil, and Madame Bernhardt sent her the following message: "To the adorable Farrar, may the sun always shine on your way, my young friend. May good fortune be your guardian angel, may all the lyres always sing in our [sic] voice."[51]

Always striving to improve her impersonations, Miss Farrar apparently agreed with those critics of her first act portrayal, because one year later a reviewer wrote: "Miss Farrar has greatly improved her interpretation of the role, which she sang last season for the first time. She has lost much of that childish petulance which debased the part in the first act from the realm of the violent jealousy a great woman might show into one of a spoiled, petted young girl who knew not life's big moments at their real worth. She was much more serious and carried more poise in the first act and her second was the work of a great actress."[52]

Still another commented: "Miss Farrar not only has no respect for traditions when they are senseless, but has a way of changing her own conceptions, improving them from year to year. This change and growth made themselves felt last night in many details ... one felt a certain maturity in her conception which was not there last year. At the end of the first act her excess of real jealousy, contrasted with the earlier coquettish jealousy expressed to her lover—an emotion slyly stimulated by Scarpia—was a rare piece of good acting."[53]

Also, as Miss Farrar matured in her portrayal of the Roman diva, she attempted to refrain from forcing her voice during passages of vocal and dramatic intensity. "She sang with warmth and beauty of voice,"[54] reported *Musical America* of Miss Farrar's Tosca on January 4, 1913. According to the former Metropolitan Opera tenor, Frederick Jagel, who as a student had attended many of Miss Farrar's performances at the Metropolitan, her singing of the famous second act aria was "the most appealing I have ever heard—bar none."[55] That she never completely overcame her inclination to allow the emotion of the moment to override her vocal control, however, is attested to in her statement: "Tosca always offered a disastrous temptation to unleash temperament to the detriment of vocal discretion; the results were often irregular and they generally favored the temperamental side!"[56]

On November 13, 1917, the soprano's histrionic and vocal talents were put to a severe test. One half hour before curtain time, Miss Farrar was informed that Ricardo Martin, her leading tenor for that evening's performance, had been taken ill and was to be replaced by Paul Althouse, who had never sung the role publicly. They had not rehearsed together, and Miss Farrar only had time to say, "Take my hand when you're in doubt, and I'll tell you what to do."[57] She "not only sang and acted her part but whispered instructions to Althouse as to where he should stand and how she should [sic] move in good season for him to be ready. She did not miss a single cue, either her own or Cavaradossi's."[58] Miss Farrar saved the performance and confirmed a claim made in 1901 by a Berlin critic that nothing could shake her confidence and repose on stage.[59] Tosca was Miss Farrar's last new role for the 1909-1910 opera season.

After spring and summer operatic performances in Paris and Berlin, followed by her first major American concert tour in the fall, she scored a great personal success at the Metropolitan Opera on December 28, 1910, as the Goose Girl in the world premiere of Englebert Humperdinck's fairy-tale opera, *Königskinder*. Humperdinck, head of the Master School for Musical Composition in Berlin, was renowned for his first opera, *Hansel and Gretel*, composed in 1893. Aside from his operatic works, he also wrote incidental music for plays presented at the Munich Court Theatre, as well as Berlin's Deutsches Theater, Kammerspiele, and Volksbühne. He had composed the musical accompaniment for Elsa Bernstein's *Ernst Rosmer*, which had its premiere in 1897 in Munich. Fascinated by this fairy-tale, Humperdinck eventually developed his incidental music into its present operatic form and named his composition *Königskinder*.

Geraldine Farrar as the Goose Girl with her flock, 1916.

This romantic fairy-tale concerns the adventures of a beautiful Goose Girl, who has been put under the spell of a wicked Witch. The Goose Girl and her geese have been forced to live in the German forest of Hella with the witch. One spring a wandering Prince finds the young maiden and begs her to follow him into the world. Although she has fallen in love with the handsome stranger, the spell prevents her from leaving the forest. In frustration, her royal lover throws his crown at her feet and continues on his journey. Eventually, the Goose Girl escapes into the world and goes in search of her young princely admirer. Soon, she arrives at the city of Hellabrunn, whose inhabitants have been informed by the witch that the first person to enter the city gate after the stroke of noon during the Hella Festival should become their ruler. At the twelfth stroke of the clock, the gates swing open and reveal the Goose Girl surrounded by her flock and wearing the prince's golden crown upon her head. The young Prince, who has been working as a swineherd in the city, rushes to embrace her. The enraged and disappointed people of Hellabrunn chase them from the city and burn the witch at the stake. Hungry and lost, the children wander through the forest, until one winter day, they arrive back at the witch's hut but now inhabited by a woodchopper and a Broommaker. In exchange for the prince's crown, the Broommaker gives the young pair a poisoned loaf left by the witch. Wrapped in each other's arms, the Prince and the Goose Girl die in the drifting snow. The children of Hellabrunn, led by a minstrel who had believed the young couple to be the rightful rulers of the city, discover the bodies and bear them away for burial.

Humperdinck's lyrically declamatory and often folk song–like music, as well as Elsa Bernstein's simple fairy-tale figure of the ill starred Goose Girl were ideally suited to the talents of Miss Farrar. Concerning "this sweetest of roles,"[60] she wrote: "What woman had not rather be a Goose Girl in a dreamy fairy-tale, than a Tosca in black, bloody tragedy, or a heartbroken Madame Butterfly, lying dead among the cherry blossoms? ... I love the simple story, the ineffably sweet music, the real children on the stage—and the geese. There is no great psychic stress, nothing neurotic, nothing sensational, nothing exotic or unwholesome. Perfect simplicity breathes in every line. It is human and lovely.... Pure pathos takes the place of tragedy."[61]

Although the Kaiser had wanted *Königskinder* for the Berlin Opera, the Metropolitan had requested it first, and as Professor Humperdinck commented; "You were the first to ask for 'The Children of Kings' and that is all there is to that."[62] The famous German composer was present at the rehearsals and the premiere, but, unlike Puccini in 1907, he refrained from advising Miss Farrar on how to interpret her role in his opera.

Geraldine Farrar was enthused over her new role and stated that "the

Goose Girl is a lovely, innocent figure from a fairy-tale, the embodiment of all that is good and pure. It is not an easy part to act, for the singer must lay aside all her sophistication."[63] Because the Goose Girl was "simple, and direct in outline, a beautiful, legendary figure of fairyland appeal," the diva had to refrain from "any extraordinary effects, or theatrical tricks, and reside in her feeling of spiritual faith and tranquility."[64] In an interview, Miss Farrar commented that "it is such a relief after the modern sophisticated operas, with their complicated, sensual themes. It was, too, a great delight to me to find how easily I fell into the spirit of the work.... And then the story is so dramatic, and to me the dramatic is always of first appeal."[65]

It was this appeal of the dramatic that caused Miss Farrar to request a flock of real geese on stage instead of some mechanical creatures suggested by Professor Humperdinck and the stage manager. Miss Farrar said, "I felt the opera would lose much of its atmosphere if I had to lead in a crowd of such uninteresting objects. I felt sure that real geese could be taught to behave, and I said so."[66] Philip Crispano, assistant property man, purchased twelve white geese and two gray ganders from the Gansevoort Market in New York.

The birds were ensconced in the property room on the top floor of the Metropolitan Opera's storehouse. Another assistant property man, George Henry, became their trainer. He had a tank of water installed in the back part of the property room so that his feathered "artists" could paddle and float between lessons in stage deportment. The long-suffering Henry taught the hungry geese to eat out of his hand and to obey commands by rewarding them with kernels of corn. One goose became quite tame, and Miss Farrar was going to place the golden crown around his neck in the first act. But the bird squawked so loudly in a rehearsal that Professor Humperdinck decided a "property" goose would have to be shoved out from the wings at the appropriate moment.

Miss Farrar related that the birds were not given anything to eat until they came upon the stage and were "pretty hungry by that time, and in a bag at my waist I have a store of corn. I can tell you those geese know that corn is there, and they don't leave me for an instant. Whenever I want them to come specially near I surreptitiously drop a few grains, and they come, and there is no hesitancy about their coming, either. When I want them to go I close my pouch and a stage hand in the wings holds out a handful of corn. It doesn't take many seconds then for them to get after the new bait."[67]

A reporter at one of the rehearsals wrote: "They came out promptly when Miss Farrar clapped her hands and recited from the score 'Come here, come near. How do you like me?' They turned and nodded their heads when she sang 'Look at me, on every side. Am I not fair?' They toddled about with a naïveté that any soprano might envy while the two kings' children sang their first love duet, and when Miss Farrar clapped her hands and cried, 'Go, you have taken him from me,' they shambled in to the wings without a moment's hesitation."[68]

Professor Humperdinck was heard to remark, "I suppose people will come to see my geese instead of coming to hear my music."[69] But Geraldine Farrar commented that she knew "of no more charming moments in any opera than those in which the Goose Girl stands on the stage, at the beginning of the second act, with her geese—these few exquisite moments of silence against the web of instrumental music spun by the orchestra—and she sings not a phrase! The power of magnetic conveyance of illusion."[70] Unlike Humperdinck, Miss Farrar saw that the production's oral and visual elements supported and enhanced each other.

Aside from the novelty of live geese on the stage, there also was a chorus of forty young children in the second and last acts. Apparently, Miss Farrar was impressed with their enthusiasm, stating publicly, that they were "all of them little actors and actresses, and all doing their best to make the opera succeed."[71] Shortly after the premiere, the Society for the Prevention of Cruelty to Children informed the Metropolitan Opera that, although young people could appear on stage, they could not sing in the opera. According to the law, children with special permits were allowed to act, but not to sing and dance on stage. Many tears were shed by the children, but from then on the women's chorus sang their music while they stood mutely by.[72]

As usual, Miss Farrar took great care in the selection of her costumes. She discussed them with a reporter, saying:

> "I see that you are looking at my costume, and wondering why it is silk crepe. Well, it looks like wool from the front. I've had three costumes made for the part, and none of them would do at all. You see, if wool is used, then it doesn't hang well; neither does linen. Besides, both these materials would muss while I am lying about on the bank and sitting at the pump.
>
> This final costume is none other than my third act *Tannhäuser* costume....[73] I had the sleeves cut off, the neck changed, the bottom made ragged and the material dyed.... Now, this is my last act dress."
>
> Miss Farrar pulled from the wall a robe of green, covered with straws. The leaves were fashioned of felt and carefully dyed in reds, purples, and yellows.
>
> "Frau Humperdinck asked me about my clothes for the part. When I told her that my first act dress was of silk crepe, I could see that she shuddered a bit. And then, without thinking exactly how it sounded, I described my last act costume as being made of Autumn leaves fastened together with straws. A few moments afterwards I realized that she must have visualized such a costume as Eve might have worn after the feast of apples."[74]

On December 28, 1910, there were many empty seats at the premiere of Humperdinck's *Königskinder* because the opera had not generated much interest with the general public. One viewer recalled: "Those who attended, however, witnessed one of the most delicate, charming and winsome characterizations ever seen on the American stage."[75] Miss Farrar wrote that "when the curtain rose upon the idyllic forest scene, with the Goose Girl in the grass, the geese unconcernedly picking their way about, now and again spreading snowy wings, unafraid, the house was simply delighted and applauded long and vigorously."[76] At the end of the opera, the diva received a tumultuous ovation for her portrayal. She also caused a sensation by appearing for her final solo curtain call with a fluffy white goose in her arms.

The press concurred that the Goose Girl was one of Miss Farrar's most skillfully rendered characterizations. One reporter wrote:

> Even Madama Butterfly is not a more congenial or touching role for Miss Farrar than this new one, which suits her both vocally and dramatically. From her first appearance under a great tree, rosy, beautiful, delicately blooming in spite of the Witch's cruelty, to her last under the same tree, when fate had been even more cruel than the Witch, and the lovely child was changed to a pale, sad-eyed woman, she touches every heart. Miss Farrar conveys very beautifully this mental development from girlhood to womanhood through love and suffering, and, weak as she has become from hunger and cold, her courage still holds out to cheer her beloved one. It would be difficult to decide where she is most winning, in the first act, when she is tending her geese and feeding them, or later, when she sees a man and a lover for the first time in her life; in the second, when she appears at the gate, crowned with her face glowing with an inner light; or in the third, when, almost dropping from exhaustion, she dances in the snow in an attempt to make the King's Son forget their misfortunes.[77]

Another critic stated: "Miss Farrar as the Goose Girl was truly what everyone expected—a positive marvel. No one could image a more beautiful characterization than she made of this simpleminded wonderfully poetic part. Not for a moment did she try to exploit her beautiful voice, in every instant she lived and breathed and sang the real character of the Goose Girl. One forgot that she was singing and only absorbed and appreciated the marvelous beauty of the sincere expression of this simple herder of the geese."[78]

Still another reporter wrote: "Miss Farrar has done nothing during her entire Metropolitan career that surpasses her Goose Girl. Every changing mood with which the three acts are filled she depicted with unerring ability by gesture, facial expression and subtle modulations of the voice."[79]

Her second act entrance caused the most comment, since the public and press were "distinctly thrilled at the sight of the great gates of the town swinging wide at the last stroke of noon to disclose the expected queen—

the Goose Girl clear in the cool sunshine against the ground of grassy hill and driving cloud."[80] Of this same scene, another reporter declared: "What a picture she makes when the gates are thrown open and she stands there, in the strong sunlight, with her attendant flock, and the golden fields as a background, while the people who have been awaiting a prince howl in derision."[81] Even the *Tribune's* staid Henry Krehbiel enthusiastically recorded that "with what exquisite charm Miss Farrar was likely to invest so romantic a heroine the artist's admirers might easily have guessed; but it is doubtful if any imagination ever reached the figure which she embodied. She was a vision of tender loveliness, as perfect in poetical conception as in execution. Memories of the picture which she presented walking through the massive town gates followed and surrounded by her white flock will die only with the generation that witnessed it."[82]

Memories of this beautiful moment did live on, because nearly thirty years later, Oscar Thompson recalled that "unforgettable is the picture she made standing in the huge town gateway of the second act, with flowing golden hair to her knees, on her head a simple golden crown such as a child would make of paper, and her flock of white geese crowding about her."[83]

There were no dissenting voices among the members of the press concerning Miss Farrar's vocal and dramatic portrayal of the Goose Girl. In this role, she avoided any tendency to overact or to force her voice. "Miss Farrar has never reached the note of sincerity that she does in this role," summarized the *Musical Leader*, "and the simplicity of her dramatic action leaves her voice in its natural beautiful condition. She shows what many have long suspected, that her great powers could only manifest themselves when she eliminated the personal element and gives herself, her true self, to the character as she does in this part."[84]

For the next six years, Miss Farrar's eloquent portrayal resulted in *Königskinder* becoming one of the Metropolitan's most popular productions. But in 1917, along with all German works, it was dropped from the company's repertory, so that "the public might rest assured that it [would] contain nothing to cause the least offense to the most patriotic American."[85] Miss Farrar's thirty-nine performances of Humperdinck's lyrical heroine made such "an indelible impression"[86] that even in 1954, Helen Noble, a former Metropolitan Opera staff member, wrote: "Many times I have wished that I might have heard Farrar do *Königskinder*. She must have given a remarkable performance in this opera, because for years I heard people at the Met rave about it. They would say to me: 'Oh, Helen, if you could only have heard Farrar as the little Goose Girl! She was wonderful! She was so lovely!' It must have been so, and how I regret that it was before my time."[87]

During a matinee of *Königskinder* in 1912, apparently two of the geese interpreted the orchestral sounds "for the call of the wild."[88] Just as the Prince was about to reveal his life's story to the Goose Girl, the two birds broke away from the flock and headed towards the prompter's box. Without hesitating a moment, Miss Farrar pursued the delinquent geese. After grabbing one by the wings and the other around the middle, the diva carried them into the wings and soundly wacked them with her herding stick.

Three months after the world premiere of Humperdinck's *Königskinder*, on March 29, 1911, Miss Farrar sang the role of Ariane in the first American performance of Paul Dukas' opera, *Ariane et Barbe-Bleue*. The libretto is based on a symbolist drama of the same name by the Belgian playwright, Maurice Maeterlinck. In 1897 Dukas had attained fame with his symphonic scherzo, "L'Apprentri sorcier." Ten years later, his only operatic composition *Ariane et Barbe-Bleue*, was produced at both the Opéra Comique and the Paris Opéra.

Ariane et Barbe-Bleue concerns the attempts of Bluebeard's latest bride to liberate his former five wives from their dungeon prison. Bluebeard has given Ariane the keys to seven rooms in her new home but has informed her that she may only open six of them. After having opened the doors of the six rooms full of jewels, she unlocks the seventh door, behind which are the lamenting former wives of her cruel husband. Ariane leads them up out of the dungeon into the sunlight, where they joyously bedeck themselves in jewels. Suddenly, they are interrupted by rebellious peasants, who drag in a wounded and bound Bluebeard. Left in the custody of Ariane, the bigamist believes that his wives will kill him for his cruelty. Instead, they slavishly care for him refusing to follow Ariane out into the world and freedom.

Like Maeterlinck's play, Dukas' opera is a satire on the feminist movement. But by minimizing the script's subliminal symbolism, the drama can also be performed as a fairytale. Miss Farrar chose the latter interpretation, since she had little interest in or sympathy with suffragettism[89] and its zealots. Their fanatically intense and often vehement manner was completely alien to her own. Explaining her decision to a reporter for the *New York Times*, she said:

> "There are two ways of regarding Ariane.... One can take every sentence, every action, to have a symbolic meaning, and the work becomes an allegorical satire on the feminist question. It isn't exactly a suffragette matter, it is larger than that. The question is whether women aren't as intelligent as men, equal to them in every way; whether they should not be allowed to think for themselves, to know the truth, and to proceed logically from it. One gathers, however, from the play that Ariane is the exceptional woman. The other way of looking at it is simply to consider the drama as a fairy story, and a very pretty one at that, with forbidden doors, and cascades of jewels, all of the action taking place in a faraway castle in a faraway land." Miss Farrar said that for stage purposes this should be her conception of the play.[90]

Maeterlinck and Dukas conceived of Ariane as a zealous feminist, who escapes from the stronghold of male domination after having failed to convert the other women to her viewpoint. Miss Farrar regarded her as simply an unusually beautiful, highly intelligent, and extremely curious woman. Concerning her equally viable interpretation of this rather ambivalent role, Miss Farrar commented:

> There are some women ... who are so great in themselves that no matter how weak they may be physically they are able to conquer everybody about them. Ariane was such a woman. She not only had great physical beauty, which is often mentioned in the piece, but great intellectual beauty. She was never afraid of Blue Beard, and she never was in love with him. It seems at times as if she were not interested in him but only in those women. Sometimes I wonder if it were not mere feminine curiosity which led her through that forbidden door, only she was more courageous than the other curious women.
>
> The drama may also be considered as a tract on how to hold a husband once you have him. It may be observed that although Ariane goes and the other women remain that Ariane is the only one of them whom Blue Beard wants.
>
> Why did she marry him? It may have been a marriage for position or freedom or what not, but it is certain that she does not love him, and from the moment that she enters his palace she has but one purpose in mind, and that is to discover all his secrets, to know the truth at all costs. She frees her foolish sisters, to no avail. The point is that they can only free themselves through themselves. When she sees that they do not want to be free, she has no further interest in them. Blue Beard remains unchanged....
>
> It is very sad when you stop to think that probably in a week all these five women will be back in their subterranean vault and Blue Beard will bring back another wife.[91]

Ariane et Barbe-Bleue is not so much an opera, as a symphonic work with chorus and solo voices. At first, Miss Farrar rejected the role of Ariane as unsingable.[92] Its low vocal tessitura lies mainly in the middle and lower registers, with only occasional ascents into the normal soprano upper register. Finally, she agreed to sing the part, after Dukas had consented to make changes in the score, by raising those low passages to which she had objected. Since much of the dramatic action is verbal rather than physical, Miss Farrar had realized that the vocal line should lie within a range permitting her to place "the essential emphasis upon diction."[93] She even devised a method of half singing and half speaking the notes, so that the text could be clearly understood. This method of vocal production, however, placed a strain on her voice. For several days after a performance, she was unable to sing roles such as Mimi or Juliette, which demand a smooth pure tone and line.

The dramatic action was generally static in nature and vocal problems resulted from words being set to notes whose rhythmic and intervallic values made them difficult to sing. Therefore Miss Farrar based her portrayal of Dukas' indomitable heroine on simplicity and nobility of manner and movement. "I have no intention of making Ariane a forcible woman," said Miss Farrar, "that is, no intention of doing so by means of gestures. I shall make as few movements as possible. It would seem to me ridiculous to do otherwise considering the way the music is written. But through the words and by the expression of my face I shall try to denote her power."[94]

Miss Farrar took great care in the selection of her costumes for this role, because she felt that each garment should symbolize a particular aspect of Ariane's character. Following a rehearsal of this work, she explained to a correspondent:

> Maeterlinck's Ariane is a symbolic figure. You must not confine her too closely to any particular time. She is medieval, she is modern; but, more than all, she is essentially feminine...
>
> In the first act, which shows Ariane coming home as the new bride of Barbe-Bleue I have dressed her in robes that are Oriental in their effect, and gold is the prevailing tone. That seems to symbolize the triumphant, dominating Ariane. A golden headdress and golden sandals complete the costume.
>
> For the second act, in which Ariane discovers and releases the poor imprisoned wives, the dress is white, with touches of gold. It seems to fit the mood of the liberator.
>
> And in the last act, the robe is pink and embroidered with figures that look like scorpions.... The pink robe and the emerald jewels on the robe and in the shimmering headdress symbolize the hope and energy of Ariane, who escapes from the bondage of Barbe-Bleue.[95]

The fundamental conception for these costumes, which were designed and made for Miss Farrar by her Parisian costumer, came from Asian sources. "The stage settings seem to have caught their glamor from the Arabian Nights," claimed Miss Farrar, "and it is from rare editions of that wonderful work that I have drawn some of my ideas."[96]

According to the *New York Times*, the sets for *Ariane* were "finely designed, with an effect of architectural solidity, of indefinite period."[97] Unlike his predecessors, Gatti-Casazza was keenly interested in both the visual vocal aspect of operatic productions. He placed special emphasis upon lighting. "It seems better to err on the side of having things seen than to have them not seen at all," he commented, after refusing to comply with Maeterlinck's suggestion that "a great deal of darkness"[98] should be employed in the presentation of his work. Parisians might have accepted the shadowy lighting of Dukas' opera in 1907, but Gatti-Casazza was convinced that the singers' faces should be seen in the opening scene and that New Yorkers "would not sit for twenty minutes in utter darkness"[99] at the beginning of the second act. A new era was dawning and famous scenic designers such as

Joseph Urban, Boris Anisfeld, and Norman Bel-Geddes were to create exciting sets for Metropolitan Opera productions.

The critics were mixed in their opinions of Miss Farrar's latest portrayal. H. J. Peyser of *Musical America* and William J. Henderson of the *New York Sun* enthusiastically endorsed her performance. Henderson wrote that Miss Farrar was "a gorgeous saffron clad figure,"[100] who interpreted the libretto superbly and sang the music compellingly. And Peyser concluded:

> First honors among the singers must go to Geraldine Farrar for her wonderful Ariane. One is almost at a loss where to begin and where to end the praise which should be showered upon her. To mention the beauties of her impersonation would be to recapitulate every incident of the opera. Miss Farrar occupies the stage from the beginning to the end, yet not a moment passes without some detail of subtle beauty striking the beholder. Her calm defiance of Blue Beard as he first questions her temerity, was superbly expressed. As she kneels over the women in the cave, the candle light illuminating her face, she presents one of the most exquisite pictures ever seen on any stage. In the last act her look of half-sorrowful, half-contemptuous pity at the weak, dependent, vacillating wives of Blue Beard conveyed a world of meaning, infinitely more eloquent than words.[101]

Henry Krehbiel of the *New York Tribune* and Carl Van Vechten, however, disapproved of Miss Farrar's impersonation. According to Krehbiel, Miss Farrar's portrayal was an unsuccessful attempt to imitate the dramatic gestures and elegant poses of Mary Garden,[102] the foremost exponent of modern French lyric heroines. Van Vechten maintained that the role of Ariane requires "plasticity and nobility of gesture and interpretation of a kind with which Miss Farrar's style is at variance."[103]

Taking the middle ground, Richard Aldrich of the *New York Times* commented: "She is singularly successful in embodying the radiant grace, dignity and tranquil courage of this woman whom nothing can turn from her purpose. There would be more repose and more potency if she were more sparing of her gestures and poses, however graceful and plastic they are.... Her French diction is excellent and she does much to make her enunciation carry through the house."[104]

Despite clear diction, intelligent textual interpretation, effective costumes, and moments of great visual beauty, Miss Farrar's portrayal succeeded only partially in conveying the simple nobility and subtle power of the fairy-tale figure Ariane. Her frequent posturing and often excessive use of elaborate gestures—the very thing she had intended to avoid—marred her presentation.

Ariane et Barbe-Bleue was not popular with the general public and was withdrawn from the repertory of the Metropolitan Opera after only seven performances. Apparently Miss Farrar agreed with the public's lack of enthusiasm, because she wrote: "I cannot say that I am much in sympathy with the vague outlines of the modern French lyric heroines; 'Melisande' and 'Ariane' I think can be better entrusted to artists of a less positive type."[105] She was too forceful and realistic a performer for the abstruse characters of symbolist drama.

Miss Farrar did not add another role to her now extensive repertoire until the 1911-1912 Metropolitan season. On January 3, 1912, she performed the role of Rosaura in the first American production of Ermanno Wolf-Ferrari's opera, *Le donne curiose*. One of the early twentieth century's most popular composers, Wolf-Ferrari was noted for his lyrical and melodious comic operas, based on fairy-tales by the seventeenth century French poet, Charles Perrault, and on dramas by William Shakespeare, Lope de Vega, Molière and Carlo Goldoni.

The basis for the libretto of Wolf-Ferrari's *Le donne curiose*, which had its premiere in 1903 in Munich, was an eighteenth century comedy of the same name by Goldoni. The opera concerns four Venetian women's stratagems to invade a gentlemen's club from which ladies are excluded. Suspecting that their husbands or fiancés may be delving into alchemy, or indulging in the pleasures of gambling and love-making, the four inquisitive ladies obtain a key to the clubhouse. To their surprise and delight, they discover that the men are merely conversing, while enjoying an excellent dinner.

The youthfully romantic role of the beautiful and conniving Rosaura once again permitted Miss Farrar to reveal her great charm and talent for lyric comedy. "Miss Farrar as Rosaura," wrote Aldrich in the *New York Times*, "was a vision of demure and mischievous beauty"[106]; and the *Musical Leader* added that she "represented a young girl of tender years, and there could be no more captivating, more beautiful or more winsome than she."[107] Mischievous she was, and on one occasion the singer brought sudden life into the first act by pinching the tail of the usually docile silken haired white dog in her lap. The New York critics agreed that Miss Farrar was "delightful"[108] in this role, which she sang with exceptional purity of tone and style. The theatrical exaggerations that had marred Ariane were entirely eliminated in Rosaura.

Miss Farrar's next new impersonation at the Metropolitan came nearly a year later during the 1912-1913 season as Susanna in another Wolf-Ferrari opera, *Il segreto di Susanna*, which had its premiere on December 13, 1912. Adapted from Enrico Golisciani's brief one act comedy, *Le secret de Susanne*, Wolf-Ferrari's comic opera was first performed in 1909 in Munich. The opera dramatizes the unsuccessful attempts of a young nineteenth-century Piedmontese countess to prevent her husband from discovering that she smokes. Public and press were fascinated by the sight of Miss Farrar smoking a cigarette during her aria in praise of nicotine and blowing "a puff toward the orchestra"[109] during her first curtain call at the opera's conclusion. "Farrar Fine as Susanna"[110] captioned the *New York Tribune*, and the *New York Times* reported that she was an "ideal" interpreter of the cigarette-smoking heroine. Concerning her singing of Wolf-Ferrari's lyrically melodious music, the *New York Times* concluded that she "gave much pleasure."[111] Van Vechten claimed that she sang with "Mozartean purity."[112] Both vocally and dramatically, Miss Farrar was well suited to the ingénue roles of Mozart and Wolf-Ferrari.

Like her performances of Zerlina and Cherubino in 1908 and 1909, Miss Farrar's portrayals of Rosaura and Susanna had disclosed the diva's pronounced comic talent. She revealed even more versatility in her next new portrayal, that of the five-part composite characterization of Louise in Gustave Charpentier's opera *Julien*, which had its American premiere on February 26, 1914. Charpentier's opera displayed the entire gamut of her impressive histrionic gifts.

The 1913-1914 Metropolitan season had not begun auspiciously for Miss Farrar who was suffering from a severe attack of bronchitis. An exhausting schedule of incessant operatic performances, annual spring and autumn concert tours, rehearsals, private study, and travel, combined with "the handicap of a delicate throat,"[113] insomnia, and a chronic nervous stomach condition, had gradually undermined her strength and health. During a performance of Gounod's *Faust* on November 29, 1913, Miss Farrar lost her voice. "When she reached for the high B at the end of the Jewel Song," recalled the author, J. A. Haughten, "only a raucous sound came out."[114] Frustrated and furious, Miss Farrar flung her hand mirror into the wings. After having turned her back on the audience, which was applauding in sympathy, she motioned them to desist.[115] "She sang the Garden Scene in half-voice," concluded Haughten, "declaimed the Church Scene, and then gave up, relinquishing the Prison Scene to Rita Fornia, the Siebel of the cast."[116] After a month of rest, Miss Farrar had regained her voice and resumed an active schedule of operatic performances and rehearsals for Charpentier's *Julien*.

First performed on June 4, 1912, at the Opéra Comique, *Julien* was supposedly a sequel to Charpentier's popular opera *Louise,* which had brought immediate fame to its long-haired, frock coated composer. The symbolic and declamatory *Julien* is really an expansion of the picturesquely Bohemian composer's 1892 symphonic drama, *La Vie du poète*, into a four-act opera with prologue. However, it does feature the same two principal characters and repeats certain melodic themes from the musically lyrical and theatrically realistic *Louise*.

In a series of dream-like but often realistically portrayed sequences, the allegorical libretto of Charpentier's *Julien* depicts the moral and physical

Enrico Caruso and Geraldine Farrar in *Julien*, 1916.

disintegration of an idealistic young poet. The five different manifestations of his mistress, Louise, conform to her lover's changing fate. The composer's preface states that except for Louise in the prologue, "the characters surrounding Julien are not so much real beings as a representation of his extemporized stages of consciousness. Some of them intervene merely as the momentarily animated reflection of a desire, a regret, a weakness, a memory."[117]

In the opening prologue, the happy young lovers are living in Rome, and the contented Julien falls asleep with Louise tenderly bending over him. In this dream, the young idealist sets out on a pilgrimage to the Temple of Beauty. After having promised to be true to his vision, he receives a blessing from the Vision of Beauty. Soon disillusioned by the world which has rejected his vision of paradise, Julien flees to the country and meets a young peasant girl who reminds him of his lost love, Louise. After having spurned her offers of love, the hapless young poet journeys on to his grandmother's home in Brittany. She advises him to seek solace in prayer and warns him to beware of pride. Instead, he curses heaven and turns to a life of dissipation, ending in a drunken stupor at the feet of a Parisian prostitute.

Except for the sibylline Vision of Beauty, all of the other four characterizations comprising the composite heroine of Charpentier's *Julien* demand a realistic rather than a stylized form of presentation. Vocally, the brief five roles are composed for the lyric soprano voice. Histrionically, the parts differ radically. The performer is required to portray successively the beautiful and devoted Louise, the statuesque and beneficent figure of Beauty, a simple and romantic country girl, the poet's affectionate and devout old grandmother, and finally, a drunken and dissipated Montmartre grisette.

This composite impersonation proved a tour de force for Miss Farrar. The diva commented that she "had five roles, sang about two phrases in each, and undressed more and more until the degradation of the last act."[118] Each of her characterizations was a distinct entity, clearly differentiated from the others. As Louise, she was tender and affectionate with her fervid young lover. While as the Vision of Beauty, she addressed her new worshipper in oracular tones, majestically raising an arm in approval above the poet's prostrate form. Before disappearing, she slowly blew him a kiss in benediction. Her dramatic contrast was most marked as the gruesome Parisian prostitute. Miss Farrar devised a hideous laugh for this impersonation and danced "an insinuating dance ... all the while puffing the end of a cigarette."[119]

Although she disliked this "hodge-podge" of an opera, claiming that she had "no work at all,"[120] the press was united in its approval of her portrayal. "In the composite five roles Miss Farrar acted as she had done at no previous occasion here," wrote the reviewer for the *New York Herald*, "displaying versatility and dramatic abandon."[121] "Her triumph in this opera," commented William J. Henderson for the *New York Sun*, "is in the scale she sweeps from the sweet Louise and the gentle peasant to the really grisly Grisette."[122] Richard Aldrich for the *New York Times* reported: "Miss Farrar is supposed to fill no fewer than five parts, or at least a part with five different manifestations ... and Miss Farrar fulfills it with accomplished skill and a wide variety of expression that gave plausibility to each of her appearances."[123]

The critics were especially interested in her realistic portrayal of the Parisian prostitute. "She was superb in her wild recklessness"[124] wrote the reviewer for the *New York Herald*. Richard Aldrich found her impersonation "hideously realistic,"[125] and Henderson reported: "In this last guise she makes the wreck of the ideal one thing really terrible. She has added to her gamut of expression a laugh which she might have learned in the regions of Dante's *Inferno*." At times, admitted Henderson in his review, he had found Miss Farrar's acting exaggerated, "erratic," but in her portrayal of Charpentier's grisette, he declared: "She is an artist to her fingertips."[126] Even though she detested "the repellent characterization of the guttergirl"[127] in *Julien* as intensely as the role of Nedda, she now had attained sufficient artistic maturity to suppress personal aversions in order to portray degeneracy with appropriate realism.

In addition to her superb acting, Aldrich reported that "she did much excellent singing,"[128] and the *New York Herald* wrote that "she sang beautifully."[129] Despite the excellence of Miss Farrar's portrayal and the presence of Enrico Caruso in the role of Julien, the opera was not popular with the public. It was dropped from the repertory after only five performances. "At least there was never talk of revival, thanks be,"[130] was Miss Farrar's final comment on Charpentier's second and last operatic composition.

After witnessing Miss Farrar's realistic portrayal of the Paris prostitute, several members of the press suggested that she was ideally suited both vocally and dramatically for the role of Bizet's Carmen.[131] Bizet's opera had not been performed at the Metropolitan since 1908, when Maria Gay's "vulgar"[132] portrayal (q. v. Chapter III, p. 59) of the Spanish gypsy had shocked the New York public and press. *Carmen,* however, was a popular work, and by 1914, New Yorkers again were ready for another production of this opera. Gatti-Casazza suggested an immediate revival of Bizet's opera for Miss Farrar, and she accepted his offer with alacrity. Ever since seeing the great Emma Calvé as Carmen in 1896, Miss Farrar had wanted to sing the role. The essentially medium vocal tessitura of Bizet's Carmen is best suited to the mezzo voice, lying rather low for that of a soprano. Miss Farrar realized that she would have little difficulty in singing this role, due to the exceptional richness of her middle and lower registers. Already she had demonstrated her ability to sing mezzo roles in her successful performances of Thomas' Mignon and Massenet's Charlotte. "As for the acting and looking," she later commented, "well I smiled into ... a mirror, and blew myself a kiss of congratulations."[133] At the end of March, the projected revival had to be postponed until the following season because Miss Farrar's physician had advised the diva "against the strain which rehearsal for the work would bring on her." She had not been in the best of health since her attack of bronchitis and needed all her strength "to keep her in proper condition for the rest of the season."[134]

Following Miss Farrar's concert tour after the conclusion of the Metropolitan's 1913-1914 opera season, she sailed for Europe to fulfill engagements in Berlin. Also, she intended to take a rest cure at Salsomaggiore, Italy, since Caruso claimed the spa's waters were "particularly favorable to singers' throats."[135] Miss Farrar was forced to cancel her operatic performances that summer in order to recover from measles and a chronic stomach condition. Her convalescence in a Munich sanatorium was suddenly interrupted, when on July 28, 1914, war was declared in Europe. As soon as Miss Farrar was strong enough to travel, she made plans for her return to the United States. After a futile attempt to sail from Amsterdam, she traveled by rail to Naples, since Gatti-Casazza had managed to book tickets on a British liner for various members of the Metropolitan. The elegantly clothed diva found the German and Italian customs authorities thoroughly cooperative. But "many gold francs" were required to convince the Swiss train conductors that she genuinely was "an harassed opera singer, and not royalty, incognito, bent on strange errands." Gatti-Casazza was relieved to greet his leading prima donna, and during the ship's journey through waters infested by German submarines, often facetiously remarked that he relied upon her "Berlin connections" should they ever encounter one of those "sea monsters."[136]

Arturo Toscanini was also on board and suggested the role of Carmen to Miss Farrar for her first appearance of the 1914-1915 opera season. The cast was to include Enrico Caruso as the gypsy's jealous renegade lover, Don José, and Pasquale Amato as the fascinating toreador, Escamillo, José's rival for Carmen's affections. Now fully recovered from her nervous stomach condition, Miss Farrar "jumped at the idea,"[137] and daily rehearsals were conducted by Toscanini in the ship's dining room.

Before appearing as Car-

Geraldine Farrar as Carmen, 1914 (Library of Congress, Music Division).

men, Miss Farrar had hoped to spend some time in Spain studying gypsies and native dancers, as well as seeing "places where the atmosphere would lend an authentic note."[138] But she was unable to visit Carmen's homeland, because of a busy rehearsal schedule at the Metropolitan Opera House and private sessions in her living room to perfect certain scenes with Caruso and Amato. Miss Farrar possessed a lively imagination and claimed that she had a "natural feeling for this role, so grateful in its dramatic impulse, so physically animated in song and movement."[139] Her portrayal was to be a distinctly original creation rather than a copy of past interpretations. Unlike Calvé, Miss Farrar was coquettish instead of intensely sensual. She emphasized Carmen's mischievousness, exuberance, courage and preoccupation with fate, instead of her wantonness. Conscious that French opera demands an elegance of performance, she refrained from the vulgarities that had marred Maria Gay's portrayal.

In an article entitled "The Psychology of Carmen," Miss Farrar informed the Boston music critic, Frederic Dean, that Carmen's character was so complex that each interpreter "probably sees 'something' that others have not seen ... and that is her individual Carmen.... Prosper Mérimée is quoted as saying that 'the psychology of Carmen is the psychology of Life.' If this be true, then every expression of his variable heroine will be a new expression of Life. So why should the procession of Carmens ever end?"[140] Miss Farrar then set forth her own views of Carmen:

> Personally, I do not believe Carmen to be the wanton that some would have her. Her beauty, her position, her race compelled her to be what she was. Admiration she demanded and obtained as freely as the flower demands and absorbs the sunshine that gives it life. The mere indifference of José aroused her—truly womanly—sense of injustice and pique. Homage was her birthright. And she proposed to have it—obtain it as she might. Fate threw her into José's path and her charm proved effective. The mere man fell to the fascination of the mere woman. José did Carmen a good turn and she repaid him in the only coin she possessed—herself. But, proud woman that she was and proud of her conquests, she could not help despising a man and especially a soldier who threw away honor, position—everything that life held for him—to become her slave—to follow where she led.
>
> It was natural, also, that she should be attracted by the strength and courage as well as the brilliance of the toreador. Here was a dominating personality—a lover who would beat her—kill her, probably—if she were unfaithful to him, but who would never cringe and cry and beg her to return to him after she had ceased to love him. Carmen knew that her passion for José would not last and as it ebbed away she could not understand why José failed to realize the change and accept it....
>
> Carmen also knew that death was inseparably connected with her new love. Her cards had so warned her, ... they never lied to her. And so resignedly, willingly, joyously, she went forth to her fate, for in it was bound

a greater love, ... a union with a man more worthy of her, ... I call Carmen a "high priestess," and she was. This is the crux of the story. This is the key to the psychology of her character.[141]

Geraldine Farrar stated that Prosper Mérimée and Georges Bizet believed female gypsies were the descendants of the priestesses of the golden voiced Egyptian moon god Thoth, inventor of the arts, sciences, soothsaying and magic. Carmen was more than just a beautiful gypsy girl; she was a seeress of fate accepting her destiny as inevitable and making no attempts to avoid it. This element of fate was present in Carmen and José's first meeting, which Miss Farrar described as follows:

> "Carmen! Carmencita!" proclaimed the youths of Seville as their queen and favorite swaggers upon the scene, in the stage version of the story, and from that moment she dominates the play as she dominates the hearts of her admirers. There is one, however, who does not even feel her power—who does not even see her. And upon him are concentrated all her powers of fascination. For Carmen claims all hearts; universal must be her allegiance; no one may escape her lure. And when José remains sublimely unconscious of her beauty—of her very presence—the others ... officers and men ... are brushed aside. Selecting the most intimate thing she has about her—the rose that is being kissed by her own warm mouth—Carmen flings it against José's cheek—and rushes off.... Carmen must become the dominant factor in the heart of this Basque soldier.[142]

The diva then pointed out:

> As the story progresses, see also how clearly the idea of the Seeress is brought out. The fate of the world lies in Carmen's hand—why not see what it may have in store for herself? With perfect faith in the future as it shall be told her among the shuffled spades and hearts, she deals her cards anxiously and with many forebodings—and once realising the message moves on to her destiny as one who knows and delights in knowing.[143]

At the conclusion of the article on Carmen, Miss Farrar contrasted the gypsy's death as related in Mérimée's book and as dramatized by Bizet and his librettists, Henri Meilhac and Ludovic Halévy, in the opera.

> In the original story, you will remember, Carmen willingly accompanies José Maria to the woods and there meets death at his hands as her punishment, possibly, but as the only outcome of her infidelity and the only fulfillment of her life....
> In the opera this is changed for mere theatric interest.... But the idea is the same. It is the climax, the only end possible for this Fate-driven woman.
> And so, Carmen openly challenges José to do his worst, laughs at his threats, ... and flings his ring into his face as he plunges his knife into her heart. It is a dying but still defiant Carmen that stumbles across the threshold of the arena in which her toreador is receiving the plaudits of the public. The toll is paid.[144]

Miss Farrar thought that Carmen was "less a singing than an acting role" and that the performer "first of all must absolutely look her part."[145] "When she dashes onto the stage," claimed the diva, "her appearance alone must be so exciting and magnetic that every man will edge forward on his chair and scheme how to venture past the stage door Minotaur with his orchids."[146] "The seduction of the eye," she concluded, "must be instantaneous upon her first appearance."[147] Therefore, Miss Farrar took great care in the selection of her costumes, which, due to the war, were now designed and made for her in New York by the house of Bendel. Her wardrobe for this opera consisted of colorful long dresses with "V" shaped necklines and flounces on the skirts, overlaid with fringed floral shawls. On her bosom she wore a bouquet of roses, and for the festive last act outside the bullring added an ornamental comb to her hair.

On November 19, 1914, Geraldine Farrar captivated her audience. Her next fifty-seven performances of Carmen were sold out. The critic of the *New York Herald* wrote:

> It was the happiest role that the prima donna ever has sung here.... Her impersonation was free from exaggerations, devoid of all freakishness. She did not slam furniture about the stage, did not drop combs, did not posture before the mirror—in short, she threw to the wind all of the conventional stocks in the trade of the usual every day, rubber stamp Carmen.
>
> She is light hearted, dances Spanish dances in a manner that would reflect credit on a premiere danseuse [she even had added a dance to the lively flamenco-like music that concludes the Seguidilla aria at the end of the first act], flirtatious one moment; sinister, fatalistic the next. Her moods flit with the whirl of time and are clearly registered with the audience. All in all, she is a very satisfying Carmen.[148]

Equally enthused, another critic reported:

> Farrar's Carmen was distinctive for Carmen is not so much a singing role as it is a living role, and Farrar gave herself up to her conception of the part with an abandon that was consummate. Her Carmen was at once an instrument and a plaything of fate....
>
> Farrar had gone deep into the part, and her conception was complete, even to the costuming—which in itself was distinctive, so that her appearance was as little akin to Calvé's as is her personality.
>
> The subtle tones of her performance became more and more effective as the opera progressed, and the audience knew at the last that they had been vouchsafed sight of an artist.[149]

Henderson of the *New York Sun* and Aldrich of the *New York Times* were not so exuberant. Although Henderson found her a "vision of loveliness, never aristocratic, yet never vulgar, a seductive, langorous, passionate Carmen," he felt that her acting was slightly "artificial."[150] Aldrich claimed that there was "a certain lack of rude elemental force in this sophisticated maiden, sometimes too prettily coquettish, too little of the soil." Nevertheless, he admitted that her portrayal was "unquestionably" both "captivating" and "interesting." He was convinced that as Miss Farrar entered "more deeply into it, it will gain in some of the essential attributes that belong to the character."[151] Only five months later, the Philadelphia press observed that she "imparted too much of the street Arab"[152] to her impersonation of Carmen. Apparently, by the end of April 1915, Miss Farrar had overcome even the histrionic artificiality objected to by Henderson. Following Miss Farrar's Carmen on April 28 in Atlanta, Georgia, the music critic, Louise Dooly, wrote that regarding "the criticism of Farrar's first performance of Carmen ... the studied details have become a coherent character, and the impersonation has now the spontaneity which is the inevitable mark of the work of genius."[153] Dudley Glass commented: "How Farrar does act Carmen! She throws herself into it, lives it, breathes it. She ... casts her own personality aside. Geraldine Farrar is left in the dressing room. Only Carmen is on the stage! That is why Geraldine Farrar, pride of American opera lovers, is at the top most peak in her profession."[154]

There were several dissenters, such as the authors Oscar Thompson and Carl Van Vechten, who felt that Miss Farrar's portrayal was "not a very Spanish one"[155] and lacked "atmosphere."[156] Both admitted though that their views were contrary to "popular opinion."[157] Miss Sylvia Blein, the French housekeeper and companion to the diva, attended forty-five performances of *Carmen* and maintained that Miss Farrar's portrayal was "very Spanish."[158]

Vocally, Henderson declared that she sang the role "better than any one since Emma Calvé,"[159] and Krehbiel commented: "Miss Farrar has approached her task with full regard for its difficulties, of its traditions, of its artistic demands, and she has paid special attention to the music itself, and to how it should be sung."[160] Even Van Vechten admitted that the role lay "well"[161] in her voice. Carmen became one of Miss Farrar's most popular portrayals in a production whose "elaborate and picturesque"[162] settings had been designed by Hans Kautsky of Vienna.

As the 1914-1915 opera season advanced, Miss Farrar again began to suffer from nervous tension due to her busy schedule at the Metropolitan. Succumbing to a bronchial attack, she was forced to cancel several performances in mid–January 1915. She had recovered sufficiently by the 25th of that month to sing the role of Catherine Huebscher in the world premiere of Umberto Giordano's opera, *Madame Sans-Gêne*. The composer had granted performance rights to the Metropolitan Opera in 1914.

The Italian libretto, based on a French play by Victorien Sardou and Emile Moreau, was written by Renato Simoni and is set in Napoleonic

France. Catherine Huebscher, a vivacious and beautiful young laundress, becomes the Duchess of Danzig and scandalizes Napoleon's court by her constant breaches of etiquette. Napoleon commands the Duke to divorce her. Eventually he pardons her after she presents him with his unpaid laundry bill from the days of the revolution as well as proves the innocence of his supposedly unfaithful wife.

Miss Farrar enjoyed the role of Catherine Huebscher "for its acting comedy"[163] and spent many hours perfecting her portrayal. She rehearsed the first-act laundry scene until she had mastered the technique of singing in one rhythm and ironing in another. According to the music critic Howard Taubman, it made a most "effective stage picture."[164]

Although Miss Farrar's portrayal was acclaimed by the New York operatic public, the press generally maintained that she overemphasized the heroine's vulgarity. Richard Aldrich of the *New York Times* wrote:

> Miss Farrar has an abundance of the mirth, humor, the good fellowship, and something of the natural simplicity and forthright directness that are essential qualities in representing Sardou's heroine. She expresses the quick changes of emotion, and there are suggestions in her impersonation of the tears that are sometimes near to laughter in it. She is broadly humorous in her expression of the gaucheries of the Duchess in her new surroundings, of her irritation and impatience at the restrictions they impose on her. It may be questioned whether the humor here is not a little too broad, a little too much verging on the ridiculous....
>
> Miss Farrar is an attractive figure in the part. Her command of facial expression stands her in good stead. A little more restraint in some of her too obvious scenes would enhance the value of an impersonation which, as it is, will doubtless be much admired and much enjoyed.[165]

Less generous in their appraisal of Miss Farrar's impersonation were Carl Van Vechten and William J. Henderson. "Too rude, too vulgar,"[166] concluded Henderson; and Van Vechten claimed: "In *Madame Sans-Gêne* she is often comic, but she does not suggest a bourgeoise Frenchwoman; in the court scenes she is more like a graceful woman trying to be awkward than an awkward woman trying to be graceful."[167]

It was noted that Miss Farrar sang Giordano's mellifluous, undistinguished lyrical music "with much vigor and whole-heartedness"[168] but that "the effects of her indisposition had not wholly left her."[169] Despite the critics general lack of enthusiasm, the production remained a popular success at the Metropolitan for nearly three seasons. Miss Farrar performed the role of Catherine nineteen times.

Following the premiere of *Madame Sans-Gêne*, Miss Farrar resumed her busy schedule of concert engagements and recordings for the Victor Gramaphone Company. But by the spring of 1915, her voice was "temporarily crippled"[170] from overwork. Absolute quiet was essential for her recovery. She was forced to give up all vocal activities for several months. "It was in the midst of this discouraging condition," wrote Miss Farrar, "that motion pictures were suggested to me."[171] Realizing that silent films offered her an activity with no vocal demands, she enthusiastically agreed to make three motion pictures in Hollywood during the summer of 1915.

By now, Miss Farrar was firmly established as the "pet child"[172] of the Metropolitan's public. Her portrayal of Madama Butterfly was "always good for a sold-out house."[173] Under Gatti-Casazza's management since 1908, she had added twelve roles to her repertoire and scored great personal successes in all but one of them—the symbolic figure of Dukas' Ariane. Miss Farrar had almost eliminated the artificiality which had often marred some of her earlier performances at the Metropolitan. In addition, she had learned to portray degeneracy with telling realism. Also she had proved equally effective in lyric comedy. Versatility was one of her outstanding characteristics. Her pronounced pantomimic ability had been refined over the past seven years through the constant practice of her art. This talent was to prove of inestimable value in her next "venture"[174]—motion pictures.

◆ FOUR ◆

Hollywood, 1915–1920

With the introduction of feature-length motion pictures to American audiences in 1912, Hollywood producers, such as Adolph Zukor and, later, Jesse L. Lasky, began to purchase the film rights to successful plays and novels. Leading Broadway stars—Mrs. Minnie Maddern Fiske, Henrietta Crosman, Leonore Ulric, James O'Neill, James K. Hackett and John Barrymore—were engaged to perform in these productions. Although the feature film was established as an accepted form of entertainment by 1914, it did not attain respectability until the latter part of 1915. These stars of the legitimate stage had been afraid that acting in the movies might tarnish their reputations. They would not allow their names to be mentioned in any publicity connected with films.

Jesse L. Lasky had purchased several successful plays from David Belasco and was looking for a way to overcome the prejudice against motion pictures. On April 23, 1915, Morris Gest, Belasco's son-in-law and a friend of Miss Farrar's, invited Lasky to attend a performance of *Madama Butterfly* at the Metropolitan Opera House. While watching the adulation of Miss Farrar by her devoted fans at the end of the opera, the film producer suddenly got an idea. He asked Gest to introduce him to the famous American prima donna and said to her: "I don't know whether you have ever seen a motion picture, but my company makes them, and I'd like to persuade you to do the story of Carmen for us. (I knew it was her favorite role.) We have no trouble securing famous plays and engaging their stars ... but they're always afraid acting in a movie will hurt their stage prestige. I could see by the ovation you got today that your prestige is such that whatever you do, your public will accept it as right."[1]

When Miss Farrar asked him if he really thought she "could turn the tide,"[2] he assured her that other stars would follow her lead. He offered her the largest salary ever paid to a film star by the Jesse L. Lasky Feature Play Company. The producer also agreed to provide the services of their best director, "a private railroad car for her journeys between coasts, a two-story house in Hollywood staffed with butler, cook, maid, a limousine and chauffeur, a private bungalow at the studio equipped with grand piano as well as other amenities, an augmented orchestra on the set for mood music worthy of the reigning queen of the opera, living expenses for the star and her entourage, and billing as 'Miss' Geraldine Farrar [stage stars but not film stars were accorded this distinction]."[3]

The proposal from Lasky came at a most opportune time, because Miss Farrar needed a period of complete vocal rest at the end of the 1914-1915 opera season. Due to the war, she no longer had summer engagements in Europe and was fascinated by "the novel and the unusual,"[4] feeling that "motion pictures seemed to suggest a new medium for dramatic expression."[5] But above all, Miss Farrar "adored to act."[6]

The directorate of the Metropolitan Opera House did not approve of opera singers making motion pictures. Miss Farrar was informed that she should remember she was "the greatest American prima donna—a star of the Metropolitan Opera Company." It was argued that if people could see her in the films for fifty cents, they would not be willing to pay six dollars to hear her sing at the Opera House.[7] Nevertheless, she accepted Lasky's offer and was the "first personality in motion picture history to receive what has since become known as 'the full treatment.'" A red carpet was laid in the Los Angeles

Geraldine Farrar on the porch of her Hollywood home, 1916.

Sante Fe Depot from the train to her chauffeur-driven limousine. After being greeted by the mayor and by school children throwing blossoms in her path, Miss Farrar was escorted to her house where "every room was banked with flowers."[8]

She had agreed to make three motion pictures that summer—*Carmen*, *Maria Rosa*, and *Temptation*. Although Lasky had promised Miss Farrar that her first appearance before cameras would be in her favorite role of Carmen, the company's leading director, Cecil B. DeMille, decided it was unwise to let "Geraldine Farrar learn a new art and hazard her reputation by appearing first in *Carmen*." DeMille realized that there were decided differences between stage and film techniques, explaining in his autobiography:[10]

> The best actor still has things to learn and unlearn when he comes before a camera; and that, I felt, was particularly true of one coming from grand opera, where the tradition is to over-act and where the glorious music can carry or cover a certain amount of less than glorious acting if necessary. On the stage, an actor is trained to project himself, his character, his actions and his thoughts, to an audience the nearest of whom is thirty feet away from him. To be effective his projection must reach and grip the people sitting in the last row of the top gallery. They must be moved by voice and gesture. They cannot see the actor's eyes. But the camera can, ruthlessly, infallibly. You cannot lie to a camera. That is in part what I mean by the motion picture's ability to photograph thought. Until an actor learns to use his eyes and the slightest flickering change of facial expression to project what is in the mind of the character he is playing, the motion picture audience will not believe him; and they will be, as usual, right.[9]

The prominent film director recommended that Miss Farrar be allowed "to cut her motion picture teeth" on a film version of Wallace Gillpatrick and Guido Marburg's stage play, *Maria Rosa*. It had been adapted for the screen by William B. DeMille, brother of Cecil B. DeMille, a well-known playwright of that time. Since it had been announced that Miss Farrar was to make her film debut in *Carmen*, DeMille suggested that *Maria Rosa* could be released after *Carmen*. Then it would have "all the values of the experience"[10] she would have gained in the filming of *Maria Rosa*.

DeMille's suggestion was accepted, and since Miss Farrar had brought her Bendel-created costumes for all three productions, the filming of *Maria Rosa* commenced almost immediately. The story is set in the Catalonian Mountains of Spain and concerns the rivalry of two men for the affections of a fiery and beautiful young peasant girl, Maria Rosa. One of the men commits a murder for which the other is convicted and imprisoned. Although the heroine is really in love with the prisoner, she finally marries the villain after he has convinced her of his rival's death. On the wedding day, however, the convict returns and secretly visits Maria Rosa. In a fury, she murders her treacherous new husband and is reunited with her true love.

The melodramatic role of Maria Rosa was ideally suited to the talents of Miss Farrar, who was supported by Wallace Reid as her handsome film lover and by Pedro de Cordoba as the villain. DeMille soon realized that the diva had a natural talent for motion picture acting. Rather than imposing his conception upon her, he "tried to help her bring out her own best performance,"[11] allowing Miss Farrar to evolve her own extemporaneous actions and dialogue. Concerning her work with DeMille on this film, she wrote:

> Mr. DeMille's long and varied experiences in the legitimate theatre gave him an uncanny reading into his actors' psychology. Thus, with me, he outlined briefly the scenes, their intended length, the climax—and with the minimum expenditure of precious energy in preliminaries, set his cameras at all angles to catch the first enthusiasm of a scene, which spontaneous impulse was always my best interpretation. We were not cautioned to beware of undue emotion, disarranged locks, torn clothing, etc. We were allowed free action as we felt it; so we acted our parts as if we were engaged in a theatre performance, and I believe, for this reason, we had real expression and feeling ... at any rate, Mr. DeMille understood my enthusiasm and left me to express natural impulses wherever my feeling prompted them.[12]

One of the most dramatic scenes in the film version of *Maria Rosa* was the reappearance of the heroine's supposedly deceased admirer. Maria Rosa has fled to her room after the wedding breakfast. As she sits gazing forlornly into her mirror, the reflection of the man she loves appears beside her own image. Startled, she slowly turns and finds her love standing before her. The *New York Times* reported that "the amazement, mixed with joy and incredulity of the girl ... is skillfully portrayed by Miss Farrar."[13] As in the opera, Miss Farrar placed special emphasis upon facial pantomimic detail in the films.

Following the completion of *Maria Rosa*, Miss Farrar and DeMille commenced work on *Carmen*, with Wallace Reid as the jealous lover, Don José, and with Pedro de Cordoba as the valiant toreador Escamillo. The film's scenario was to have been based upon the libretto of Bizet's opera but the copyright owners demanded such an exorbitant fee for the film rights that the Jesse L. Lasky Feature Play Company decided to work from the Prosper Mérimée novel. It was then adapted for the screen by William B. DeMille. Cecil B. DeMille wrote that "some of the characters and some of the situations were different in the book and opera, but Carmen was Carmen in both; and it was Geraldine Farrar as Carmen that the public ... was avidly awaiting."[14] The film concludes with the opera's final scene, and Carmen is stabbed by her discarded lover in front of the arena instead of in a deserted wood.

Miss Farrar requested music during the filming of her scenes because she "was so accustomed to orchestral accompaniment for certain tempi and phrasing, ... and felt [she] could better pantomime the rhythm of the effects."[15] She sang and spoke her role in French or Italian, and "sometimes good American slang phrases—a product of the studio—added 'punch' to the piquancy of the situations. There was no curtain to go up! The director-general replaced the harassed stage manager and gave the signal; 'Camera, Go!' No fiery leader overwhelmed [her] with the feverish tempest of his orchestra; just a watchful operator warily turning the crank of his machine, while [she] evolved her scenes."[16] From then on, Miss Farrar always had a small orchestra on the set to inspire her. She claimed that its "soulful throb did more to start my tears than all the glycerine drops or onion more frequently employed by other less responsive orbs."[17]

Soon other performers requested musical accompaniments for their scenes, and the number of musicians allotted each artist became "bones of contention."[18] Pauline Frederick, another Lasky film star, objected to having only one violin while Geraldine Farrar had two or three. But although Samuel Goldwyn pointed out that Miss Farrar's "operatic tradition demanded this excess of string stimulation" and that Miss Frederick had formerly performed without any musical accompaniment at all, the obdurate actress demanded the same privileges as her colleague. Eventually, mood music on the sets became "an almost universal feature"[19] in silent film Hollywood.

A highlight of Miss Farrar's film version of *Carmen* was the first act fight scene between the gypsy heroine and another girl in the cigarette factory. In the original story, there is a quarrel among the cigarette girls, and DeMille expanded "the argument into a full-blown brawl."[20] He cast Jeanie Macpherson, his head scenarist and a highly competent actress, as the young woman who wrestled with Miss Farrar. According to DeMille:

> Jeanie was game for anything, and, as I have said, Geraldine needed little direction. We had rehearsed a very convincing bout, but I noticed that something was not quite according to the rehearsal. Geraldine's first haymaker had knocked Jeanie's wig askew. Jeanie was much too good a trouper to stop before she heard the director's "Cut." She merely put up one hand to hold her wig in place and went after Geraldine with the other. Geraldine, too excited to notice anything was wrong, with her mind only on giving the scene all the realism she knew I wanted, waded in, and the two hot-blooded Spanish cigarette girls did their Scots and Irish ancestors proud, rampaging back and forth across the set, with Jeanie frantically holding on to her wig with one hand and vainly trying to defend herself with the other. Jeanie and I were perhaps the only two people on the set who knew that her gyrations had one object: to keep the wig from flying off in the middle of the scene. But it photographed, as Jeanie knew it would, as if Jeanie, terrorized, were desperately trying to protect her head from Carmen's furious assault; and it made Geraldine look like a one woman whirlwind.[21]

The bullring scene at the film's climax anticipated DeMille's future use of spectacle. The Lasky Company obtained special permits from the Los Angeles city government to construct an entire bull-fighting arena which "in every particular was ... a duplicate of some of the famous bull-fighting rings in Spain." Twenty thousand people were present at the filming of this scene that depicted "every feature of a gala day, including the gatherings at the exterior of the bullring, the march of the matadors, toreadors and picadors, the arrival of Miss Farrar as Carmen and of Pedro de Cordoba as Escamillo ... on the way to the bullring several hundred children lined the path, strewing roses in front of Miss Farrar."[22] The Lasky stars and executives, dressed in Spanish costumes, sat in the stands, and Jesse L. Lasky appeared in the box with Miss Farrar.

Two weeks after completing the film version of *Carmen*, Miss Farrar started work on her third motion picture, *Temptation*. It was an original photo-drama written by Hector Turnbull, a member of the Lasky writer's department and a former drama critic for the *New York Tribune. Temptation* was Turnbull's first scenario for the screen and concerns the "trials, troubles and tribulations" of a young prima donna in her "long hard fight to the top."[23] Miss Farrar portrayed the melodramatic and highly emotional role of Rénee Dupree who is tempted to sell herself to a lecherous impresario in order to save her dying composer sweetheart. The young singer is spared, however, by the villain's death and by her beloved's sudden miraculous recovery. The happy couple go on to fame and fortune.

The Lasky executives were confident that Miss Farrar would succeed as a film star. Their faith was confirmed at the gala opening of *Carmen* on October 2, 1915, in Boston before an audience of 2500, including Miss Farrar, her parents, Mayor James M. Curley, Samuel Goldwyn, Mrs. Morris Gest, and Mrs. David Belasco. A symphony orchestra and three singers performed selections from Bizet's opera in an arrangement written specially for the film's Boston run.[24] A reporter for the *New York Herald* wrote: "Carmen on the screen as presented here probably marks an advance in motion pictures. Every movement on the screen applauded. At the conclusion Miss Farrar to rise and bow her acknowledgement of the applause."[25] The diva told a *New York Times* correspondent that "she was thrilled as if she had left her seat and actually was acting on the screen."[26]

When the film opened in New York City on October 31, 1915, at the Strand, the *New York Tribune* reported:

> It is a pity that Geraldine Farrar can sing, for she is a remarkable movie actress, and in a democracy the public has a right to demand that her talents shall be exercised for the many of the picture theatre rather than the few of the opera house.

Undoubtedly Miss Farrar has never acted as well as she does in the screen version of *Carmen* which opened yesterday at the Strand Theatre. Moving pictures, of course, offer histrionic opportunities unknown to the operatic stage. Nice touches which would be lost in the Metropolitan Opera House are visible to everybody in the theatre where Geraldine Farrar plays close up for the camera men.... As Carmen smiled and died a pet theory of our own sickened. We have often maintained that there were tricks of the moving picture trade which could not be mastered by a newcomer and that no novice could act with the skill of the trained picture player. Geraldine Farrar can. She was born, perhaps, with a camera man and a director within call. Her best work is done in the close-ups, which try the soul of the untrained, and never have we seen an actress in moving pictures who so roundly justified the advance of the camera man.... Her Carmen is passionate, cruel, humorous and courageous. She loves and she fights two-handedly. For several moments we feared for the last remaining garment of the rival cigarette girl during her struggle with Carmen. Miss Farrar plays a thousand feet of film with one side of her face marred by mimic scratches. But there is no marring the beauty of a Carmen who smiles as Miss Farrar does. One is quite ready to condone the folly of Don José.[27]

The critic for the *New York Herald* also mentioned the fight scene, stating that "this passionate fight caused a dispute before the censors in Philadelphia, when in the confusion of a general encounter the clothes of the cigarette girls began to disappear, the pictures become startling. But just when one thinks it is about time to 'sit up and take notice' the scene changes." He went on to say that "Miss Farrar always was a good pantomimist in the opera and her facial expressions were attractive. These features of her work are always apparent. From the start to the finish of the picture she occupies the center of the screen, and some of her striking personality seems to have found its way into every scene."[28]

Miss Farrar's facial pantomime was likewise commented on by a *New York Sun* reporter who wrote: "Her banter with the cigarette girls was eloquently expressed by her facial emotions ... and if there ever was a symptom of agony and death from a stab wound it was graphically depicted on Miss Farrar's face for the benefit of the public." Of her characterization he added:

> A Spanish cigarette maker is, to judge from what the audience witnessed yesterday, a combination of tigress and light weight slugger, with a tendency to go about at all times in a state of undress. Miss Farrar emphasized the physical, not to say the bestial note in the gypsy, as these pictures reveal her idea of Carmen to a degree that leaves little else in the woman's character. She lays about with the vigor of a longshoreman when she does not care for the addresses of a swain and bites and scratches her fellow employees like a tigress.[29]

The critic for the *New York World* agreed that Miss Farrar stressed the physical aspect of Carmen's character, stating that "when she isn't in somebody's arms or about to be kissed she is involved in a fight or mix-up of some sort, and her 'go' with her rival 'lady friend' in the cigarette factory is realism of the Nth degree.... Miss Farrar makes her part vivid and red blooded. It is real acting."[30] The *New York Times* correspondent also commented on Miss Farrar's histrionic ability: "Let it be said that among the movie actresses she is one of the best.... She does more than make faces at the camera; she knows that in acting for motion pictures, she must do more than go through the motions. And she does ... she brings to the richly colorful performance a degree of vitality that animates all the picture and offers a good illustration of the difference between posing and acting for the camera."[31] In a similar vein, Lesley Mason for *Motion Picture News* wrote:

> She is not a great prima donna appearing in her most successful role. She IS Carmen. She lives the part. Every gesture is one of Carmen's own; every play of the feature is, you feel, as Carmen would have looked; every action, every decision is made in the exact mood you are sure governed this woman who would walk through fire and not be harmed, who loved love, but not her lovers, whose one ambition was absolute power over men, not for their sake, but for its own.
> The abandon of Farrar's Carmen, the overflowing life, energy and power of her characterization exhilarates, while it irresistibly charms. It requires but a few minutes of her conquering vitality to convince the onlooker that she could impose her will, upon any man, under any condition and at any price. All that the facts and foundations of the story require you to believe of Carmen, you accept as possible and true, because Farrar is what she is as the personifier of the gypsy maid.[32]

Miss Farrar's motion picture portrayal of Carmen was an unmitigated success, due to the intensity and realism of her acting. The new film star requested that her movie be shown throughout the country at popular prices because "she wanted to appear before the masses who were unable to see her in concert or grand opera."[33] It became the Jesse L. Lasky Feature Play Company's biggest money-maker. It also aided in taking "the curse off movie work for stage personalities." Now they not only allowed their names to be mentioned in connection with films, but they also demanded "the full treatment" with newspaper publicity and interviews.[34] The stars of Broadway no longer scorned the motion picture "as an undignified and despicable form of activity." It was gaining acceptance as a valid means of dramatic expression.[35] Miss Farrar's appearance in films encouraged attendance by the much sought after carriage trade. Movies were becoming fashionable instead of merely popular.[36]

In 1916 Miss Farrar's two other films, *Temptation* and *Maria Rosa*, were released. *Temptation* was first exhibited on January 2 at the Broadway Theatre in New York. The *New York Times* recorded that "in sharp contrast to *Carmen*, the first of the Farrar films, *Temptation* is a specimen of modern photo-drama, as opposed to a version of some drama, opera, or story adapted for the screen. Unquestionably it will be pronounced a fine picture by movie audiences, for it abounds in strong emotional scenes."[37] The reporter for *Moving Picture World* stated that "coming at a time when Miss Farrar's film version of *Carmen* is breaking all records as a feature attraction throughout the country, announcement of the release of Temptation has evoked the keenest interest among motion picture men and the public.... That many of the incidents which comprise the play have been taken from Miss Farrar's own personal experiences, lends no small amount of interest to the production. Many of the scenes reveal for the first time publicly the manner of life and artistic business behind the scenes of a great opera house."[38]

Maria Rosa opened on May 7 at the Strand Theatre in New York, and one reviewer reported: "Geraldine Farrar is seen at her best in this meritorious film. The story enabling her to fulfill her task to the best advantage."[39] According to the *New York Times*, the film was "as good, if not a better motion picture than *Carmen*." The *Times* critic then added that although Miss Farrar was "a hit in *Maria Rosa*" and "skillfully portrayed" many of her scenes, she was unable "to suggest in her facial expressions the sterner emotions." He concluded, "Sometimes fleetingly hate, terror or deep sorrow is reflected in her face, but always it is driven away by her irresistible smile."[40] Miss Farrar had been well advised by Cecil B. DeMille to "cut her motion picture teeth"[41] on *Maria Rosa*. In her following films, she had learned to express both joyous and serious emotions.

Following the completion of Miss Farrar's third film for the Lasky Company, she left California to fulfill several months of concert engagements prior to her February 1916 return to the Metropolitan Opera Company. Before leaving Hollywood, however, she had accepted Lasky's offer to make additional films the following summer. Lasky, Goldwyn, and DeMille realized that the prima donna possessed an exceptional talent for motion picture acting. She was able to portray emotional melodramatic roles with telling realism.

During the filming of the motion picture *Maria Rosa*, Miss Farrar had met the handsome Dutch actor, Lou Tellegen, at the Lasky studios. Tellegen had starred on Broadway in the original stage version of this drama and served as consultant for the film. In 1912 and 1913 he had toured the United States as Sarah Bernhardt's leading man. After a brief courtship, Geraldine Farrar and Lou Tellegen were married on February 8, 1916, at her home in New York. A month later, Miss Farrar's first autobiography *Geraldine Farrar: The Story of an American Singer by Herself* was published. It had been a busy year. Following the diva's performances at the Metropolitan and her annual spring concert tour, she and her husband returned to Hollywood. Miss Farrar spent two months filming *Joan the Woman*, and Tellegen made his debut as a film director.

In the spring of 1916, DeMille cast Miss Farrar as Joan of Arc in his first historical picture, *Joan the Woman*. Following David W. Griffith's 1915 *Birth of a Nation*, this was to be the most spectacular film yet made in Hollywood. Delighted with the opportunity to portray one of her favorite heroines of history,[42] Miss Farrar informed DeMille that it would be "the greatest work of her life."[43]

The Jesse L Lasky Feature Play Company had suggested to DeMille the filming of a picture on the life of Joan of Arc. The executives felt that "at this particular moment in the world's history, or, rather, in the thought of the public, the story of Joan of Arc would have a greater appeal than at any other time. France, the country she had saved for eternity, was fighting for its existence ... and reports frequently came from Europe that French soldiers believed they saw the figure of Joan in the midst of battle, leading and encouraging them to deeds of greatness."[44] DeMille's head scenarist, Jeanie Macpherson, was selected to write the screenplay. She chose the title, *Joan the Woman*, because "she wanted to emphasize the humanity of Joan of Arc rather than project the conventional, and so frequently false, image of the saint."[45] According to DeMille and Miss Macpherson, Joan should be "portrayed as a strong peasant girl, with a sense of humor and human sympathy, ever faithful to her Voices, but tempted and fearful too—

Geraldine Farrar as Joan the Woman, 1917 (Library of Congress, Music Division).

a woman of flesh and blood, whose heroism was as much in her victory over herself as in her victory over the English."[46] Although Miss Macpherson based most of the film's incidents on actual events in the martyred saint's life, she added a love story to bring "out the womanly qualities of the great Joan."[47]

The motion picture's opening scene takes place in an English trench during the First World War. A British soldier, commissioned to make a dangerous night raid on the German trenches, finds an old sword and dreams of Joan of Arc. The saint, appearing before him, bids him "do and die, that his sin against her centuries before [might] be effaced."[48] The story of Joan's life then follows. It includes her visions as a peasant girl in Domrémy, her appearance before the Dauphin Charles at Chinon, the Battle of Orléans, the coronation of King Charles VII, her capture at Compiègne, her imprisonment and trial, and, finally, her burning at the stake in Rouen. Added to these events, however, was the saint's supposedly innocent love affair with an English soldier named Eric Trent, whom she had twice rescued from death at the hands of the French. Bitter over her rejection of his marriage offer, Trent aids the unscrupulous Bishop Cauchon in Joan's capture. Finally, overcome by remorse for his betrayal, Trent hands her a cross of twigs at the stake. Following Joan's martyrdom, the film returns to the opening scene in the British trench. The young officer awakes. Inspired by the thought of Joan's great sacrifice, he willingly gives up his own life in the destruction of a German trench. The part of the young soldier in the introduction and the epilogue was played by the same actor (Wallace Reid) who portrayed Joan's English lover in the main body of the film. This added continuity to the photo-drama.

Joan proved to be Miss Farrar's favorite movie characterization. According to the opera singer, she spent "as much thought and energy in making live again—if only on the shadow stage—the blessed Maid of Orléans, as upon any of [her] opera creations."[49] She was pleased with Miss Macpherson's scenario and commented to a reporter: "Emphasis was given to the womanly traits of the character making her out a woman first and a soldier second. That is what the immortal Joan must have been.... Joan of Arc was simply a wonderful, beautiful woman, possessing a soul of feminine greatness which for all time will be an inspiration to every woman of the world."[50]

In portraying her role, Miss Farrar found DeMille's direction "inspiring."[51] As with *Maria Rosa*, *Carmen*, and *Temptation*, he never demonstrated a scene for his actors. Instead, he explained it, and then allowed them to improvise. The prima donna claimed that the cast was completely absorbed in the production. She recalled that during off hours they frequently remained in character and spoke in the archaic speech used on the sets, which were authentic replicas of medieval French villages, castles, battlements, and churches.

Miss Farrar gained fifty pounds in order to wear an eighty-pound suit of aluminum armor. She could only bear it a few minutes at a time.[52] Like a medieval knight, Miss Farrar was lifted onto her white charger by two men. Once the horse ran away with her during a battle scene, and thereafter DeMille supplied a double for the long shots. No double was used for the close up shots and DeMille "posted specially skilled riders to surround Geraldine Farrar and protect her from being unhorsed or injured."[53]

In addition to bearing the eighty-pound suit of armor, Miss Farrar had to carry a large sword and heavy three-and-a-half-yards-long banner. The latter "had a terrific pull"[54] as it flapped in the breeze when she charged into battle. To mount the walls of Orléans, she used a heavy scaling ladder planted with her own hands after she had stood for hours in the moat with cold water up to her shoulders.

"I think I have never in any picture seen anything more beautiful and heart-lifting," wrote the reporter, Nell Brinkley, of this battle sequence, "than the scene of the riding forth of Joan and her army, across the plain at a measured pace that quickens and quickens, a silent, vast troop of horse, shoulder to shoulder, armed, lances a forest with the leaves of their pennants rippling in the sun, the dust like the surf clouding each horse's hoofs, an oncoming sea, before it, a white horse and its rider standing in her stirrups with the banner of France straining from her hand."[55]

For the sake of realism in the dungeon scene, Miss Farrar allowed little brown-dyed mice to follow a trail of sugar laid upon her body "to entice them to dramatic deeds."[56] And for weeks her arms bore lacerations and bruises from the torture scene.

At the film's climax, she was placed in the middle of burning oil tanks "whose spectacular flames together with the clouds of rolling smoke, gave a perfect illusion." Miss Farrar's clothing, skin, and hair were fire-proofed with an inflammable fluid. Cotton saturated with ammonia was placed in her nostrils and mouth to prevent inhalation of the gaseous vapors.[57] Cecil B. DeMille wrote of this scene that "Geraldine Farrar ... stood amid the smoke and flame until the very end of the scene, when, of course, a dummy made of wood was substituted for the actual burning of Joan's body. Geraldine wrote later that it was a 'truly terrifying' experience; but she did not weaken for a second until, standing aside after her part was over, she saw the dummy being burned where she had stood a short time before. Then she had to go to her dressing room and be sick. That was how thoroughly she had put herself into her role."[58]

Despite the many discomforts and dangers connected with the filming of *Joan the Woman*, Miss Farrar never complained. She stated: "I would no more think of having someone substitute for my 'physically violent' scenes in the movies than I would think of letting another sing my top notes at the opera. If I cannot do a thing absolutely and completely, I do not want to do it at all."⁵⁹ Miss Farrar lived her part so intensely that "when the bugles shrilled for the charge and maneuvers, [she] couldn't help thrill, and forgot [her] fears, [her] inexpert horsemanship—everything, in fact save that [she] was actually the Maid bent on [her] holy errand."⁶⁰ Her fortitude was admired by everyone, including the cowboy extras hired for the battle scenes. During one of the long delays on the set, an extra asked if she did not mind the heat and the long waits, to which Miss Farrar replied: "I'm too interested all the time to know what's happening on the outside of me."⁶¹

On December 25, 1916, *Joan the Woman* had its premiere at New York's Forty-Fourth Street Theatre. The movie industry, wishing to appeal to the carriage trade as well as to the photo-play fans, specified that "in handling a Farrar film it is well to keep advertising along dignified lines in accord with the reputation of the star."⁶² Great care was taken with all publicity, displays, and décor for this motion picture. Instead of the usual colored pictures and electric lighted figures, the theatre's lobby contained paintings of famous episodes in the life of Joan of Arc and the walls of the auditorium were hung with long red curtains frosted with lilies. A single candle burned on stage while a bell was rung and the house was bathed in a dim blue light in order to create the atmosphere of a French cathedral's interior.

Joan the Woman was hailed as "the high-water mark of picture production"⁶³ and declared "the principal achievement of Cecil B. DeMille as a motion picture producer and director ... and at this moment is the most talked about and widely discussed amusement and artistic entertainment in the land. *Joan the Woman* has raised the whole standard of motion picture producing. It has taken the sting of childishness from a great art and clothed it with respectability and power."⁶⁴ The critic for the *New York Sun* claimed that this film was "the most interesting and spectacular ever seen in New York."⁶⁵ The motion picture reviewer, Peter Milne, also acknowledged the film's worth and added:

> But through it all, because of the magnificent inspirational performance of Geraldine Farrar you feel inspired yourself. It is because of Miss Farrar as the Heaven-sent Joan, that the picture possesses such remarkable balance. The first half of the picture runs to the spectacular, the second gives you the tragic downfall of Joan. After the thrills and sensations of the battle to switch to a story of personal interest is a difficult test to apply to even the most accomplished star. Miss Farrar rises to the occasion triumphantly and in truth saves the picture from being top heavy. *Joan the Woman* is a triumph for Geraldine Farrar.... *Joan the Woman* deserves to rank as a true classic of the screen.⁶⁶

Equally impressed with Miss Farrar's convincing performance as Joan, the critic for the *New York Herald* wrote that "she has merged her personality into the character of the Maid completely. Her Carmen on the screen was just a sketch compared with this faithful work. She assumed the virtuous and resolute bearing of Joan even in the wild fields of Lorraine, where she had been a solitary girl, and not once did she deviate from the quiet sincerity of the Maid as she moved through most stirring scenes."[67]

The submergence of Miss Farrar's own personality in her portrayal of the French saint was also commented upon by a New York music critic, who stated: "Miss Farrar utterly submerges all traces of twentieth century qualities. As Joan she is revealed as a sturdy, tireless, vigorous peasant of the far-removed past." He then said it was not at all surprising that the diva was selected as "an ideal Joan," since she possessed "physical beauty of a rare and lustrous type, dramatic temperament that [had] been developed by the greatest authorities in the world, and an understanding of gesture and posing that make her work in the field of opera far removed from that of the usual prima donna." In conclusion, he even ventured to add that "the Joan of Miss Farrar may really be considered the crystallization of all her dramatic experience."[68]

In similar vein, another reporter stated: "Over at the Metropolitan Opera House I used to sit in the gallery ... and have watched the boys cheer and whistle when Geraldine Farrar would play Tosca or Mimi or Butterfly. Say, they should see this remarkable woman in *Joan the Woman* and really know what she can do in the way of acting. Tain't enough that she can act; she can ride a horse like a veteran, fight like a bull-dog, love like a queen and die like a martyr."[69] "In this role," concluded a colleague, "Geraldine Farrar has surpassed her fame as a singer and won new laurels as an actress."[70]

The press agreed that Miss Farrar had succeeded in endowing her characterization of the fervid French saint with a genuine humanity. Her portrayal was noted for its realism or lifelikeness.

Prior to leaving Hollywood in mid September of 1916, Geraldine Farrar and Lou Tellegen had renewed their contracts with the now named Famous Players–Lasky Corporation (later to become known as Paramount Pictures) for the summer of 1917. After the prima donna's concert tours and operatic performances, she and Tellegen returned to California. Miss Farrar and DeMille made two more pictures together — *The Woman God Forgot* and *The Devil-Stone*.

In *The Woman God Forgot*, which concerns Cortez's conquest of Mexico in the sixteenth century, Miss Farrar was again cast in a period spectacle. The Famous Players–Lasky Corporation wished to capitalize on her success in the historical film, *Joan the Woman*. This time she portrayed Tecza, an

Aztec princess, who saves her Spanish lover by betraying her father Montezuma's empire to the invading forces of Cortez. Regarding this role, Miss Farrar wrote:

> Her unusual appeal lies in the romantic mysteries of the Aztec race. We all know they represented the highest form of civilization among the natives of the American continent at that period.
>
> Careful research into many and sometimes mythical chronicles of this ancient people revealed in Tecza, the daughter of Montezuma, a personality peculiarly adaptable to a unique characterization.
>
> Such a close study of this character was required for a historically correct portrayal that I was put on my mettle to actually live the life of this woman of a dead race in her conflicting loves for Alvarado, the Spanish captain, and her own people.[71]

Geraldine Farrar as Tecza, 1917 (Library of Congress, Music Division).

For the famous battle scene between the Aztecs and the Spaniards, DeMille built a two-hundred-foot-high pyramid that covered an area of over two square miles. One thousand people participated in the battle and Miss Farrar led the attacking Indian warriors. DeMille also constructed a huge pool and garden which were enclosed in a fifty foot high and four hundred foot long fine wire netting to prevent the escape of several thousand rare water fowl inhabiting the lush green foliage. "My girl attendants rose from the water like nymphs," related

Miss Farrar, "while hundreds of gay birds fluttered about us, in sweet song."[72]

The film opened on October 28, 1917, and the motion picture critic E. T. Keyser reported that "the cast fitted their parts, but the star, Geraldine Farrar, was born for hers. All through the picture she was the barbaric princess, sometimes loving, often sad, sometimes vengeful, but always just below her greatest gentleness was the suggestion of the ruthlessness of the savage woman of high estate."[73] The *New York Times* commented that Miss Farrar "poses in the trappings and mountings of Aztecs, and in a variety of ravishing costumes demonstrates anew her fitness for the screen."[74] In *Joan the Woman* and *The Woman God Forgot*, Miss Farrar proved highly effective as a realistic interpreter of both historical and fictitious melodramatic heroines.

Miss Farrar's next film, *The Devil-Stone*, concerns the vicissitudes of Marcia Manot, a beautiful Breton fishermaid, who has discovered an enchanted emerald. At one point in the movie, there is a flash-back, and Miss Farrar appears as one of the jewel's former owners, the ancient, cruel Norse Queen Grenalda. In this sequence, she is shown seated upon a throne "with two vicious wolf hounds at [her] feet."[75] The *New York Times* wrote of this film that "it is only by its enlistment of the services of Miss Farrar that it differs in any particular from several dozen other films. First in the garments of a fisherwoman, then in a convenient vision, and later as a woman of wealth, Miss Farrar is given the opportunity for the depiction of three varied types and all of them she renders interestingly."[76] As she had already demonstrated in opera, she was beginning to reveal in films, that she could achieve personal artistic success despite mediocre music, librettos or scenarios.

Following the completion of *The Woman God Forgot* and *The Devil Stone*, Miss Farrar did not renew her contract. Her husband had failed as a film director and had been fired by the Famous Players–Lasky Corporation. She and Lou Tellegen signed with Samuel Goldwyn, who had just established his own company with studios in Fort Lee, New Jersey. During the next two summers, Miss Farrar made seven motion pictures for the Goldwyn Company—*The Turn of the Wheel, The Hell Cat, The Stronger Vow, The World and Its Woman, The Flame of the Desert, Shadows* and *The Woman and the Puppet*. Of special interest to her motion picture admirers were the films *The World and Its Woman, The Flame of the Desert,* and *The Woman and the Puppet*, since all three featured Miss Farrar's husband as her screen lover. Unlike *Carmen* and *Joan the Woman*, the scenarios for these seven photo melodramas were of mediocre quality. Great emphasis was placed upon sensational scenes. In *The Flame of the Desert*, Miss Farrar, dressed in a ball-gown, rode bareback on an Arabian steed across the desert at midnight summoning a troop of British cavalry to suppress an Egyptian uprising. She, however, did not approve of these society dramas and had requested in a 1918 letter to Samuel Goldwyn "material in modern dress that has guts in it, like *Tosca*."[77]

Hoping to capitalize on her success as Carmen, Miss Farrar was again cast as a high-spirited Spaniard in *The Hell Cat*, *The Stronger Vow*, and *The Woman and the Puppet* in which she danced "with alluring abandon"[78] in a Seville wharf cafe. The studio's publicity department stressed "that the star is in a class by herself in the delineation of Spanish roles." It advised those promoting the films to announce that "she is the best Carmen who ever appeared in this famous opera."[79]

Aside from the indifferent scenarios, Miss Farrar was "discontented with any leading man who was not Lou Tellegen." Unfortunately, her husband's good looks did not carry well on the screen.[80] Jealous of his wife's success, he attempted to steal scenes from her in their three joint films. Samuel Goldwyn recorded that "while they were playing together on a set Tellegen would frequently try to arrogate to himself the most advantageous focusing of the camera.... 'Take him that way,' we whispered to the director, 'and then we'll throw away the negatives. The ones we'll keep will be those where Farrar is played up.' ... Time and time again she tried to bring him into the conspicuous position he so much desired."[81] Miss Farrar tried to attain star billing for her husband, but Samuel Goldwyn flatly refused her request. She later admitted that he was right. Miss Farrar maintained her high standards of acting despite Lou Tellegen's ill humor both on and off the sets.

The Moving Picture World wrote that "Miss Farrar's first two Star Series releases, *The Turn of the Wheel* and *The Hell Cat*, have unquestionably marked the diva as one of the greatest portrayers of intensely dramatic roles."[82] The *New York Times* reported of her beautiful and fiery Irish-Spanish rancher Poncha O'Brien in *The Hell Cat* that "Miss Farrar is undoubtedly one of the best emotional actresses on the screen, and one who can look as handsome as any. She was reported to have said recently that she 'took her motion picture work seriously.' Most persons will admit that she can be forceful even while in a frivolous frame of mind."[83]

The same newspaper commented on *The Turn of the Wheel*, in which Miss Farrar portrayed Rosalie Dean, a wealthy young American tourist at Monte Carlo, that it "is considerably more engrossing than the common run of film plays. Either that, or Miss Farrar lends interest and distinction to the tale by her striking appearance and unfailing poise."[84]

Miss Farrar's portrayal in *The Stronger Vow* of Dolores de Cordova, a passionate Spaniard, torn between her duty to avenge her brother's death and

Geraldine Farrar as Rosalie Dean, 1918.

her love for the man who may have murdered him, was praised by the *New York Times*. The reviewer stated that the film "pleased chiefly by the acting of Miss Farrar ... with the exception of Miss Farrar, the characters do not look Spanish. They act well, but are obviously Americans in Spanish costumes; Miss Farrar, by her appearance and acting, makes her character ring true."[85] The *Chicago Tribune* wrote that "Miss Farrar blossoms forth most effectively as a Spanish senorita ... she plays as well as she sings."[86] Another reporter said of her Spanish senorita that "Geraldine Farrar has a character which unquestionably is well suited to her personality. In the role of a high-spirited Spanish woman she has plenty of opportunity to act with dramatic force and to display the intensity which is so much a part of her personality, on the stage as on the screen."[87]

Of her last film with the Goldwyn Company, *The Woman and the Puppet*, the *New York Times* commented:

> Those who have followed Miss Farrar's screen work need be told nothing of what she does in *The Woman and the Puppet* except that she is more intense, more intemperate, and more magnetic, it seems, than ever before. And into her headlong acting she introduces a number of dance scenes with accelerating and in one instance somewhat startling effect.
>
> Whatever else may be said about *The Woman and the Puppet* by way of praise or condemnation, it cannot be denied that she puts into it life and spirit that it could not have without her, even with the satisfactory acting of the other members of the cast.[88]

Although her last two films with Goldwyn—*The Flame of the Desert* and *The Woman and the Puppet*—were artistic successes, they were financial failures. "Geraldine Farrar continued to interest," wrote the author, Daniel

Blum, "but she never touched the heights of popularity she reached in her first picture, *Carmen*."[89] The diva was famous in large cities where she had performed in opera or concert. But she was unknown in the small towns whose film attendance was of prime importance to the motion picture industry. When Goldwyn informed Miss Farrar in mid-winter of 1920 that her films were no longer financially successful, she consented to terminate her contract with his company. Goldwyn wrote of their final interview:

> I went to Miss Farrar and asked if she did not think it might be better to stay off the screen for a year.... She was prompt to perceive my meaning, and with head up she took it.
> "Very well!" said she promptly, "... Only don't you think that perhaps it would be better to quit entirely? If you think so say so, Mr. Goldwyn, and we'll tear up the contract here and now."
> It was hard to tell her, but I did, that I thought this course might be wiser for us both. Thereupon, without another word and with the most gallant look in the world, she destroyed the contract which had meant two hundred and fifty thousand dollars.[90]

The termination of Miss Farrar's film contract with the Goldwyn Company in 1920 was not the end of her Hollywood activities. She soon accepted an offer from Pathé to appear in several films. The first in this proposed series was a motion picture entitled *The Riddle: Woman*, an adaptation of Carl Jacoby's stage play of the same name. Miss Farrar portrayed the melodramatic role of Lilla Gravert, a young bride, who is being blackmailed by a former lover, until his murder at the story's conclusion. Although Miss Farrar brought "the principal character, Lilla, to life as a definite, dynamic individual," the film was a failure due to an inferior scenario and poor photography.[91] The diva immediately cancelled her contract. According to Samuel Goldwyn: "She saw that it was infinitely better to be remembered by the pictures of her prime than to go on to a lusterless close."[92] In both motion pictures and opera, Miss Farrar wished to be remembered as a star, who had retired at the height of her powers, and not as a "defunct canary."[93]

Perhaps if the studios had supplied Miss Farrar with better scripts and had not merely sought to repeat her earlier roles, she might have maintained her success in films. This might also have been true if she had stayed with Jesse L. Lasky. He seemed to use her more intelligently than either Goldwyn or Pathé.

By the time she had concluded her cinematic career in 1920, American stars of the legitimate stage no longer disdained to "stoop to the degradation of the films."[94] The screen appearance of such a distinguished artist definitely aided in creating an aura of respectability for this new form of dramatic expression. "The fact of it is," concluded Goldwyn, "that Geraldine Farrar's chief value to the picture-producer lay in the publicity she brought."[95] Like her colleague and friend, Sarah Bernhardt, who also performed in films during the second decade of the twentieth century, Geraldine Farrar was a trailblazer in this thriving new industry.

In addition to the publicity value of her appearances in the films from 1915 until 1920, she had proved very effective as the heroines of melodramas and historical spectacles. They demanded highly dramatic and intensely emotional portrayals. Miss Farrar excelled in this theatrical style of performance. Her cinematic acting was noted for both intensity and realism. Added to these qualities was her exceptional pantomimic talent which enabled her to translate speech and thought into visual action. "Geraldine Farrar's facial expression," wrote the *New York Sun*, "is sometimes potent in explaining the scene."[96] Her portrayals were lifelike and relatively free from theatrical exaggeration. Although she was best known for her impersonations of fiery Spaniards, Miss Farrar's finest film characterization was undoubtedly her human and moving portrayal of Joan the Woman.

Her fifteen years of incessant practice, developing and perfecting her art of dramatic expression for the operatic stage, was of inestimable value to her work in the films. In turn, her experience in motion pictures was to enrich her operatic performances from 1916 until her retirement in 1922.

✦ Five ✦

At the Metropolitan Opera, 1916–1922

"I believe that my own art profited immensely from this work in silent pantomime,"[1] wrote Miss Farrar of her career in motion pictures. Following her first summer in Hollywood, she incorporated certain elements of cinematic realism into her operatic portrayal of Bizet's *Carmen*. In the opera's first act, she introduced the Spanish gypsy's brutal scuffle with a fellow cigarette factory-worker. Miss Farrar engaged a chorus girl to wrestle with her. On the evening of February 17, 1916, the diva caused quite a stir. After dashing down the set's center stairs with her clothes in rags and with a scarlet wound on her left arm, she seized, kicked, and floored her opponent. The young woman's mass of long hair had been arranged so that "it fell in cascades and flowed and writhed about so that it gave murderous impressions."[2]

The unsuspecting Enrico Caruso was the next object of Miss Farrar's new realistic stage business. Instead of throwing her rose at Don José, she "allowed her hand to continue with the gift and presented ... a blow on the cheek that could be heard all over the house."[3] Caruso simply rubbed his cheek. But in the third act, reported the *New York Times*:

> Miss Farrar's acting became so fervid as to bother Caruso in his singing. His friends say he was exasperated. At any rate, he decided the only way he could get his voice heard was to subdue his fellow artist. So he grasped her tightly in both arms and, in spite of her struggles, held her in a grip which she could not loosen. When Caruso finished Miss Farrar half broke away and was half pushed, and she fell violently to the floor. The fall was thought by the audience to be part of the regular business, and it was to a certain extent; but such emphasis had not been insisted on at the rehearsal.[4]

The famous tenor objected to these innovations, commenting: "Hollywood tricks! ... What does she think this is? A cinema?"[5] The press echoed: "Cinematographic exaggerations."[6] In succeeding performances, Miss Farrar never again slapped or struggled with Enrico Caruso. She did retain the first act fight scene between Carmen and the cigarette girl. It eventually became a traditional piece of stage business in every production of that work. Miss Farrar caused more commotion that same year, when she whistled parts of the Seguidilla in the opera's first act.

The press generally disapproved of Miss Farrar's new pieces of stage business, but they did commend the diva for the added emotional intensity of her portrayal. "Miss Farrar has now brought her performance of the role to a point of more animation and power than last year," wrote the *New York Times*, "and has made progress in the direction of building it up to a more consistent whole along the lines in which she conceives the character."[7] Henry T. Parker of the *Boston Evening Transcript* asserted that she had become one of the finest and most individualistic interpreters of Bizet's fate-driven heroine. By the fusion and projection of "tones" and "histrionic means," Parker claimed Miss Farrar achieved "a Carmen that added its own incarnating and propulsive power to the Carmen of Bizet's opera clearly apprehended, vividly imagined and thoroughly assimilated."[8] Following a performance of this work on April 5, 1916, at the Boston Opera House, Parker described Miss Farrar's portrayal of the Spanish gypsy as follows:

> The close-plaited black hair framing the face; the slightly swarthy and impassive mask that in repose suggested a conscious and baleful fascination and then suddenly became animate with gust after gust of mood or impulse; the contrasting movements of grave and a little dour self-absorption, the occasional instants of clear physical elation (as when Carmen descends with Escamillo before the bull ring) all suited the character; while the fluency and the vividness of Mme. Farrar's mimique and the clear force of her gesture—sparing and incisive rather than careless and voluble—as excellently served. Her dresses—above Carmen's purse and world, as the dresses of Carmen always are—added pictorial quality to an outward semblance that accorded with music and text and drew not a little from Mérimée's novel.... This Carmen plied her first fascinations upon José a little mechanically till indifference irritated and quickened her; let fly a savage temper upon the offending cigarette girl; and mocked as she lured the soldier to release her. This same Carmen played with lazy wantonness in the tavern until the bullfighter's coming interested her and finally kindled physical attraction and gratified vanity, in a blending that Mme. Farrar artfully suggested; took the returning José a little for granted and for the pastime of the instant until his hesitations enkindled her will. It was not this Carmen's way to let men go unmastered. Yet in the interchanges with José, an implication seemed to steal out of the impersonation that is rather of Mérimée than of Bizet, so far, in his opera. For a moment Carmen was the dour Carmen that sees Fate somehow creeping upon her out of what otherwise is but an ordinary amour.
>
> So, astutely Mme. Farrar led her personage into the scene over the cards in the mountains where that Fate looks as dourly into her own eyes, where,

indeed—a well-imagined stroke—it stands beside her in the restless José uneasily watching, his hand almost upon her. As Mme. Farrar seems to conceive of the character—and with warrant from text and music, novel and opera that call it into histrionic being—this glimpse of fate fills Carmen with an acrid wantonness and pride of will. In such mood, she surveys Michaela [sic], the "pure" and puppet-love; flatters the bullfighter; exasperates José; strikes and thrusts in natural physical expression of the perverse and scornful temper within her. Both pride and wantonness swell out of her coming with the bullfighter to the acclaiming crowd. With a perverse patience or an acrid flash of scorn this Carmen dourly endures José's entreaties. Fate hardly flashes upon her eyes or screams in her tones till its knife is in her back.[9]

Parker maintained that the role of Carmen was ideally suited to Miss Farrar's temperament and histrionic abilities, and that the medium tessitura of Bizet's music permitted the diva to display the "uncommon sensuous beauty" of her rich middle register. He noted, however, that she frequently forced the upper tones of her voice, which then became "pale" and "thin."[10] This dangerous tendency, probably due to excessive emotional intensity and to overemphasis of the middle and lower registers, had been observed earlier that season in a *New York Times* review of Miss Farrar's Carmen. This same article had also expressed an opinion, often to be repeated during the next three years, that on numerous occasions Miss Farrar substituted histrionic excellence for poor vocalism. "A large part of the audience will overlook these matters," stated the *New York Times*, "since in her acting she emulates the busy bee and is always providing something to occupy the eye if not to soothe the ear."[11]

During the next six years, Geraldine Farrar performed Carmen over forty times to sold out houses. Howard Taubman wrote of this particular production that "Farrar and Caruso in *Carmen* constituted one of opera's best sellers of all time."[12]

Aside from Miss Farrar's performances of Carmen in the 1916 opera season, she also repeated her interpretations of Madama Butterfly, Tosca and Madame Sans-Gêne. It was not until the following season that she added a new role to her operatic repertoire. On February 26, 1917, she sang the title role in the Metropolitan premiere of Massenet's opera, *Thaïs*. The work had first been performed in 1894 at the Paris Opéra. The libretto, based on a novel of the same name by Anatole France, was written by Louis Gallet. The opera concerns a fourth-century Alexandrian courtesan, who under the influence of a Cenobite monk, becomes a nun. The monk, however, falls in love with his convert.

According to the press, Miss Farrar's portrayal of the voluptuous Egyptian prostitute lacked forcefulness and conviction. "Her Thaïs had interesting moments," commented Henry Krehbiel in the *New York Tribune*, "but of the great courtesan it possessed not a trace." Flirtatious rather than seductive, Miss Farrar gave more "the impression of a Manon"[13] than of a Thaïs, concluded the *Tribune's* critic. Agreeing with Krehbiel, Richard Aldrich of the *New York Times* added: "The part does not seem to call forth her best powers. She only dimly presents the swift litheness and graceful activity, the incessant play of plastic pose, the rich suggestiveness of facial expression that seem to be suggested as the charm of the courtesan in her unregenerate state. An unceasing intensity and poignancy of dramatic style are needed to show forth the changing phases of emotion through which she passes, but Mme. Farrar was rather heavy and rather limited in her expression of it."[14] W. J. Henderson of the *New York Sun* also found Miss Farrar's courtesan an unconvincing portrayal, stating that "her Thaïs ... bravely labored to be shamelessly seductive, but was obviously doomed to sanctity from the instant of her first appearance on the stage."[15] In addition, he criticized her costumes as "unduly conservative."[16] Apparently Miss Farrar took note of the latter comment, because at her next performance she appeared in a gown described by Henderson as "entirely ... skirt. From the waist up it is exclusively Miss Farrar and two small groups of jewels ... inconspicuous, but essentially located."[17] Early in her career, the diva had learned that "to [her] profession the subject of dress was as important as the subject of voice."[18] Despite the change in costuming, Miss Farrar's Thaïs remained an unsatisfactory portrayal because of her inability to portray intense eroticism. Also her singing of Massenet's lyrical music was marred by the stridency of her strained upper register. "She was in exceedingly poor voice"[19] had become a frequent commentary on her performances at the Metropolitan.

Her next new portrayal after Massenet's Thaïs came nearly a year later during the 1917-1918 opera season. She performed the title role in the American premiere of Pietro Mascagni's opera *Lodoletta* on January 12, 1918. The libretto was Gioacchino Forzano's adaptation of Ouida's (Maria Louise Ramé) short story, *Two Wooden Shoes*. First performed in 1917 in Rome, the opera dramatizes the tale of a beautiful and naive young Dutch village maiden, who falls in love with a French painter named Flammen. He is suddenly recalled to Paris but promises to return and marry Lodoletta. Instead of waiting, however, she follows him. After watching him through a window celebrating New Year's Eve with a lively party at his home, Lodoletta leaves her shoes on the doorstep. She then collapses in the snow from hunger and exhaustion. When Flammen opens the door, he finds his beloved dead.

Miss Farrar's performance of the innocent and trusting Lodoletta won the press's approval. The *New York Times* reported: "Miss Farrar was ... never so naive, and withal graceful, as if the *Goose Girl* were suddenly become a swan."[20] Unfortunately, Miss Farrar's singing of Mascagni's essentially lyrical music was hampered by an attack of bronchitis, and she was forced to cancel all vocal engagements for a week following the premiere. She requested Gatti-Casazza to delay the second performance of the work until her return to the Opera House. Instead, he cast the American soprano Florence Easton as Lodoletta. Miss Farrar refused to sing the role again.

Not until the beginning of the 1918-1919 season did Miss Farrar add another new part to her operatic repertoire. It was the title role of Puccini's *Suor Angelica* with the exquisite aria "Senza mamma." The libretto for *Suor Angelica* was an original composition by Giaocchino Forzano and concerns the tragic suicide of a young seventeenth century French nun. Suor Angelica's aristocratic family have forced her to enter a convent after giving birth to an illegitimate child. During a visit, her aunt informs her of the infant's death. Once left alone, Suor Angelica swallows poisonous herbs. Realizing she has committed a mortal sin, she prays for forgiveness. Suddenly the Virgin appears with Angelica's child and pardons the dying nun.

Suor Angelica was a histrionic success for Miss Farrar but a musical failure for its composer. Puccini's lyrical music was criticized for monotony of tone. Regarding the diva's portrayal, James Huneker of the *New York Times* stated: "The piece has one role, which is played with histrionic beauty by Geraldine Farrar.... Her sentimental nun was lovely to gaze upon"; while the same critic wrote of Puccini's opera that it "plays fifty-five minutes, but it seems double that time, despite the art of Geraldine Farrar."[21] The *New York World* concurred, commenting that "Miss Farrar did her share by Puccini to a most admirable extent, but her individual success—and it was one of the most consistently fine operatic achievements to her credit—could not carry the work as a whole beyond the possible operatic limits."[22] Vocally, it was reported that she "was in better voice than usual."[23] Miss Farrar performed the role eleven times at the Metropolitan. It was stated in *The International Cyclopedia of Music and Musicians* that her "personal charm and vivid characterization galvanized a puppet character into life."[24]

One month after the world premiere of Puccini's *Suor Angelica*, Miss Farrar performed on January 24, 1919, the melodramatic role of Orlanda in the first American production of Xavier Leroux's opera, *La Reine Fiammette*. The composer was the leading professor of harmony at the Paris Conservatoire from 1896 until 1919. The libretto for this musically dramatic work, first performed in 1903 at the Opéra Comique, was adapted by Catulle Mendès from his own play of the same name. It is set in Renaissance Italy. Cardinal Forza wishes to get rid of Queen Fiammette, who is also known as Orlanda. He persuades a young man named Danielo to stab her, claiming that she had caused the death of Danielo's brother. Just as he is about to murder the Queen, Danielo recognizes her as someone with whom he had been in love when she was in a convent. For failing to assassinate Orlanda, Danielo is condemned to death. But before his execution, he is informed by the Queen that she is innocent of his brother's death. He then unsuccessfully attempts to kill the Cardinal, who immediately orders the beheadings of both the young man and the Queen.

According to the New York press, the Metropolitan's production of Leroux's opera was chiefly notable for the sets of the Russian artist Boris Anisfeld and for Miss Farrar's costumes. "The scenery is more attractive than the music," stated Huneker in the *New York Times*, adding that "Miss Farrar as Orlanda ... was a lovely creature, sumptuously garbed."[25] Leroux's music was condemned as "feeble,"[26] and Mendes' characters were described as "colorless."[27] Aside from such brief comments as "The character was not a difficult one to compass for such an actress of her attainments," or "She sang with dramatic intensity,"[28] little was said of Miss Farrar's portrayal. Anisfeld's massive "riot of reds"[29] canvas drapes dominated the stage. Attempting to "stand out"[30] from these sets, which Huneker claimed "thrilled the optic nerves,"[31] Miss Farrar had her costumes embroidered with diamonds and pearls to catch the spot lights. One of the diva's most dramatic costumes consisted of "a ceremonial cloth-of-gold dress, edged with ermine," to which she added "a vivid red wig ... with jewel-entwined braids" and a "heavy silver crown."[32] The opera was withdrawn from the repertory after only four performances because of the public's lack of interest. Miss Farrar ruefully commented that the work was "chiefly notable for its indifferent music and her superb costumes."[33]

For the remainder of the 1918-1919 Metropolitan season, she was plagued by attacks of bronchitis but insisted upon fulfilling her exhaustive schedule of operatic and concert performances. In addition, she frequently appeared at Liberty Loan rallies to disprove rumors that she favored the German cause. By April of 1919, she was suffering from serious vocal problems, resulting from incessant forcing of her upper register and from singing when she was ill. In the late spring of that year, Miss Farrar underwent surgery for the removal of a vocal cord polyp. The operation was a success. After a summer of film-making and a fall concert tour, the diva returned to the Metropolitan Opera Company in November of 1919. Her voice had regained much of its former beauty, and she refrained from forcing the upper tones.

By 1920, Miss Farrar had the largest following of any artist at the Metropolitan[34] and the Opera House's box-office "treasure trove."[35] Gatti-Casazza referred to her as the public's "pet child."[36] She was adored by people of all ages and statuses. But from the very outset of her career, Miss Farrar had appealed especially to the young generation of females who thought of her as "the great Glamour Girl of her era."[37] Mary F. Watkins wrote in the

Woman's Journal that "the thing grew into a cult ... the demonstrations at her performances attained the distinction if not the dignity, of a rite."[38] Throughout America these young women formed fan clubs. They greeted their idol ecstatically and showered her with flowers wherever she appeared in opera or on the concert stage.

Following the First World War, many of these young fans were adherents of the social protest movement and displayed their defiance of convention by wearing flapping unbuckled galoshes. These young women were referred to as "flappers." In 1920, W. J. Henderson of the *New York Sun* christened Geraldine Farrar's youthful admirers "the gerryflappers." Henderson defined the term as follows: "What is a gerryflapper? Simply a girl about the flapper age who has created in her own half baked mind a goddess which she names Geraldine Farrar."[39] On January 16, 1920, several hundred enthusiastic "gerryflappers" attended the first Metropolitan production of Ruggiero Leoncavallo's opera *Zazà* featuring Miss Farrar in the title role.

This opera had a checkered career. The libretto, written by the composer, was based on a play of the same name by Pierre Berton and Charles Simon. Leoncavallo's score made frequent use of vocal declamation. *Zazà* was a failure at its first performance in 1917 at Milan's Teatro Lirico.

It concerns the amorous adventures of a Parisian cafe singer, Zazà, and her lover, Milio Dufresne. Dufresne calls on Zazà in her dressing room and is seduced by her. She becomes his mistress without knowing that he is a married man. Hearing that he has been seen in Paris with another woman, she calls at her rival's home. She is deterred from making a scene by the disarming innocence of Dufresne's little daughter, Toto. After returning home, Zazà confronts her lover. Dufresne admits that he really loves his family more than he loves her. She renounces him, sending him back to his wife and child.

Geraldine Farrar as Zazà, 1920.

In 1899 Miss Farrar had attended a performance of the stage play *Zazà*. It had been produced in New York by David Belasco, with Mrs. Lesley Carter in the leading role. In 1920 Miss Farrar turned to Belasco for advice on her portrayal of Zazà. According to the diva, the famous director came "to the house where her colleagues were good enough to work in unison, to put real drama into this opera the music of which is not particularly remarkable without such underlying intention."[40] On the day of the premiere, Belasco sent Miss Farrar the following message: "Dear marvelous Geraldine Farrar. Your performance of Zazà is wonderful. Full of life pathos tragedy. Every throb of my heart will be for you and your triumph."[41] Miss Farrar's performance of the tempestuous, but also selfless music-hall singer proved to be one of her career's greatest achievements. The diva had turned Leoncavallo's musical failure into a histrionic success. When asked why *Zazà* had failed before she sang the lead, Miss Farrar replied:

> I can only say that it is a role which depends altogether on the true, convincing interpretation of the heroine by the singer. It calls on more than melodrama, there is genuine feeling, genuine emotion underlying the theatric character of Zazà when she realized what she might have been, confronted by little Toto in the third act, instead of a vulgar hussy! ... The singer who can make her audience feel that the emotions she is portraying are real, can make the figure from the libretto live in voice and action, must always carry her part to success.[42]

During the first act dressing room scene, Miss Farrar caused a furor. Following David Belasco's directions, she perfumed her bloomers with an atomizer, while changing clothes down to her chemise. Belasco then had the tenor run his hands down her momentarily naked spine. In the highly emotional third act, reported J. G. Huneker of the *New York World*, Miss Farrar opened "the sluices of the tearducts" as she "stifled her agony [in broken ejaculations], muted her vocal woe and looked so despairingly lovely [lying on the sofa while Toto played Cherubini's 'Ave Maria' on the piano]."[43]

The critic described her portrayal in detail:

> Zazà in the role of Geraldine Farrar is a sensation. She reawakened last night, did this disreputable but interesting drab of the old play by Pierre Berton and Charles Simon, and as her latest incarnation occurred on the boards of the Metropolitan Opera House, you may hazard without fear of contradiction that the naughty lady sang. She did. She had taken possession of the physical habitation of Geraldine Farrar; therefore, she was beautiful, therefore she was reborn with a golden throat.... It was Geraldine Farrar who was the entire show; a new "Jerry," and it may be admitted without per-adventure of a doubt, a Geraldine who will enthrall the town for a long time to come.... Musically speaking, *Zazà* is dry rot, hardly worth a critical match to set it afire. But it serves in its insincerity and unoriginality to accompany the thrice insincere story of the scarlet heroine who would a-wooing go.

Last year we noted the tendency in the art of Miss Farrar toward the dramatic stage. The entire season her voice was under a cloud. The sluttish psychology of Zazà is not difficult for an actress of her technical abilities. In sustained power it is thus far the most brilliant of her roles.... Miss Farrar is a singing actress, and luckily enough for her hearers, she is in her old vocal form this season.... She is Zazà. Zazà is Farrar. Réjane played it in a more literal, too literal key, as befitted the theatre. Mrs. Carter was alternately shrill and tigerish. Miss Farrar cuts nearer the essential bone of a feverish, artificial character.

She is dazzlingly vulgar when the scene demands that commodity, she is intense when she whirls off his feet the weak Dufresne, tragic at his defection, and wonderful, because unaffected, in her suffering when at the home of the man. There are genuinely pathetic moments in the interview with Toto.... That the fine Italian hand of David Belasco may be detected in the shaping of her interpretation is a further proof of Miss Farrar's knowledge of herself.... Despite its score Zazà is human in the hands of Geraldine Farrar.[44]

Max Smith, another member of the New York press, also acclaimed Miss Farrar's performance, stating:

Every one will want to, and should want to, make the acquaintance of Geraldine Farrar's portrayal of the title role. Decidedly, it is the most sincerely felt, convincing and moving impersonation this remarkable singing actress has ever put to her credit. More than that it stands out as one of the most remarkable histrionic achievements by any woman—which does not exclude the incomparable Mary Garden—on the contemporary lyric stage.

Many playgoers whose memory encompasses more than a few years will recall the Zazà of Mrs. Carter—a very striking performance. Yet it is not going too far to say that Miss Farrar in spite of the restrictions imposed by the demands of synchronous singing and miming, outstripped that highly emotional, if none too intelligent actress. Even David Belasco, it would seem, admits this. In the presence of the writer he remarked, at any rate, that without venturing to express any opinion of her vocal accomplishments, he could not ask for a finer embodiment of the character....

It was in the third act [Zazà's visit to Dufresne's home] ... that Miss Farrar reached her climax of her remarkable achievement. In the scene with Dufresne's little daughter ... she gave so pathetic a delineation of the conflicting feelings awakened in Zazà through the innocent appeal of her lover's child, and of her change of heart, only the most callous person in the audience could remain unmoved.

A careful and intelligently thought out performance it was which she gave in this memorable scene, finely elaborated in details of facial expression, of pose, of gesture, of restrained, tremulous, tearful, vocal modulation....

A certain artificiality has clung persistently to many of Miss Farrar's impersonations—to most of them indeed, ... In Zazà, however, she is the woman inspired, the woman actually suffering the agony which she translates to eye and ear through the medium of her art.[45]

Like Huneker and Smith, W. J. Henderson observed that Leoncavallo's opera previously had been a failure:

But last night ... the magic kiss of Miss Farrar had awakened it from a long sleep.... Miss Farrar's scarlet ladies rise quickly before the memory.

But not till last evening did Miss Farrar emerge into the glare of the footlights as a real siren. Never before did she reach the abandon of the creature of absolutely uncontrolled passion....

The play and Miss Farrar are the things, not the music.... Her impersonation is the opera. Let it be added that it is a work of art. She plays skillfully along the gamut of emotions.... Miss Farrar usually improves in her roles. However, it might be hazardous to modify last evening's impersonation. The master hand had touched it, the hand of Belasco. It is unlikely that Miss Farrar will alter it to its benefit.[46]

There were those, however, who did not feel that scarlet ladies were fit subjects for dramatic treatment. They criticized Miss Farrar for appearing in such a work and also for the realism of her portrayal. Henry Krehbiel, music critic for the *New York Tribune*, wrote:

The only question involved, so far as this review of last night's production will be concerned, is of the influence of the play upon the lyric drama. That influence, which we conceive to be vicious, will not interfere with the popular success of the opera. On the contrary, it will enhance it.

Should such things be hid? Shall consideration of dignity or propriety (conventions, both), prevent a prima donna from exhibiting her skill in impersonating a demi-rep who has risen to the dignity of a song-and-dance performer in a variety show? Not if she can add a feather to her crown of popularity.[47]

Krehbiel was appalled by the "flagrant realism in her shameless exhibition of vicious animalism in the scene in which she wins the embraces of Dufresne in the first act." The critic attributed these touches of realism to Belasco, commenting: "The ingenious and formative hand of Mr. Belasco was evident in Miss Farrar's acting, and the reflected halo, if that be the proper term, of Mrs. Lesley Carter in her crown of Titian red hair."[48] Echoing Krehbiel's aversion to the realism of Miss Farrar's impersonation, another member of the New York press said: "Evidently the conception of the authors required that Zazà should be represented as a very shameless, frivolous, coarse, sensual creature.... Would it not have been better art and fully as effective to suggest by song, word, gesture, the kind of woman Zazà must have been?"[49]

The most severe censure of Miss Farrar's Zazà followed a performance in Atlanta, Georgia, on April 27, 1920, during the Metropolitan opera's spring tour. Prior to her appearance in Atlanta, Miss Farrar had asked the head of the Atlanta Music Association how far she should go in the first act of Leoncavallo's opera. Colonel Peel had told her to "go the limit."[50] Miss Farrar then "sent notes to her friends suggesting that they sit on one side of the stage in order not to miss the undress show. The rush to left side, front row seats was noticeable."[51] The Atlanta newspapers protested vehemently against the diva's scant apparel. And on May 9, Dr. John Roach Straton, pastor of New York's Calvary Baptist Church, preached a sermon in Atlanta on the "iniquities" of New York City. He singled out for special mention the "prostitution of art" in the New York theatres. Dr. Straton referred to Miss Farrar's performance of Zazà in Atlanta stating: "The South ought to guard herself against the abominations that are perpetrated under the name and camouflage of art, and that have already debauched some of our Northern cities."[52] To this general eruption of moral outrage, Miss Farrar responded: "What on earth did they expect Zazà to be—a Seventh Day Adventist? It's rubbish to say I shocked them in the theatre. The operagoers of the South are just as sophisticated as those up north."[53] Zazà became one of Miss Farrar's most popular roles, but the Association never invited her back to Atlanta.

She ignored such censure. On February 16, 1921, Miss Farrar sent David Belasco a recent review of the opera and asked, "Why haven't you a twin-brother who typifies for opera what your genius creates for the theatre? No production has the flame of *Zazà*. Your interest and advice were incalculable to us and I like to feel it has the 'Belasco stamp.'"[54] He graciously replied: "I received your letter and the *Zazà* notice. Yes, indeed, I rejoice with you that it continues to please but how could it help doing so when presented by such an artist."[55]

Histrionically and vocally, Miss Farrar's performance of the flamboyant French cafe singer was one of her finest and most realistic portrayals. In fact, it was so realistic that the diva's father always remained in the lobby smoking a cigar until the first act disrobing scene was over. Her acting was free from artificiality or theatrical exaggeration, and her singing was no longer marred by forcing of the upper register. "She has never sung so well for years," wrote Huneker in the *New York World*, "as she does the meretricious music of *Zazà*. She positively melts or thrills."[56] "Zazà," concluded Richard Aldrich in the *New York Times*, "suits the extremes of her temperamental qualities as an actress, the gayety and recklessness of the singer in her element in the unbridled freedom of the coulisses, the amorous passion, the oppression of grief in the later scenes, in all of which she gives a forcible and sympathetic portrayal."[57] Dramatic realism, naturalness of movement and gesture, as well as ease of vocal production were the keystones of Miss Farrar's impersonation. "In *Zazà*," wrote Frederick Jagel, "she was fabulous."[58] Miss Farrar's ability to handle untoward situations on stage, such as a crying child in *Madama Butterfly* or delinquent geese in *Königskinder*, was also demonstrated one evening during a performance of Zazà. In the second act, the tenor lead, Giovanni Martinelli, sat down rather quickly on the sofa instead of embracing

Miss Farrar as prescribed. He hissed at her that one of his suspender straps had just given way. Miss Farrar "draped herself over him in the most beguiling fashion, herself taking the initiative properly the tenor's." The following day, the press censored her for "submerging her partner in original if dubious innovations in acting."[59]

The following two years, 1921 and 1922, proved most eventful in the career of Miss Farrar. She added the roles of Louise (Charpentier's *Louise*, 1921) and Anita (Massenet's *La Navarraise*, 1922) to her repertoire and began to contemplate retirement from the Metropolitan Opera at the end of the 1921-1922 season.

Since their first meeting in 1907, David Belasco had often suggested that she forsake opera for drama.[60] In 1921 he offered her the leading role in Melchior Lengyel's and Lajos Biro's play, *The Czarina*. After careful thought, Miss Farrar returned the script to Belasco with this note:

> It has taken me twenty years to establish myself on the lyric stage, abetting any dramatic powers I may possess by my particular vocal efforts; the risk of impairing this by adopting the dramatic recitation of the theatre with no technique in this line, is not to be considered lightly.
>
> *The Czarina* is no production for an amusing tryout, but a creation of months involving great responsibilities on both sides, in such a novel venture for me.... There has always existed in my hopes that some day, some how, I could realize my dream of a dramatic creation under your guidance.... But in this case of *The Czarina* we can't hold her over till I'm eighty, can we?
>
> I feel I am right to speak openly in this way to you, yet the disappointment is keen—but—what a woman to play.[61]

With regret, David Belasco accepted her decision and wrote:

> Your charming letter received and I perfectly understand. Of course you couldn't—now that I come to think it over. But it's too bad—for you are the "one and only" for the part. I could hold it over till you're eighty—as you suggest—but the authors might object (they are very unreasonable). You know that I admire your genius, beauty and popularity too much to really wish to rob the Metropolitan of a great song-bird—but all the same, I am selfish enough to yield at times to an overwhelming desire to see your plumage on my stage.[62]

While considering Belasco's offer, Miss Farrar was rehearsing the title role of Charpentier's *Louise* for the Metropolitan's first production of that opera on January 15, 1921. The diva invited the famous director to the dress rehearsal, since she greatly valued his judgment, but Belasco was unable to attend.

Charpentier's dramatically realistic opera was first performed in 1900 at Paris' Opéra Comique. It concerns the love affair of a young Parisian seamstress and an aspiring painter, Julien. The youthful artist wants to marry his neighbor, Louise, but her parents refuse permission. Torn between love for Julien, and duty to her parents, Louise finally elopes with her lover. Hearing that her father is dying, she returns home and nurses him back to health. When her parents demand that she remain with them, she refuses and goes back to Julien in Montmartre.

Henry Finck of the *New York Evening Post* felt that Louise was one of Miss Farrar's finest characterizations. But Richard Aldrich of the *New York Times* queried her dramatic identification with the role, writing: "As for how far she reproduces the essential nature and emotions of the Parisian girl that Charpentier drew, there may be some questions."[63] Agreeing with Aldrich, W. J. Henderson of the *New York Sun* added that her "clothes, shoes, and stockings"[64] belied the Montmartre sewing girl. Miss Farrar had objected to the "shirtwaist-sailor hat-pompadour effects" of the Paris premiere and had costumed her character in "simple but well-cut little silk frocks." Disturbed by Henderson's criticism, Gatti-Casazza voiced a diplomatic objection to the diva's costumes. Miss Farrar ignored his suggestion, claiming that the dresses she had selected best suited her "slender and elastic figure."[65]

Opinions again differed in regard to Miss Farrar's vocal performance. Finck found her singing outstanding, and Henderson and Aldrich considered it disappointing. Despite adverse criticism by the press of Miss Farrar's undistinguished singing and inappropriately elegant representation of a basically proletarian figure, the general public delighted in her portrayal. She performed Louise fourteen times during the 1920-1921 and 1921-1922 seasons.

Not until ten months after the Metropolitan premiere of Charpentier's *Louise* did Miss Farrar perform another new role. At the beginning of the 1921-1922 season, she sang the part of Anita in a revival of Massenet's opera, *La Navarraise*, on November 30, 1921. First produced in 1894 at Covent Garden, Massenet's opera had been a successful vehicle for the histrionics of Emma Calvé. The melodramatic libretto, written by Jules Claretie and Henri Cain, was based on Claretie's story *La Curette*. During the Spanish Carlist War (1837–1839), Anita, a beautiful young Navarrian orphan, is in love with a Royalist sergeant, Araquil. His father forbids him to marry her since she has no dowry. Learning that a reward has been offered by the Royalists for the murder of the Carlist general Zuccaraga, Anita enters the enemy camp and kills him. Araquil, who has followed her, is mortally wounded in an attempt to rescue her. Both escape Zuccaraga's guards, however, and return to the government camp. Anita claims her reward, but her horrified lover dies knowing that she is a murderess. Losing her reason, Anita collapses on Araquil's body with shrieks of maniacal laughter.

According to Henry Krehbiel of the *New York Tribune*, Miss Farrar's portrayal of Massenet's highly emotional heroine lacked the tragic power of

Calvé's impersonation.[66] In a less critical vein, Richard Aldrich of the *New York Times* also compared Miss Farrar's impersonation with that of Emma Calvé's, writing: "Mme. Farrar did it in her own way, needless to say, effective in a more conventional operatic fashion and lacking the horrific thrill of the elder singer. She made a striking figure as the peasant woman of Navarre, however, and denoted vividly the rude gusts emotion and passion by which she is swept."[67] Henderson of the *New York Sun*, on the other hand, found her portrayal "consistent, well-planned and theatrically effective."[68] But all of the New York critics agreed that she sang the role well. Miss Farrar admitted that she was dissatisfied with her portrayal of Anita, complaining to Henry Finck of the *New York Evening Post* that she had been unable to "get even one full rehearsal for *La Navarraise*."[69] Massenet's opera was not popular with the public and was withdrawn from the Metropolitan's repertory after only four performances.

Miss Farrar began to prepare for her retirement from the Metropolitan at the end of the 1921-1922 season for various reasons. Often she had said that she intended to retire from the operatic stage at the age of forty because "it is possible to dash on the stage as Carmen with all the verve of youth at twenty-five. It is a far less active dash at forty-five. The young Butterfly can get down on her knees and bob up again without difficulty. It is a far less active and effective Butterfly after forty." Miss Farrar began to note in her performances occasional "less brilliant effects" in "voice and action." Therefore she decided to terminate her career at the Metropolitan, since "the distressing vision of prima donnas overstaying their artistic prime gave [her] the horrors."[70] She was again suffering from nervous tension due to overwork and the emotional strain of a prolonged acrimonious divorce suit. Her marriage to Lou Tellegen had failed and she was charging him with multiple adulteries. "Mr. Tellegen," stated Geraldine Farrar, "had the perception of a moron, and no morals whatever."[71] He finally agreed to Miss Farrar's terms in 1923. She had discovered his French criminal record. In 1934 Tellegen was to commit suicide by stabbing himself seven times in the left side with a pair of dull dressmaker's shears. When a reporter phoned Miss Farrar for a statement, she "replied tartly: 'I have nothing to say and am not interested.'"[72]

When Miss Farrar consulted her family physician, Dr. James Russell, concerning her chronic stomach condition and insomnia, she asked him: "Why do my nerves bother me so, Jimmy?" Russell replied: "Perhaps they are telling you it is time to stop."[73] Aside from her doctor's advice, the diva was also "rapidly tiring" of her "well-worn repertoire."[74] Season after season, she was required to repeat the same roles because the management realized her portrayals of Carmen, Madama Butterfly and Zazà guaranteed sold-out houses. The Metropolitan Opera House had become "a treadmill"[75] to this highly creative artist. Despite her dramatic temperament, she was unable to develop into the heavier roles, due to the lyric quality of her voice. Furthermore, her position as the leading prima donna of the Metropolitan Opera was being challenged by a talented, beautiful and fascinating young soprano from Vienna. Maria Jeritza had scored a great success as Tosca on December 1, 1921. By January 1922, Gatti-Casazza had not offered Miss Farrar a contract for the following season, whereas in the past she had always been approached for a renewal months in advance. In the middle of that month, she accepted Charles Ellis' offer of an extended concert tour later that year. When Gatti-Casazza approached her with the offer of a new contract, she "quietly told him it was too late."[76]

Miss Farrar's retirement was officially announced on January 19. Four days later, following a performance of *Madama Butterfly*, she asked the audience what role they wished to hear her in at her farewell performance. The crowd shouted back "Tosca! Tosca!" and the diva replied, "That is something I cannot regulate, but I hope you will write to the management and express your desire."[77] Despite the pleas of her many friends and admirers for Puccini's opera as her farewell role, the management announced that Miss Farrar would make her final Metropolitan Opera appearance as Zazà on April 22. The public was disappointed in this decision. When Gatti-Casazza had conferred with Miss Farrar on the choice of her farewell role, she had commented: "Anything you want. What's the difference, since the public knows me in all my roles."[78]

Following the last performances of her various roles, Miss Farrar was wildly cheered by sold-out houses. She was inundated with flowers thrown from all parts of the auditorium. A reporter for the *New York Times* recorded that at the conclusion of *Tosca* on April 11, the shout of the house "rose to a yell like a Yankee home run cheer ... and Farrar in furs dashed from the stage door to her open automobile, which her friends had banked with wreaths and bouquets. The singer tossed flowers to right and left as she drove through the throng with her secretary."[79] After Carmen on April 17, Miss Farrar invited the Gerryflappers to her dressing room and gave them souvenirs from her stage jewels and costumes. Two days before her final performance at the Metropolitan Opera House, she gave many of her costumes to members of the company and her wigs to the chorus. She also presented gold bracelets to the telephone operators and the costumer, as well as gold watch chains and fobs to some of the house attendants.

April 22 arrived, and the *New York Tribune* reported: "The center of such a demonstration as has never before been known in the annals of the Metropolitan Opera House, Geraldine Farrar left that institution forever yesterday afternoon, after sixteen years of service." Many hours before the performance started, the auditorium was filled to capacity. Disappointed admirers hysterically attempted to bribe ticket-holders and house officials in order to gain admittance. Several times police were summoned to clear the various entrances of the opera house.

The performance commenced at 2 P.M., and the *New York Tribune* reported that Miss Farrar "put her heart and soul" into it and "never was ... more eloquent in song and action." At the conclusion of the first act, she was showered with bouquets. According to the *Tribune*, as the opera progressed, the "activities of the 'Gerryflappers' [who] all carried Farrar pennants ... were redoubled." Following the second act, a banner proclaiming: "None but you, Jerry! From the Gerryflappers!" found its way onto the stage. And at the end of the third act, the diva was presented with "a crown of pearls and emeralds, which she set upon her head, and a golden sceptre, ... conveyed to her across the footlights upon a red velvet cushion."[80] At this point, a huge American flag standing in a basket of American beauty roses was placed next to Miss Farrar. *The New York Times* stated that the audience, "moved by a sudden impulse, rose to pay tribute to the fame this American singer had won." Deeply moved by this demonstration, Miss Farrar "lifted a corner of the flag and pressed it to her lips and was hailed with shouts of 'bravo!'" The *Times* then added that at the opera's conclusion, when Miss Farrar as Zazà

> ... fell swooning on the floor ... people jumped to their feet, calling for her, and from every part of the lower floor men and women and girls ran forward until there was a solid mass of faces looking at her and cheering as she appeared.... She raised her arms and the house became silent.
> "Twenty years ago I slaved that achievement might be mine," she said. 'That I might be a prophet in my own country, but I never thought it would be like this. There are two folks down there in a corner who are probably shedding a tear now, two who gave everything that I might have my start, but I think that their parents' hearts are proud of this moment.
> "I don't want a tear shed in this house today," she added and was interrupted by a sobbing flapper who cried, "I c-c-can't help it, I've wept bushels," while the crowd roared with laughter.
> "I am leaving this institution because I want to, but that does not mean farewell to you," she continued, "I have many plans. I see on this side a dear man whom perhaps you have not seen, David Belasco. He is a very tempting person, he has whispered in my ear, but we will keep our secret a little longer. These have been sixteen years of happiness, such great happiness, that if I died tonight I would not regret it. I love you all dearly, but we are weary, and we must say good-bye."[81]

The closing lines of Miss Farrar's speech as recorded by the *New York Times* differed slightly from the *New York Tribune's* version which quoted her as having said, "I want to thank not only every one in this auditorium, but every member of the company, every gentleman and lady in the chorus and every member of the house staff for helping to make these sixteen years happy, and I ask you to let this be good-bye for the present, because I can find no more words to express what I feel." Her speech was interrupted "again and again by cheers, cries of 'you deserve all, this,' and other lauditory comments from all parts of the house."[82]

Gatti-Casazza had forbidden the staff to remain backstage after the performance, probably in an attempt to lessen the farewell demonstration for the star who had challenged his authority in 1908 and had rejected his offer of a contract in 1922. A secretary reported, however, that "one and all we pushed and crowded onto the stage to be with Farrar as she turned from her final curtain. We trampled upon the thousands of blossoms that had been thrown to the stage by the wildly shouting demonstrative audience that did not want to let her go ... chorus, ballet, staff, technicians, electricians, stagehands, porters—one and all we surrounded our idol on the stage. Such weeping, such cries of admiration and affection and regret and good wishes."[83] Gatti-Casazza's peremptory order was completely ignored by the Metropolitan's backstage staff, who idolized the "kind, friendly, appreciative of favors, generous"[84] Geraldine Farrar.

The *Tribune* reported that outside the Opera House, "the crowd, which began to gather at 4:30 o'clock, had reached mob proportions by six.... The street was packed from wall to wall with a solid mass of humanity several thousand strong." All were awaiting Miss Farrar. She was borne through this "ocean of wildly cheering humanity" on the shoulders of Phil Crispano, the Metropolitan's property man, and Charley Matterhorn, a stage hand, to her Cadillac touring car which was filled with flowers and flying Farrar pennants "from every vantage point." The diva, wearing her tiara, was placed on the rear seat between the big American flag that had been presented to her and a huge scarlet satin heart bearing the silver tinsel inscription: "The Public's."[85]

Flowers, confetti, and paper streamers were hurled down from the crowds on the fire escapes and roofs of nearby buildings. The *New York Times* commented that everyone "shrieked and waved" as Miss Farrar, "like a carnival queen, waved kisses and dodged flowers." Planning to pull her car up Broadway, enthusiastic stage hands had attached a rope to the wheels, but it became entangled, and traffic was stalled for nearly five minutes. "The crowd eddied around her car," concluded the *Times*, "while four husky policeman ... [pushed] emotional admirers off the running board as fast as they climbed up. Farrar waved and smiled and threw kisses to them all. The flag waved and the tiara shone. Excited men worked at the rope. At last it was clear, a toot on the horn hastened by a fussy police car behind, the automobile party forsook the rope and shot up Broadway at the head of a trailing procession of Gerryflappers two blocks long."[86] As the diva's limousine, escorted by four motorcycle policemen, turned off Broadway and proceeded toward Miss Farrar's home on Seventy-Fourth Street, the local traffic officer laughingly called out: "Well, what have you done now, Miss Farrar?"[87] Geraldine Farrar's sixteen-year reign as the "Queen Bee" of the Metropolitan had ended.

During her farewell speech, Miss Farrar hinted that she might appear under David Belasco's management. On April 24, Belasco sent her some flowers and the following message:

> All Hail! What a wonderful day! I did not send you flowers on Saturday as I knew that you would be inundated with them; but I am sending you some roses to-day to greet you when the others fade. I was indeed proud of you on Saturday and I took great delight in seeing the audience acclaim and love you (and no one loved your artistry more than I). We need you—a native American—on the stage of our own dear land. It thrilled me when I heard you speak of my whispering to you. My name, to me means so little, inspired me when I heard it on your lips.[88]

It was reported by the press that Miss Farrar would appear at the end of the 1922-1923 musical season in a new play which was to be selected by Belasco and "especially adapted to her art."[89] In a *New York Times* editorial on April 29, the problems to be faced by the diva in turning from opera to drama were discussed:

> The chasm between operatic and dramatic acting, which Geraldine Farrar is to span, is no longer so wide as once it was. Step by step with the development of the theatre intime opera has become near and human, less exclusively a matter of voice and orchestra and more thoroughly saturated with the atmosphere of actual living—the realized scene. Even in the pieces of the older repertory the gigantic strut and the sweeping, pivotal gesture which once comprised the singer's plastic repertory have been tamed and subdued.... There remains, however, a chasm, especially in the case of an artist whose first triumphs were scored in the opera houses of Germany and who has for sixteen years scaled her histrionism to the antres of the Metropolitan.
> Dramatic Miss Farrar has always been, even to the detriment of song.... To an artist of Miss Farrar's accomplishments the trick of scaling down a performance presents no difficulty.... So far as the conditions under which Miss Farrar has labored permitted, her histrionism has been admirably modern, unfailingly intelligent in adapting means to ends. And she is to have the guidance of David Belasco, master of artistic detail and crowd psychology. The experiment will be beyond question interesting, and contains promise of gain for the theatre. Never before has a star of such magnitude attempted to pass from opera to drama.[90]

After much consideration, however, Miss Farrar renounced all ideas of turning to the spoken drama, explaining:

It is true that during opera days my first concern and interest was the drama, seconded by voice. But to undertake a speaking career would have needed even all the preparation and years I have devoted to lyric utterance, where melody was my real expression. I am, by nature, a character type, and that dramatic repertoire is of another generation that burned out in glory with the passing of Sarah and Duse. If I have the speaking voice of color, it is not for the modern drawing-room roles or the limited compass of the fashionable offerings. A repertory theater might have interested my energy and stirred my imagination, but the horror of consecutive seasons in one successful role would have driven me to suicide. There is again the reluctance to capitalize a standard won in one field in the hazardous essays of another.[91]

Geraldine Farrar was content to be remembered as one of the Metropolitan Opera's greatest singing actresses.

♦ Six ♦

The Transition Years, 1922–1935

For the next two years after Miss Farrar's retirement from the Metropolitan in 1922, she completed a series of concert engagements. Then, from October 1924, until April 1925, she toured with her own opera company, performing an adaptation of Bizet's *Carmen*. Rather than presenting an abbreviated version of Bizet's opera, Miss Farrar wrote a new libretto in English, based on Mérimée's novel. She set it to musical passages from the opera. Aside from creating this "operatic fantasie,"[1] she designed the costumes and simple drape sets. She also aided her manager, C. J. Foley, in auditioning singers for the company, which consisted of soloists, a small orchestra, and a limited number of chorus members and ballet dancers.

Carmen was to be the first in a projected series of adaptations with which the diva intended to popularize opera in America. She believed that modern operatic productions were "too magnificent for the average person to care for." Thus the basic story lines had become obscured by excessive scenic spectacle, massive choruses, and augmented orchestras. "Opera," commented Miss Farrar to a *New York Times* correspondent in 1924, "strives to tell life's stories. With the aid of music the stories should be made supremely moving, but they have not been. There has been such exaggeration that the senses cannot grasp the fundamental idea and great art is lost except to those who have a definite background of musical education. The others are afraid of opera, are overpowered by it and choose any other amusement in place of it."[2]

Miss Farrar hoped to win the interest and support of those who found opera boring, confusing, or even ridiculous. The tour was both an artistic and a financial success. But once again the diva was suffering from severe nervous tension and was forced to take a complete rest during the summer of 1925.

While on vacation, Miss Farrar prepared adaptations of Puccini's *Tosca*, *La bohème* and *Madama Butterfly*. To her disappointment, the publishing house of Ricordi refused to grant performance rights, and she abandoned her project.

Instead, she accepted an offer in August 1925, from Alfred E. Aarons and A. L. Erlanger to perform the part of Zorika in a revised version of Franz Lehar's operetta, *Romany Love*. The plot concerns a young Rumanian woman torn between her love for a wealthy landowner and the romantic attraction of his gypsy half-brother. But after only one performance on November 24, 1925, in Hartford, Connecticut, Miss Farrar withdrew from the production, due to a nervous breakdown and dissatisfaction with her role. She claimed it had been so abridged that "the most prominent part of her contribution" was the billing of her "name outside the theatre."[3] The production, which was to have opened early in December on Broadway, closed.

Miss Farrar convalesced for the next two years at the Ridgefield, Connecticut, farm of her recently widowered father and vacationed in Europe. Her beloved mother had died in 1923. In October 1927, Miss Farrar returned to the concert stage performing as a Lieder singer until her retirement on November 22, 1932. Explaining her decision to retire from concertizing at the age of fifty, she stated in the *Saturday Evening Post*: "We are all pretty well fed up with those so-called farewell tours upon which the final curtain never drops until the undertaker is standing in the wings. We are only too well acquainted with the tragi-comic figure of the aging star, in diamond dog collar and rejuvenated tresses, tottering to a defiant last stand in the curve of a grand piano. And in my case this amounts to a nightmare. So, quite simply, I am escaping from the tyranny of the theatre in order to see the world before I need spectacles."[4] As in opera, so in concert, Miss Farrar felt it best "to get out when people enjoy you and not pity you."[5]

Although she had now retired from both the operatic and concert stages, her voice was again heard in 1934. This time it was on radio as the intermission commentator for the Metropolitan Opera's Saturday matinee broadcasts. Frequently interlarding her words with vocal illustrations, Miss Farrar related the operas' plots, commented on the performances, and interviewed many of the company's stars. She even persuaded Gatti-Casazza to speak a few words in farewell at the end of the 1935 opera season, when he retired as general manager of the Metropolitan. Gatti-Casazza's brief statement had been written by Miss Farrar, and after adding a few extemporaneous words in Italian, the impresario enthusiastically kissed the cheek of his former leading prima donna.

♦ SEVEN ♦

Retirement, 1935–1967

At first Miss Farrar lived a contented retired life in her spacious Ridgefield, Connecticut, home Fairhaven and then moved to a smaller residence Les Miettes in 1954. Her activities were varied, including traveling abroad, gardening and entertaining or corresponding with her extensive circle of friends. Frederick Jagel recalled: "My wife Nancy and I attended her New Year's Eve parties. Geraldine officiated at the piano and we would all sing an aria or song to her accompaniment. Finally at the stroke of midnight, Geraldine would lead us all in a stirring 'auld lang syne.' She was really an exceptional woman—jolly, a fine colleague, but a prima donna at that."[1]

Geraldine Farrar composed, arranged, and edited songs, as well as wrote her second autobiography *Such Sweet Compulsion*. Her musical compositions and writings entitled her to memberships in the American Society of Composers, Authors and Publishers and the Society of American Arts and Letters. In addition, she attended musical and theatrical performances and especially enjoyed the New York Yiddish theater, easily understanding the dialogue because of her fluency in German.

During World War II, she was a volunteer for the American Red Cross translating correspondence between soldiers and their non English reading or writing parents and later served as chairman of Ridgefield's American Red Cross chapter. Miss Farrar also was a member of Ridgefield's War Price and Ration Board, was a ground observer in the American Women's Voluntary Service of the Army Air Force and was a member of the American Women's Volunteer Service Transport, providing her chauffeured car for taxiing children to school outings. At the age of seventy-five, she dismissed her chauffeur and learned to drive a blue Ford Thunderbird.

Geraldine Farrar was a trustee of Boston's New England Conservatory of Music and gave her opera scores to their library. Her seventy years of priceless memorabilia, however, was presented in 1954 to the Library of Congress. Mr. Edward M. Waters, chief of the Music Division, conducted the negotiations with Miss Farrar and received an autographed copy of her second autobiography at the conclusion of his first visit to her home. When he returned a year later to finalize the presentation, he asked her why she had refused Richard Strauss' invitation to sing the role of Salome at the premiere of his opera in Berlin. "Mr. Waters," she replied, "if you had read the book I gave you last year, you would know the answer to that question." Recalling the incident many years later, he said with a chuckle: "She was very sharp!"[2]

Beginning in the late 1930s, Geraldine Farrar was to prove an advocate for African American classical singers. In 1939 she joined Jasha Heifetz, Walter Damrosch, Leopold Stokowski, Lawrence Tibbett, Kirsten Flagstad and Frederick Jagel in publicly protesting the Daughters of the American Revolution's forbiddance of the African American contralto Marian Anderson to perform in Washington, D.C.'s Constitution Hall. Then in 1945 she began knocking down walls of racial prejudice for the young lyric soprano Camilla Williams, who was to become the first African American to receive a regular contract with a major opera company—New York's City Center Opera. Miss Williams recalled:

> Miss Geraldine Farrar was a friend of Mrs. Howard G. Gilmour, whose husband was president of the Lorillard Tobacco Company. Although she lived in Ridgefield, Connecticut, Mrs. Gilmour came from my hometown, Danville, Virginia, which was noted for its tobacco markets. After I gave my final singing recital in college, one of Mrs. Gilmour's Virginia friends suggested that she arrange a concert for me in Stamford.
>
> Mrs. Gilmour didn't want me to know a famous lady was coming to my recital because she felt I would be nervous. When I got to the hall, the chairs were roped off with baby-blue satin ribbon. It was so beautiful, and all the invited guests were very important people. The blind pianist Alec Templeton was there, the George Biddles, the opera singer Marion Telva and all the wealthy retired people in the hills of Connecticut. And on a front row seat sat this beautiful, smiling lady whom I didn't know. With everything I sang, she smiled back at me. I remember she had on the most elegant velvet hat trimmed in teal and a lovely coat with a huge fox collar. She was so pretty. After the concert, everybody said: "That beautiful lady you were looking at was Geraldine Farrar!" I couldn't believe it, and afterwards she talked to me: "You have the most beautiful voice," she said, "and I'm going to write a letter to my former manager, Arthur Judson, telling him what I think about your singing."
>
> Miss Farrar did write Arthur Judson, who phoned her, because he didn't believe the great Farrar would take time to write a letter about an unknown little colored girl. When Judson confirmed it really was Miss Farrar, he was dumbfounded. She had said I should be given every opportunity for opera, because she felt I had an operatic voice. So they took me over to the New York City Center Opera Company to audition for the director, Laszlo Halasz. Since Miss Farrar had been one of the greatest interpreters of Madama Butterfly, they had thought of that role for me. The war with Japan was on, how-

ever, and it was forbidden to perform that opera. "If I ever give this opera," Mr. Halasz said, "call this young girl in to sing for me."

In 1946 he kept his promise and gave me the opportunity to sing Madama Butterfly on May fifteenth. Busloads of home folk and church folk came from Danville and Philadelphia, where I had been studying singing. My debut created a sensation, and Geraldine Farrar came out of retirement to hear me. When a reporter from *Newsweek* asked Miss Farrar if I had "the potentialities of a great Butterfly," she replied: "I would say that already she is one of the great Butterflys of our day." That's what Farrar did for me. We kept up a correspondence until her death in 1967. Sylvia Blein, the nice lady who

Geraldine Farrar and Camilla Williams, Miss Williams' debut, 1946 (Ben Greenhaus/Donald Greenhaus/Shabobba International, LLC).

was her housekeeper, told me: "Miss Farrar loved you, and your letter was on her night table when she died." I feel highly honored to have known such a great singer and human being. She had a wonderful mind and always gave me such good advice. "Keep the velvet on the voice,"[3] she wrote. "Do not push. Float your beautiful tones." I have a large collection of her letters, which I presented to the Amistad Research Center at Tulane University.[4]

Miss Farrar often sent messages to Miss Anderson via Miss Williams who had been both the first and second recipient of the Marian Anderson Award. When Camilla Williams was leaving on a 1958 State Department sponsored American National Theatre and Academy concert tour to fourteen African countries, Miss Farrar told her: "I keep your African itinerary at hand, as it is most interesting, and will serve to introduce you to a new world, new peoples, and new thoughts. You can serve as did Miss Anderson, in the capacity of friendship and good will; with your personality and sincerity, you should evoke even deeper reactions than those bestowed on an artiste."[5]

Aside from all her other numerous activities, Geraldine Farrar found time from 1945 until her death twenty-two years later to share her wisdom, knowledge, observations and vast experience as America's premier prima donna with a young pioneering African American classical singer of whom she was very proud.

At the age of eighty-five, Miss Farrar succumbed to a heart attack at her Ridgefield, Connecticut home on March 11, 1967, after a siege of bronchopneumonia and was buried with her parents in Valhalla, New York's Kensico Cemetery.

"The electric quality of her singing," wrote Harold C. Schonberg in the *New York Times*, "her beauty, her temperament, her considerable acting ability, the aura she cast, the glamour she represented, the hysteria she created at her performances—all those die with her."[6] One of the Metropolitan Opera's brightest stars had passed into history.

◆ APPENDIX 1 ◆

Theory and Practice

According to Miss Farrar, until prime donne can combine the arts of Sarah Bernhardt and Nellie Melba, dramatic ability is more essential than perfect singing in opera.[1] For those artists who were content to stand in the middle of the stage pouring out glorious tones and making as few movements as possible lest their serenity be marred, she had only contempt, finding them thoroughly boring both on and off the stage. "They never read," she wrote, "never have an intellectual reaction: food, drink and sleep seem to sum up their idea of spending the hours free from the footlights."[2] Miss Farrar was convinced that modern opera demands singing actors and actresses who are interesting and cultivated persons rather than mere vocal automatons. She had definite theories on their early training as well as the preparation and performance of roles throughout their careers.

After graduation from high school, she believed opera students should enter conservatories of music or study with private teachers. Her program of training for young singing actresses consisted of eight major steps.

First, they should study piano and voice as well as attend operatic performances to learn by observing great singers and to gain a knowledge of the repertory.

Second, they should have lessons in acting to teach them good deportment, natural movement,[3] and internal motivation of character.[4] She abhorred the conventionalized methods of the early twentieth century pseudo–Delsartian acting teachers, claiming that they taught a series of vapid mechanical gestures and poses which constricted the young artists' innate histrionic gifts.[5] Also she encouraged students of opera to frequent the theatre in order to study the techniques of famous actors and actresses.

Third, they should develop their own individuality of expression and beware lest they take on their teachers' mannerisms. Self-expression was of primary importance to Miss Farrar. She thought that the teacher's function was to instill self-reliance and the students should be encouraged to think for themselves.[6] Good instruction should bring forth the individual talents latent in students and teach them to seek from within rather than to accept from without.[7] Young singing actresses should learn confidence in their own convictions.[8]

Fourth, Miss Farrar believed that they should be fluent in French, German, and Italian. Only then could they fully and realistically interpret texts.

Fifth, they should submerge themselves in conscientious study of literature, history, and the fine arts. These disciplines would stimulate their imaginations and broaden their viewpoints.[9] Perusal of the world's "best books" was a necessity, as was a thorough knowledge of history. Also many hours should be spent studying sculpture and painting.[10]

Sixth, singers "must eat, exercise, live generally with an ever present thought of its effects on [their] voice [s] and appearance[s].... Singers must always keep in perfect working trim, just like the fencer and the football player."[11] Sufficient rest was essential[12] as was the avoidance of all vocal strain.

Seventh, they should spend at least three or four hours a day at the piano working on vocal technique in addition to learning and reviewing roles.[13]

Eighth, they should develop keen powers of observation. "The sight of a sunset," observed Miss Farrar, "or the gathering of a storm excites emotions which the ever watchful student-mind makes note of, and stores away, to be referred to when similar conditions present themselves on the stage. In the same way, human experiences of every sort serve one so constituted."[14]

Miss Farrar believed a liberal education was a useful tool of the actor's trade. But she did not approve of young singers being "cooped up" for five or ten years in academic surroundings. Instead, they should study "like hell" and "develop by doing, not bare learning."[15] In order to master the art of dramatic expression, she was convinced that artists needed to practice precepts learned in the classroom. Mere studio training would never give them the "artistic smoothness"[16] needed for a successful operatic career. The rough edges of professional inexperience could only be refined in the fire of routine. It would awaken and stimulate the singing actresses' intelligence and imagination, teaching them "economy of gesture and vocal volume."[17]

They should start out in supporting roles and then work into leading ones, first at provincial European opera houses and later at world renowned institutions such as the Metropolitan. They would become "smooth-polished"[18] through repetitive routine as well as through trial and error. She knew that practice was essential to a performer's development and thought it a disgrace that aspiring young American singers had to go abroad in order to acquire the necessary practical experience.[19]

Miss Farrar suggested that a system of municipal opera houses should be established in the United States enabling American artists to develop their talents at home. Opera companies could be organized in cities such as San Francisco, Dallas, New Orleans, St. Louis, Chicago, Cincinnati, Philadelphia and Boston. They could be staffed with local personnel: singers, conductors, musicians, dancers, stage directors and technicians. The expenses could be subsidized by municipal governments and private funds.[20]

Once these municipal theatres had been organized, a working relationship could be established with conservatories of music and reputable private teachers. A method could be devised assuring operatic appearances to the outstanding graduates. They would have developed a repertoire of six or ten roles, in addition to proving their proficiency in voice, acting, languages, history, literature, and the fine arts.[21] The young singers could receive modest monthly salaries and an additional fee for each performance. They could appear several times a week in a variety of roles, gaining experience in "many types of activity and polishing off the corners in the indispensable routine of practice."[22] Also they could appear as guest performers in other municipal opera houses. "This entire course of preliminary training," Miss Farrar suggested in an article for *Etude*, "would be calculated to occupy from three to five years of intensive work and activity, after which there still would be ample time for our hypothetical heroine to try her wings with The Chicago City Opera, The Metropolitan Opera Company, and at the larger houses of Europe."[23]

According to Miss Farrar, young singers should commence their operatic careers at an early age since from the age of twenty to thirty-five the lyric vocal artist "sings her roles with unconscious charm, she looks them, feels them, acts them best. Indeed, during that precious decade and a half she can well really *be* the very person she portrays." Although she admitted that a singer did not suddenly lose her "power on the morning of her thirty-fifth birthday," she did believe that after that age the lyric performer had "less time in which to scale her heights in the romantic roles of early youth." But even more important to Miss Farrar was an early retirement. The lyric artist would still be in full possession of her voice, looks, and charm, thus sparing audiences the pain of viewing "adipose heroines."[24] If, however, the performer's voice developed in volume to that of a dramatic singer, she could perform the "broader, heavier roles of Verdi and Wagner for an additional ten or fifteen years."[25]

Along with her theories on the training of singing actresses, Miss Farrar had decided views concerning the creation and performance of operatic roles. These theories which she preached and practiced, however, must be viewed in light of the time and conditions under which she worked. It was the era of the omniscient star and the acquiescent stage manager or composer. Like

Patti, Calvé, Chaliapin and Garden, Miss Farrar believed that a single performer should be permitted to work out his or her own stage movement and business. These artists were convinced that what they thought was right and that the unsolicited advice of others was in reality a challenge to their artistic intelligence. The American singer was advised by Sarah Bernhardt to "assimilate, my dear, but do not imitate"[26] and never forgot these words. Madame Bernhardt's counsel was the key to Miss Farrar's approach to acting, role preparation and advice to aspiring operatic actresses. Mere imitation was repugnant to her. She maintained that the artist should through careful dramatic and musical analysis of each role work out her own interpretation because "the personal must always rule."[27] She believed in an "intense personal expression"[28] and was contemptuous of singers who simply accepted some traditional conception of a role taught to them by a teacher, conductor or stage manager, instead of developing their own interpretations.[29] No singing actress, she felt, could perform a role satisfactorily unless she had worked it out from within herself. Miss Farrar always worked alone until she had given "consistent form to her own conception."[30] Once she had established her interpretation, however, she submitted it to the criticism of theatrical experts such as David Belasco and Madame Bernhardt.

In developing a role, Miss Farrar thought that the singing actress should rely upon both her "feeling"[31] and her "intelligence." The ability to create dramatic characterization was the outcome of a prolific imagination[32] which had been stimulated by "introspection, observation, and study."[33] She renounced the theory that performers' creative force emanated exclusively from personal experience, thinking it absurd to claim that they should have experienced all that they depict on stage.

Miss Farrar had an absolute distaste for decadence or vulgarity and was convinced that the performer should emphasize a character's virtues rather than vices. "In every work of art," she affirmed, "there must be a line of beauty; mere realism will never make a work live. An ugly theme, if it lives, must be treated in a beautiful manner. That is why, also a singer or an actress must strive always to express the beautiful."[34] Carmen was wanton, but more important to Miss Farrar was her courage. Similarly, Violetta was dying, but more significant than her coughing seizures was her self-sacrificing love. The repulsive features should not be eliminated from the portrayal, but the dominant impression should be one of "essential humanity."[35]

With each of her varied roles, the artist should strive to create a "responsive, impulsive human, not [a] mere [marionette]."[36] Conventionality in characterization was anathema to this actress. She demanded a distinct and highly individual personality for each role. "She is no respecter of tradition," commented a reporter in 1909, "but insists on doing everything in her own way....

Her way is usually better than the traditional one—more realistic and interesting."[37] "One has to admire Miss Farrar's versatility," wrote the critic Algernon St. John-Brenon, "the flexibility of her lyric disposition. She turns from Elisabeths to Zerlinas, from Cio-Cio-Sans to Juliets, and she invests them always with something that is new, delightful and personal."[38] Even David Belasco referred to her as "Geraldine Farrar, of many lifetimes."[39]

Miss Farrar's practices in developing her own characterizations were perhaps the clearest expressions of her theories concerning role creation. To begin the preparation of her own portrayals, she first read the libretto while mentally visualizing the characters. Then, with the plot and her own role clearly in mind, she went over the musical score, envisioning herself as the specific character either "moving about or standing still."[40] A word, a line, or a phrase of music might suggest a piece of stage business that would aid in the characterization. After many weeks of study, she would have diagrammed the blocking for the entire opera, based upon "rational,"[41] well motivated movements. Often, however, she was limited by the music and chafed against the restrictions which demanded certain actions on specific bars of music.[42]

By the time of the premiere, all of her basic movements as well as most of her gestures and facial expressions were securely etched in her mind. She placed special emphasis upon the face believing it the important feature of dramatic characterization.[43]

In addition, she established for each role a distinct and characteristic vocal color, such as an ethereally pure tone for Gounod's Marguerite, or a voluptuously sonorous quality for Leoncavallo's Zazà.[44] "One night," she stated, "I must sing a part with thick, heavy, rich tones; the next night my tones must be thinned out in quite another timbre of voice, to fit an opposite character."[45] During succeeding performances, however, Miss Farrar would often spontaneously change certain details of her original conception. She might add or delete a look, a gesture, or a minor movement. She might even alter the vocal color of a role. Realizing that the reactions of audiences varied at each performance, she believed that the actress should sense their moods— whether friendly or antagonistic. Then she should modify or intensify her "emotional appeal"[46] in order to win their approval. Although Geraldine Farrar rarely deviated in any large degree from her original blocking, she never played an operatic role in exactly the same way at every performance.

As she matured in certain roles, there were instances in which she did make significant changes in her blocking and in her overall interpretation. She completely altered the staging of the last act finales of *Faust* (1908) and *Madama Butterfly* (1910), and she eliminated the excessive childish petulance in her portrayal of Tosca.

In creating a dramatic characterization, Miss Farrar advised young artists that the ultimate aim should be the illumination of the librettist's and composer's intentions. The singing actress should study the entire score thoroughly. The role's body and facial movements should be impulses or emotional emphases resulting from the mood of the music and the text.[47] The artist should read books or look at pictures relating to the people, country, and era involved. Since every century and nation has its own physical and mental mannerisms, the singer has to be familiar with them if she wishes her characterization to convey a sense of reality.[48] She needs to know how these people dressed, walked, spoke, and thought in order to render a convincing portrayal.

Although her move from stage to films would seem to be a radical one, her theories of characterization underwent only minor change from one medium to the other. Her ideas on role development could be applied with equal success to both. The only significant difference she noticed between opera and film characterization was that her motion picture roles could be blocked during the acting of each scene. Instead of carefully diagramming the movements beforehand, she improvised each scene as it was photographed. These film impersonations were as individualistic as her operatic creations.

Her ability to create and embody distinct personalities for each one of her roles in opera and films was "intangible" or beyond human analysis. There was, she admitted, a conscious conception of the part, involving a careful study of "the costuming, local expressions and pantomimic idiom." But once the performer had become imbued with this tangible knowledge, she then had to be guided by her instincts or feelings. Miss Farrar believed these instincts or feelings were perhaps the result of some form of "unconscious self-hypnosis."[49] The artist subordinated her own personality to her subconscious in order to bring her conception of the role to the desired realization on stage.[50] Thus the actress was really "a thing of plastic fire and spirit,"[51] able to create within herself the emotions of a character.

Miss Farrar claimed that life was as real to her on or off the stage.[52] "You must hypnotize yourself," she stated, "into the belief that, for the time being, you are the person you are portraying and that the other characters with you are every whit as real as you are. If you can convince yourself of that, and of the actuality of your simulated joys, sorrows, regrets, doubts, madness, and passions, you will surely convince your audience."[53] As the curtain ascended, she attempted to cease being Miss Geraldine Farrar who had spent months preparing this particular role and strove to become that character. Instead of behaving as she herself would have behaved under the same circumstances, she sought to speak and move as the character would have done.

When on stage, she attempted to forget everything except "the magnificent pleasure of making that other person come to life."[54]

Convinced that each performance should be lived with "fire and enthusiasm,"[55] Miss Farrar asserted that she never went on stage or a film set without giving her all. "Spare nothing," she wrote in an article for the *Ladies Home Journal*, "give of your emotions, your feelings, your self." The singing actress, she stated, must mercilessly give of her own personality for the benefit of the public that came to see and hear her. Only then would the listeners respond to her performance.[56] Once the artist tries to spare herself by withholding her emotions or limiting her movements, a coldness or impersonality would appear in her portrayals. Geraldine Farrar lived her own portrayals with such fervor that a reporter for the *New York Post* recorded: "...one easily understands how the audience fall ... under the spell of this girl who feels her Marguerite, her Madame Butterfly, or anybody else that she plays; feels so intensely that she makes other people feel it, too."[57] "Be lavish and give,"[58] was her advice to the young singing actress. "If you love your art," wrote Miss Farrar in her *Ten Commandments for Opera Aspirants*, "you will work despite obstacles and love it. If you have to be prodded to it, better choose an easier gesture to express yourself. Art offers no crown for mediocrity."

From Miss Farrar's debut on October 15, 1901, at the Berlin Royal Opera House, until her retirement on April 22, 1922, from the Metropolitan Opera Company, she endeavored to practice the operatic theories she preached. Possessing a petite figure, refined features, charm, grace, a warm, sympathetic personality, and exceptional vocal as well as histrionic gifts, she was ideally suited for the lyrical "romantic roles of early youth."[59] "Personal beauty and grace of stage presence are an important factor in her favor, ... and ... in her interpretation,"[60] stated the *New York Times* in 1908. Visually and emotionally she virtually embodied the innocent Marguerite, the faithful Madama Butterfly, the youthfully passionate Suor Angelica and Juliette, the courageous Micaela, the charming and subtly flirtatious Mimi, the selfless Violetta, the saintly Elisabeth and the wistful Goose Girl. In the latter two roles, she captured their "spiritual faith and tranquility"[61]—qualities also prominent in her film portrayal of Joan of Arc. Even the alluring, wayward, and fickle Manon maintained the audience's sympathy when played by Miss Farrar. All of these beautiful young figures, who suffered in their loves, were ably impersonated by this American singing actress. She imbued them with her own grace and charm.

In the ingénue parts of Zerlina, Angela, Susanna, and Madame Sans-Gêne, Miss Farrar was equally appealing and manifesting her decided talent for comedy. This was especially evident in her impersonation of the elegant and amorous page, Cherubino. Her slim figure and graceful movements were convincingly boyish.

As for her impersonations of the flamboyant and outré Carmen, Zazà and la Fille, they were just as popular with the public. Disliking any display of distasteful qualities, she emphasized the admirable aspects of these characters. Thoroughly degenerate types, however, were anathema to her. In 1902, she was unsuccessful in her portrayal of Nedda, whom she considered "an animal."[62] Nevertheless, despite her aversion to roles of a decadent nature, by 1914 she had matured sufficiently as an actress to depict with brutal realism the drunken and debauched prostitute, la Fille. She detested this role "from her soul."[63]

Whereas she eventually succeeded in the portrayal of degeneracy, she was never able to delineate either the feline grace and animality of the famous courtesan Thaïs, or the calm strength of the imperturbable Ariane. Instead of being suggestive, she was flirtatious; and rather than being subtly forceful, she postured.

Aside from Miss Farrar's visual and emotional suitability as the glamorous heroines of the lyric repertoire, she possessed a voice of great beauty. It was sufficiently flexible for the rapid vocal passages of Juliette, and yet adequately powerful for the dramatic outbursts of Tosca and Elisabeth. She had a brilliant upper register necessary for the high tessitura of Madama Butterfly, Violetta, and Manon, as well as rich middle and lower registers required for Carmen and Ariane. In addition, she had the technical and vocal ability to produce almost limitless contrasts in tonal coloration, from the soft caressing notes of the seductive Manon, to the raucous laughs of the grisly la Fille. Despite a tendency throughout her career to force the upper register of her voice during moments of emotional intensity, she had a superb vocal technique—a fact sometimes forgotten because of her fascinating acting.[64] Never should the loveliness of her lyric voice be underestimated.

Geraldine Farrar was of the new operatic school which emphasized action over song. Dramatic interpretation was of primary importance to her. She renounced the conventional and brought genuine insight and an exceptional histrionic ability to her varied portrayals. In her attempt to attain theatrical realism, she sometimes exaggerated but learned to control this weakness.

"She was a fine actress and a lovely singer—beautiful to look upon,"[65] recalled Frederick Jagel. "She was a supreme artist whose acting and singing were perfectly integrated,"[66] added Mary Ludington, my New York singing teacher. Geraldine Farrar epitomized her own operatic theories.

◆ APPENDIX 2 ◆

"The Art of Acting in the Movies Requires a Technique Unlike That of the Operatic Stage," by Geraldine Farrar

(*Vanity Fair*, November 1918)

Mr. Tellegen really started it. It happened at the moving picture studio. As it was his first visit there, he had some difficulty in finding my dressing room. After wandering about through a labyrinth of alley-ways, he was finally guided to my door by a melody that chanced to be issuing from that corner of the studio. You see, in between "takes," I sometimes find time to study some of my operatic roles.

"Truly," he exclaimed banteringly, "you are an artist lost in a movie manufactory!"

"Not lost, *my* dear," I retorted, "an artist is not lost, but *multiplied,* in the cinema."

Then followed one of our many and endless discussions on the subject of the film drama; for, while Mr. Tellegen believes in the art of the cinema as a potentiality only, to be developed later into something artistically static, I always contend that it is already an established art, not brought to its maximum of perfection, perhaps, but moving very rapidly and surely in that direction.

One cannot blame Mr. Tellegen, however, for calling our studio a "movie manufactory." The huge, barn-like, glass-enclosed workshop looks more like a storage house for electrical lighting appliances and furniture, than a temple of dramatic art. In the center of all this mechanical confusion, the visitor is hypnotized by an island of light, so bright, that it is difficult at first, for the unaccustomed eye, to note that it envelopes an elegantly appointed drawing-room, enclosed by three walls, close to which are planted the clinical looking "broadsides," "mercury lights" and "flaming arcs," all of which contribute to the island of blinding light.

The "domelight" overhead not only adds to the luminosity, but alas, to the great heat of the place as well.

Mr. Barker, the director of my picture, "The Turn of the Wheel," which was filmed at Fort Lee during the burning days of June and July, jokingly remarked that he wore his broad-brimmed Panama hat throughout the day in order not to get sun-burned!

The great heat and excessive light, so hard on one's eyes, also acts as a disintegrating force upon one's make-up. Grease-paint and powder, diluted by perspiration, have an alarming way of disappearing in little rivulets, so that if one is to achieve the smooth and pearly complexion so alluring on the screen, one must stop every five minutes or so and repair the ravages of these artificial tropics.

Another thing that adds to the confusion is the fact that, while the scenes are rehearsed and "shot," a dozen or so electricians are constantly moving back and forth, adjusting the lights, shifting this fuse or that. Overalled, begrimed with the ear-marks of their trade, they move about with fine unconcern and a nonchalance that a debutante might well envy.

Very soon, however, one learns not to mind these conditions, and, as time goes on, one becomes oblivious to everything, except the scene one is enacting.

The dramatic technique involved in operatic acting is often complex, and nerve-taxing, by reason of its combination of singing and acting. I find that the simplicity of acting for motion pictures is a great relief to me after an arduous winter at the Metropolitan. My "movie" season is really my annual period of relaxation, for, having been blessed at birth with a super-abundance of vitality, the work at the studio seems more like recreation to me than actual labor.

Compared to the spoken drama, the opera in reality offers one a restricted sphere of dramatic expression, while the movies are quite the most unrestricted sphere of all drama. The greatest opera singers must all, in the past, have chafed under the dramatic restraint of the opera, many of them have threatened, time and again, to leave the singing stage for the speaking stage—but only in the days before the discovery of the kinetoscope.

Nothing, I am sure, would have given Calvé greater joy than to have punctuated her triumphant operatic appearances with opportunities to give full expression to her emotional genius in the movies, provided, of course, that she had a "screen" face and a "screen" personality: for one may be as beautiful as the morning star, possess the combined histrionic genius of a Bernhardt and a Duse, have the carriage and presence of a queen, and yet,

Appendix 2: "The Art of Acting in the Movies" 145

by some unexplained trick of photography, appear like a washerwoman on the screen. It is no exaggeration to say that half of our most beautiful and most talented stars of the speaking stage have proved absolute failures on the screen.

If one has the most essential of all attributes for success in the movies—a screen personality—the technicalities of acting are not so different from that of the spoken stage as one might expect. Of course, there are many little things that one must learn—not to open one's mouth wide when making the motions of speech; not to look at the camera; and always to remember, as in the pantomime, that all thought, ideas and expression must be translated into *action*.

The greatest difference, perhaps, lies in the make-up, always an important element in the theatrical profession. The size of the Metropolitan Opera House makes color-vividity an essential factor in "getting over." So, cheeks are rouged in an exaggerated way; eyelashes are heavily beaded, and the outlines of the mouth accentuated by the deepest tones of carmine. Of course, the strong "overheads," and footlights of the operatic stage, tone down these glaring effects so that a make-up that appears fantastic and bizarre when seen at close range looks perfectly natural to the audience in the opera house.

In the movies very little color makeup is used. On the contrary, any natural roses one may possess in one's cheeks, are obliterated by a heavy, creamish paste, uniformly applied. Since red, the color, photographs black, rouge on one's cheeks would give the appearance of deep hollows, on the screen. The rouge, instead of being applied to one's cheeks, is worked in very carefully under one's eye-brows, for that is where shadows are desired. Everything is based on the photographic principles of black and white. The eye-lashes and eye-brows are darkened a little, but no more cosmetic is applied than would be needed by a somewhat faded woman at a dinner party.

On the screen every little imperfection of contour or make-up is, of course, magnified, so that the aim of the player should be to look as natural as possible. What it loses in color and in sound, the photo-drama has to make up in *speed* and in *action*. By alternating the scenes rapidly, flash after flash, we are treated to a conversation between scenes and places rather than between the actors. By alternating a flash of the heroine, for instance, and a flash of the bracelet that is the clue to a dastardly murder, we have the heroine's soliloquy.

It takes anywhere from six weeks to six months of study and rehearsal, to bring an untried opera to a sufficient state of perfection for its first public performance. At every presentation thereafter, it must be reproduced faithfully in all its elaborate details of scenery, costuming, singing, acting, lighting, and stage management.

Appendix 2: "The Art of Acting in the Movies"

In the movies, it takes about six weeks to film a complete photo-drama, but, after that, thousands of copies are distributed all over the world, and more than a million performances are given, without further trouble to the actors, directors or any of the participants involved.

It is truly marvelous!

Moving picture acting is much like the acting in the so-called *commedia-dell-arte,* which flourished throughout Italy during the 16th century. A synopsis of the play—partly narrative and partly expository—was posted up behind the scenes. This account of what was to happen on the stage was known technically as a *scenario.* The actors consulted this scenario before they made an entrance and then, in acting out the scene, spoke whatever words happened to seem appropriate to them.

Technically, the same thing happens in the movies, with this difference: the action of the movie does not, like that of the spoken stage, march forward and gather momentum as it approaches its climax. Continuity of plot, while a film drama is in rehearsal, is chiefly conspicuous by its absence. Indeed, the scenes are acted bit by bit—rehearsed many times over—and, as each bit becomes perfect (in the eyes of the director), it is registered on the film and then forgotten.

Oftentimes, for practical reasons, the tail-end of the story is enacted first, and the beginning not touched until the last day of rehearsal.

And here is where the director makes himself felt. He must not only see that the plot of the scenario is logically worked out, despite the rather inverted, illogical method of rehearsal, but he must so enthuse, and hypnotize his players, that he will infallibly bring them to the creative pitch required for effective and telling acting.

If a motion picture star has this self-starting dynamo, or power of self-hypnosis within her, so that she need not rely on the director for her artistic stimulus, so much the better for her and for all concerned.

The photo-drama is the most intimate form of the drama. It brings a star dangerously close to her audience. For instance, one may see a star in the opera, or on the stage, for years, without knowing that she has a most ravishing dimple at the corner of her mouth; that her hair grows in a widow's peak; that her eye-lashes have an individual and utterly disarming way of curling upwards; that her finger-nails are exquisite, or that three or four freckles on her nose add a piquancy to her face that is extremely alluring.

There are a hundred intimate expressions of the eyes, the mouth, the hands, that can only be transmitted through the camera, and the strong and sometimes merciless light of the projection machine. And this is what the motion picture actress must clearly and everlastingly keep in mind—she is acting for an audience which is near enough to detect any insincerity of feeling; or any sham in make-up.

The drooping mouth and lifeless eye which can be hidden under colorful make-up on the speaking stage, the faint lines that one gets around one's eyes from lack of sleep—all these things an accentuated and magnified on the screen.

On the other hand, there are little movie studio secrets which are a great aid in obliterating defects of pulchritude, either temporary or permanent. Working on the principle that red photographs black, and that black (except against a light background) fades right into the atmosphere, rouge can often be successfully applied to blot out some offending portion of one's physiognomy. In order that I may not be accused of "giving away" the secrets of other film stars, I will tell a little story at my own expense. Recovering, this year, from a somewhat severe accident in Wyoming, I found that, although my nose was in its right place, and quite normal, at a superficial glance, there appeared on it, upon a more critical scrutiny, a bump, hardly bigger than the head of a good sized pin. This bump, I discovered, on the screen, impaired the vaunted straightness of my erstwhile classic feature. The first thing I did was to consult a surgeon, who assured me that it was only a temporary disfigurement, caused by a slight blood congestion. Relieved on that score, I was put out to think that I would have to stop acting before the camera until the bump had disappeared.

So I told my trouble to Mr. Barker, our director. "Oh, we'll fix *that* all right," he said. "Come here and I'll paint it out for you!"

He then covered the disfigurement very carefully with some of my lip rouge, and, although it greatly accentuated the bump in my mirror, I was soon delighted to find that, on the screen, my nose had resumed its pristine outlines and proportions.

I told Mr. Barker that I felt a little like an impostor. He said that I had no reason to feel so, because a well known and extremely beautiful movie siren had been born with a much larger bump on her nose which she had, for ten years, blotted out on the screen by exactly the same process. He also told me of another lovely star who had always obliterated a slight double chin in precisely this fashion.

It is known that blue, except the very darkest shade of navy blue, photographs white, or light gray. Therefore screen actresses who possess blue eyes, with a grayish or greenish tint, have to use various means to prevent their eyes from fading out on the screen. The method I pursue is to apply a little rouge on the top of my eyelids, the contrasting tones helping to deepen the color of my eyes on the screen. In close-ups, a piece of black velvet is held before me to look at. This has the same effect upon the eyes as looking into the darkness; that is to say, the pupils become enlarged.

Actresses who have thin mouths can often so artfully apply rouge that their lips take on the form of cupid-bows. Personally, I use no rouge upon my lips at all, for they are rather full and curved and the added color makes them appear black on the screen, a very un-beautiful shade for a mouth. I think over-rouging the lips is the most common fault of make-up among our better known screen actresses.

In asking me to write this story, the editor of Vanity Fair begged me to explain why it was that "so many film stars—whom the public know to be in the roaring forties—counting the years back to their first stage appearances, diamond robberies and divorce suits could still take children's parts so realistically that even the Gerry Society was deceived by them?" He wanted to know whether any tricks in make-up were involved in the mystery.

I think that, on that score, he is over-suspicious. The stars he refers to are merely fortunate in retaining the juvenile contours of their faces and figures.

The conventional conception of a prima donna is that of a woman who is constantly swathed in cotton, timid and hating contact with actuality and life. It is a conception which, in connection with myself, I utterly abhor. I love action, danger, movement, life. When it was first announced that I was to do *Joan the Woman*—a great many scenes in the screen version of which are really fraught with physical danger—people wondered whether I would act out the scenes with real abandon, or merely shirk the vivid action scenes altogether. When the picture was finally finished and shown, I am sure that my audiences were convinced that even in the most risky scenes, I did not do things by halves.

My second Goldwyn picture, *The Hell Cat*, was filmed in Wyoming this summer and we spent the entire month of August in this truly wild and woolly country, living without many of the necessities and comforts which even little shop girls in New York are accustomed to. Our location, Valley Ranch, was fifteen miles from the Irma Hotel at Cody, and more than once we found ourselves in far from civilized surroundings. If it hadn't been for the fact that we all entered into this expedition with a spirit of true adventure and good-natured tolerance, I am quite sure we would all have come to grief.

Several times during the very rough scenes in my various photoplays, I have been slightly injured, but never sufficiently to discourage future attempts at daring and realism. Only last summer, while we were making "The Hell Cat" I met with an accident which I thought would prove fatal to my looks, if not to my very existence. As the heroine of the drama, tied hand and foot, my only means of defying the villain was by biting him with my teeth and lunging at him with my head. During one of my most savage lunges, my face struck his head so forcibly that, in addition to my being knocked senseless, my nose was dislocated and, if it hadn't been for Mr. Tellegen's prompt and efficacious surgical ministrations, I do not know whether I would ever again have been able to face the camera, for the nearest physician was fifty miles away.

My friends often ask me whether, in acting movie dramas, I do not miss the audiences and the applause? Since the mechanics of motion pictures are what they are, perhaps it is just as well that we cannot have audiences while we work in them. But if it were only possible to give a logical and sustained performance of the completed action of a photoplay before a representative movie audience, before the camera fixes it indelibly upon the film, it would be a tremendous help.

The presence of an audience is always a great stimulus. A direct and almost electric current is established between the actress and her audience the very first minute she appears on the stage. An actress can feel the quality of her audiences, the intensity of their friendliness and interest, or, on the other hand, their unconvinced or even antagonistic state of mind. She can, in this way, gauge her public and intensify or modify her emotional appeal in such a way as to win them over. No actress knows her *metier* until she has learned to sense the mood of her audiences—and win them over, if the mood is one of antagonism.

Exactly what an actress must do to sense the varying moods of her audience, I believe no one, least of all myself, can say. All I know is that this instinct rarely fails me. Critics have often remarked that I never play a role in the same way on any two occasions, and I am sure that this is so, because I always try to adapt my interpretations to fit the mood of my audience.

When I began working in the cinema I missed this intimate and living relationship between the public and myself. At first, I kept trying to think of *imaginary* audiences, but I soon found that this rather hindered than helped me, for in the movies, one must not think of an audience at all. One must hypnotize oneself into the belief that, for the time being, you *are* the person you are portraying, and that the other characters playing with you are every whit as real as you are. If you can convince yourself of that, and of the actuality of your simulated joys, sorrows, regrets, doubts, madnesses and passions, you will surely convince your audiences.

✦ APPENDIX 3 ✦

Conversations on Geraldine Farrar with Camilla Williams, 1995–2011

Singing

Miss Farrar told Miss Williams to sing with both her head and heart, always emphasizing vocal quality over dramatic tone. When learning a new role, she should spare her voice with extensive silent study and proceed cautiously in the initial performances until she was acquainted with the theater's acoustical demands. Often vocal effects learned in a studio did not carry in the auditorium and the performer needed to avoid straining the voice in order to be heard. During necessary vocal climaxes, rather than forcing her normal tone, she should let her voice soar over the voluminous orchestra. Miss Farrar warned the young soprano against excessive use of the chest register since her voice obviously lay in her effortlessly beautiful top register. "Keep the velvet on the voice" was her constant admonition.

Miss Williams was also advised to find time for relaxation of the body, voice, nerves and mind. Since the voice reflects the singer's physical state, rest is necessary for the retention of lustrous vocal quality, freshness, mental acumen and "the nervous energy which is the propelling force for a magnetic performance." Miss Farrar constantly reminded Miss Williams to spare her emotions for the stage. Above all she must not allow the "pin pricks" of disappointment or words and actions of jealous people to depress her because the voice will suffer. Serenity of spirit and physical well-being are essential for beautiful singing. "Stay well, happy, and study, study, study ad infinitum" was a Farrar watchword. In addition, she should read all critical reviews with objectivity as to their validity and especially "examine" herself.

Butterfly

Miss Farrar advised Miss Williams to beware of this role's fatiguing physical demands and intense emotions which could tempt the young singer to force her voice over the volume of the orchestra. This would eventually lead to vocal and emotional fatigue. She constantly emphasized the need to conserve her fresh, soaring beautiful vocal quality. As often as Miss Williams performed the role, she was told never to lose its tender and appealing nature. Miss Farrar also suggested that she study *Madama Butterfly* with the soprano Marie Savage, a member of the Metropolitan Opera for thirty-one years and a teacher of operatic repertoire, who would probably remember many of Miss Farrar's own distinct actions in the role. Then "sing and act it from your OWN heart." When Miss Williams was later to perform *Madama Butterfly* abroad in German, Miss Farrar reassured her that the translation effectively conveyed the meaning and emotions of the text so just to sing it with beauty of tone and clarity of diction.

Mimi

Miss Farrar told her to perform this tender lyric role in a simple, unaffected, modest manner with lovely singing and intensity of feeling. Mimi must be shy and appealing while Musetta is arch and lively. She again recommended that Miss Williams study the role with an acting coach but then decide on her own portrayal. After closing the door at the end of the first act while singing the duet's concluding phrase ending on a high C, she advised her to sing it mezza voce "towards the back of the stage." She could then sing it with a solid sound and it would seem softer in the auditorium as well as avoiding a potentially evasive pianissimo or elusive pitch. Also it would prevent the tenor from overwhelming her on the high C. During the third act, she should maintain beautiful singing despite the vocal and emotional intensity caused by her illness and the "anguish" of quarreling with her lover. In the last act, she advised using a gentle sung tone rather than parlando and recommended at the end: "to turn her face towards the public as she caresses the muff; then let it drop slowly to the floor, to indicate that death releases the holding of it."

Nedda

Miss Farrar recommended that she avoid forcing and tiring the voice on dramatic climaxes and emphasize the high rather than the chest register of the role. Also, she warned her to let her body completely relax when she collapsed in the last act.

Micaela

Miss Farrar thought Micaela was an ideal role for Miss Williams, revealing the loveliness of her lyric voice in the beautiful first act duet and third act aria free of arduous vocal requirements.

Marguerite

Miss Farrar believed that Marguerite, like Micaela, demands exquisite singing and simplicity of manner free of emotional exaggeration. She regretted that the opera was to be performed in English because in French the vocal phrases are supported by the meaning of the words. In the final trio's three repeated ascending phrases, she advised Miss Williams "to begin in moderate style and volume, increase in intensity on the second reprise, and reserve full volume for the last phrase so the mounting scale should provide the requisite impulse for accent."

Aida

At first Miss Farrar did not approve of Miss Williams performing Verdi's Aida, convinced that the role's dramatic music was inappropriate for so tender and delicate a lyric voice. She advised her against singing anything that could potentially spoil the lovely quality of her voice which was her greatest asset and repeated her beloved teacher Lilli Lehmann's words that "you should correct immediately whatever taxes your voice." Since Miss Williams was committed to performing the role of Aida at the New York City Opera, Miss Farrar counseled her to create the necessary "required accents in fine singing" rather than forcing her voice, particularly with the Nile scene's soaring phrases.

Camilla Williams, diva and Geraldine Farrar's protégée, 1950s.

She hoped that in the future Miss Williams would be able to choose those roles best suited to the quality and freshness of her voice and sing Aida as little as possible. "Let others who will, yell to their mistaken hearts' content."

Recitals

According to Miss Farrar, recitals are complex creations involving the appropriate selection of songs as well as their representation and differentiation. She not only recommended specific vocal music appropriate to Miss Williams' vocal range but sent her albums of songs. Her choice of composers and styles was varied, including Haydn, Mozart, Schubert, Mendelssohn, Brahms, Hugo Wolf, Gounod, Dvořák, Rachmaninoff, Grechaninoff, Moussorgsky and Richard Strauss. She believed that Mozart's works should be well represented in every singer's repertoire since they require "classic style and fine singing" while aiding the spirit. She also recommended Miss Williams investigate the modern repertoire "for both artistic and business reasons."

New Fields and Audiences

Miss Farrar remained well informed on the musical scene and was an astute advisor for potential career development. Realizing that the concert field in the United States was being challenged by television and radio, she recommended that Miss Williams consider tours to Paris, Italy, Scandinavia, Japan, Australia and South Africa. She suggested adding these countries' vocal literature to her repertoire since a singer must continually investigate the potential for new musical opportunities. Miss Williams was later to visit fourteen African countries as well as Australia and Japan. "You young artists are embracing a wide area of interest, and through the medium of the arts," observed Miss Farrar, "perhaps the gentler muse may have more influence and good will than the professional diplomat."

Also she mentioned performances of secular and religious works with symphony orchestras as well as concerts alternating singing and relating of interesting personal experiences while on tour. Miss Farrar recommended the keeping of a daily diary for reference and as a record of her career in the world of music even containing observations on the challenges of singing while indisposed or the need for vocal adjustments to various sized auditoriums. She had always maintained one herself.

But Miss Farrar was not an advocate of the new mediums of radio and television which she felt were not always favorable to the singer either vocally or photographically. The vital intercommunication between the artist and the audience was lacking. It was in the hands of studio engineers and cameramen manipulating the sound and picture rather than the singers' live performances. Managers, press agents, and public demand were fostering too many "odd little talents" with "praise indiscriminate." She advised Miss Williams to avoid the new mediums.

Because Miss Williams was now a recognized performer, Miss Farrar advised her to consider working with a personal representative instead of an agency managing numerous singers and desirous of introducing new talent with its "element of surprise."

She even broached the topic of eventual teaching. It was not until after Miss Farrar's death, however, that Miss Williams was to become the first African American to join the prestigious voice faculty of Indiana University's School of Music in 1977. Geraldine Farrar was very savvy.

✦ Appendix 4 ✦

Operatic Roles

Berlin, Royal Opera

Marguerite, *Faust*, Gounod, 1901.
Violetta, *La traviata*, Verdi, 1901.
Nedda, *I pagliacci*, Leoncavallo, 1901.
Zerlina, *Don Giovanni*, Mozart, 1902.
Juliette, *Roméo et Juliette*, Gounod, 1902.
Leonora, *Il trovatore*, Verdi, 1903.
Manon, *Manon*, Massenet, 1903.
Mignon, *Mignon*, Thomas, 1904.
Angela, *Le Domino noir*, Auber, 1905.
Elisabeth, *Tannhäuser*, Wagner, 1905.
Gilda, *Rigoletto*, Verdi, 1906.

Monte Carlo, Casino

Mimi, *La bohème*, Puccini, 1904.
Marguerite, *La Damnation de Faust*, Berlioz, 1905.
Arnica, *Amica*, Mascagni, 1905.
Sita, *Le Roi de Lahore*, Massenet, 1906.
Margarita, *L'Ancêtre*, Saint-Saëns, 1906.
Queen Elizabeth, *Don Carlo*, Verdi, 1906.

Warsaw, Imperial Theatre

Maddalena, *Andrea Chénier*, Giordano, 1904.

Paris, Nouveau Théâtre and Opéra Comique

Zephirine, *Le clown*, Camondo, 1906.

New York, The Metropolitan Opera

Juliette, *Roméo et Juliette*, Gounod, 1906–1911.
Marguerite, *La Damnation de Faust*, Berlioz, 1906–1907.
Marguerite, *Faust*, Gounod, 1906–1922.
Elisabeth, *Tannhäuser*, Wagner, 1907.
Cio-Cio-San, *Madama Butterfly*, Puccini, 1907–1922.
Mimi, *La bohème*, Puccini, 1907–1922.
Nedda, *I pagliacci*, Leoncavallo, 1907–1908.
Margherita, *Mefistofele*, Boito, 1907.
Zerlina, *Don Giovanni*, Mozart, 1908.
Violetta, *La traviata*, Verdi, 1908.
Mignon, *Mignon*, Thomas, 1908.
Micaela, *Carmen*, Bizet, 1908.
Cherubino, *Le nozze di Figaro*, Mozart, 1909–1918.
Manon, *Manon*, Massenet, 1909–1915.
Charlotte, *Werther*, Massenet, 1909–1910.
Tosca, *Tosca*, Puccini, 1909–1922.
Goose Girl, *Königskinder*, Humperdinck, 1910–1914.
Ariane, *Ariane et Barbe-Bleue*, Dukas, 1911–1912.
Rosaura, *Le donne curiose*, Wolf-Ferrari, 1912–1913.
Susanna, *Il segreto di Susanna*, Wolf-Ferrari, 1912–1913.
La Beauté/La Jeune Fille/L'Aïeule/La Fille, *Julien*, Charpentier, 1914.
Carmen, *Carmen*, Bizet, 1914–1922.
Caterina, *Madame Sans-Gêne*, Giordano, 1915–1918.
Thaïs, *Thaïs*, Massenet, 1917–1919.
Lodoletta, *Lodoletta*, Mascagni, 1918.
Suor Angelica, *Suor Angelica*, Puccini, 1918–1920.
Orlanda, *La Reine Fiammette*, Leroux, 1919.
Zazà, *Zazà*, Leoncavallo, 1920–1922.
Louise, *Louise*, Charpentier, 1921–1922.
Anita, *La Navarraise*, Massenet, 1921–1922.

✦ APPENDIX 5 ✦

Silent Films

Jesse L. Lasky Feature Play Company

Carmen 1915

The gypsy Carmen seduces and deserts a Spanish soldier who kills her.
Directed by Cecil B. De Mille. Cast: Geraldine Farrar, Wallace Reid, Pedro de Cordoba, Jeanie Macpherson.
Running time: 59 minutes
(DVD available from VAI DVD 4362)

Temptation 1915

The opera singer Renee Dupree attempts to save the life of her ill lover.
Directed by Cecil B. De Mille. Cast: Geraldine Farrar, Theodore Roberts, Pedro de Cordoba, Raymond Hatton, Elsie Jane Wilson.
Running time: 60 minutes

Maria Rosa 1916

The Catalonian peasant Maria Rosa struggles to marry her imprisoned lover.
Directed by Cecil B. De Mille. Cast: Geraldine Farrar, Wallace Reid, Pedro de Cordoba.
Running time: 50 minutes

Joan the Woman 1917

The life of Joan of Arc.
Directed by Cecil B. De Mille. Cast: Geraldine Farrar, Wallace Reid, Raymond Hatton, Theodore Roberts, Hobart Bosworth Charles Clary, Tully Marshall, James Neill, Marjorie Daw, Lillian Leighton, Walter Long.
Running time: 138 minutes
(DVD available from IMAGE ENTERTAINMENT (Blackhawk Films Collection) DVD ID0509DSDVD)

Feature Films-Lasky Corporation

The Woman God Forgot 1917

Montezuma's daughter Tecza betrays her country for the love of a Spanish officer.
Directed by Cecil B. De Mille. Cast: Geraldine Farrar, Wallace Reid, Raymond Hatton, Hobart Bosworth, Theodore Kosloff.
Running time: 60 minutes

The Devil-Stone 1917

The possession of an enchanted emerald turns the Breton fishermaid Marcia Manot into the Norse Queen Grenalda.
Directed by Cecil B. De Mille. Cast: Geraldine Farrar, Wallace Reid, Hobart Bosworth, Tully Marshall, James Neill, Gustav von Seffertitz, Mabel Van Buren, Lillian Leighton.
Running time: 60 minutes

Goldwyn Pictures Corporation

The Turn of the Wheel 1918

Rosalie Dean attempts to prove the innocence of her lover in the murder of his wife.
Directed by Reginald Barker. Cast: Geraldine Farrar, Herbert Rawlinson, Percy Marmont, Violet Heming, Hassard Short.
Running time: 50 minutes

The Hell-Cat 1918

The beautiful and fiery Irish-Spanish Poncha O'Brien is a Wyoming rancher.
Directed by Reginald Barker. Cast: Geraldine Farrar, Milton Sills, Thomas Santschi, William W. Black, Evelyn Axzell.
Running time: 60 minutes

Shadows 1918

The socialite Muriel Barnes attempts to regain her reputation after the revelation of her past as the dance hall girl Cora Lamont.
Directed by Reginald Barker. Cast: Geraldine Farrar, Milton Sills, Thomas Santschi.
Running time: 50 minutes

The Stronger Vow 1919

The Spanish Dolores de Cordova has sworn to avenge her brother's murder but suspects her husband of the crime. She must choose between her two vows.

Directed by Reginald Barker. Cast: Geraldine Farrar, Milton Sills, Thomas Santschi, Kate Lester, Hassard Short.
Running time: 60 minutes

The World and Its Woman 1919

An American prima donna and a Russian prince are in love during the Russian Revolution.
Directed by Frank Lloyd. Cast: Geraldine Farrar, Lou Tellegen, Alec B. Francis, Edward Connelly, Naomi Childers.
Running time: 70 minutes

Flame of the Desert 1920

The English Lady Isabelle Channing is in love with a sheik in the middle of the Egyptian desert at the time of an uprising.
Directed by Reginald Barker. Cast: Geraldine Farrar, Lou Tellegen, Alec B. Francis, Casson Ferguson, Edythe Chapman.
Running time: 50 minutes

The Woman and the Puppet 1920

The philandering Don Mateo pursues the Spanish dancer Concha Perez.
Directed by Reginald Barker. Cast: Geraldine Farrar, Lou Tellegen, Dorothy Cummings, Bertram Grassby, Macey Harlam, Rose Dione.
Running time: 70 minutes

Pathé

The Riddle: Woman 1920

Lilla Gravert is being blackmailed by a former lover.
Directed by Edward Jose. Cast: Geraldine Farrar, Montagu Love, Frank Losee, Madge Bellamy.
Running time: 60 minutes

✦ Appendix 6 ✦

Select Discography

From 1907 to 1927, Geraldine Farrar made 174 Victor Talking Machine Company 78rpm recordings of arias, songs and duets with Louise Homer, Antonio Scotti, Josephine Jacoby, Enrico Caruso, Marcel Journet, Pasquale Amato, Hermann Jadlowker, Ernestine Schumann-Heink, Edmond Clément, Giovanni Martinelli, Giuseppe De Luca, as well as ensembles with Gina Viafora, Enrico Caruso, Antonio Scotti, Reed Miller, Harry Macdonough, Reinald Werrenrath, Gabrielle Lejeune-Gilibert and Marcel Journet. The list of these recordings may be found on the website of the University of California, Santa Barbara, at http://victor.library.ucsb.edu/index.php/talent/detail/28157/Farrar_Geraldine_vocalist_soprano_vocal.

The following CDs of Miss Farrar's recordings are available:

1. Geraldine Farrar: Opera arias (*Carmen/La bohème/Madama Butterfly*)
   Label: Pearl Gemm CD 9420

2. Farrar in French Opera: Arias (*Manon/Mignon/Roméo et Juliette/Thaïs/Les contes d'Hoffmann/Carmen*)
   Label: Pearl LC 5871 ADD NI 7872

3. Farrar in Italian Opera: Arias (*Le nozze di Figaro/Don Giovanni/Le donne curiose/Il segreto di Susanna/La bohème/Tosca/Madama Butterfly*)
   Label: Nimbus Records LC 5871 ADD NI 7857

4. Geraldine Farrar: Berlin G & T's 1904–1906; Victor electrical recordings 1927; Bell Telephone Laboratories experimental recordings 1932: Arias and songs:
   CD 1 (*La traviata/Mignon/Manon/Roméo et Juliette/Roland Von Berlin/Mefistofele/Faust/Le domino noir/Martha/Tannhäuser/Rigoletto/Mattinata/Aime-moi/Dear heart/Cherry ripe/Caro mio ben*;
   CD 2 *Le nozze di Figaro/Frasquita/Midnight Bells/Christina's Lament/*

Hame to the Highlands/Drowsy Poppies/*Serenata*/*Pur dicesti*/*Auf Flügeln des Gesanges*/The Old Refrain/Old Folks at Home/Love's Old Sweet Song/In Old Madrid/*Marie am Fenster*/*Heiden Röslein*/ Excerpts of opera performance intermission talks)
Label: Marston 52040-2 ADD

◆ APPENDIX 7 ◆

Select Radio Broadcasts

In 1934 and 1935 Geraldine Farrar was the intermission commentator for the Metropolitan Opera's Saturday matinee radio broadcasts. Excerpts of her broadcasts are available on CD:

Geraldine Farrar: Berlin G & T's 1904–1906; Victor electrical recordings 1927; Bell Telephone Laboratories experimental recordings 1932: Excerpts of opera performance intermission talks.
    Label: Marston 52040-2 ADD

Chapter Notes

Preface

1. David Belasco, Western Union telegram to Geraldine Farrar, dated November 4, 1929, included in the Geraldine Farrar Collection at the Library of Congress.

Introduction

1. Carl Van Vechten, *Interpreters and Interpretations* (New York: Alfred A. Knopf, 1917), p. 54.
2. Marguerite Mooers Marshall, "...Of Great Operatic Singers," *New York Evening World*, included in Scrapbook 1915–1930 (found in the Farrar Collection at the Library of Congress), n.p.
3. Homer Ulrich, *Famous Women Singers* (New York: Dodd, Mead and Company, 1953), p. 73.
4. Geraldine Farrar and Mary F. Watkins, "Diva's Decades," *Saturday Evening Post*, 16 January 1932, p. 91.
5. Ibid., p. 92.
6. Clara Louise Kellogg, *Memoirs of an American Prima Donna* (New York: G.P. Putnam's Sons, 1913), p. 130.
7. Ibid.
8. Ibid., p. 34.
9. David Belasco, *The Theatre Through Its Stage Door* (New York: Harper and Brothers Publishers, 1919), p. 103.
10. Bernard Shaw, *London Music in 1888–89 as Heard by Corno di Bassetto (later known as Bernard Shaw) with Some Further Autobiographical Particulars* (London: Constable and Company Limited, 1937), p. 182.
11. William J. Henderson, "Themes and Topics in the Musical World," *New York Times*, 15 April 1900, p. 18, col. 3.
12. William J. Henderson, "Themes and Topics in the Musical World," *New York Times*, 4 February 1900, p. 18, col. 2.
13. Farrar and Watkins, p. 92.
14. James Henry Mapleson, *The Mapleson Memoirs: The Career of an Operatic Impresario 1858–1888*, ed. Harold Rosenthal (London: Putnam and Company, Ltd., 1966), p. 236.
15. Peter G. Davis, "When Patti Wowed Her Fans She Really Undid Them," *New York Times*, 1 September 1974, Sect. II, p. 11, col. 2.
16. William J. Henderson, "Music," *New York Times Magazine*, 20 February 1898, p. 8, col. 1.
17. William J. Henderson, "Themes and Topics in the Musical World," *New York Times*, 8 April 1900, p. 20, col. 3.
18. William J. Henderson, "Music," *New York Times Magazine*, 20 February 1898, p. 8, col. 2.
19. William J. Henderson, "A Week's Musical Topics," *New York Times*, 17 February 1895, p. 14, col. 1.
20. Henderson, "Music," p. 8, col. 2.
21. Farrar and Watkins, p. 91.
22. "Live Musical Topics," *New York Times*, 27 January 1889, p. 16, col. 3.
23. Bernard Shaw, *Shaw on Music: A Selection from the Music Criticism of Bernard Shaw*, ed. Eric Bentley (Garden City, N.Y.: Doubleday and Company, Inc., 1955), pp. 157–59.
24. Shaw, *London Music 1888–89*, p. 183.
25. Henry E. Krehbiel, *Chapters of Opera: Being—Historical and Critical Observations and from Its Earliest Days Down to the Present Time* (New York: Henry Holt and Company, 1908), p. 97.
26. "Amusements," *New York Times*, 23 November 1871, p. 5, col. 2.
27. Henriette Brower, *Vocal Mastery: Talks with Master Singers and Teachers Comprising*

Interviews with Caruso, Farrar, Maurel, Lehmann and Others (New York: Frederick A. Stokes Company Publishers, 1920), pp. 29–30.

28. Quaintance Eaton, *The Miracle of the Met: An Informal History of the Metropolitan Opera 1883–1967* (New York: Meredith Press, 1968), p. 126.

29. Lilli Lehmann, *Mein Weg* (Leipzig: Verlag von G. Hirzel, 1913), p. 218.

30. Constantin Stanislavski, *My Life in Art* (New York: Theatre Art Books, 1948), pp. 36–37.

31. "Amusement," *New York Times,* 25 March 1890, p. 5, col. 2.

32. Krehbiel, pp. 238–39.

33. "Mary Garden, Opera Star, Dies in Scotland at 92," *New York Times*, 5 January 1967, p. 37, col. 2.

34. Ibid.

35. Stanislavski, p. 463.

36. Howard Taubman, *Opera: Front and Back* (New York: Charles Scribner's Sons, 1938), p.60.

37. Ida Cook, "In Brief: A Visit with Farrar," *Opera News*, 26 January 1966, p. 6.

Chapter One

1. Geraldine Farrar, *Geraldine Farrar: The Story of an American Singer by Herself* (Boston: Houghton Mifflin Company), 1916, p. 4.

2. Ibid., p.10.

3. Ibid., p. 27.

4. Ibid., p. 30.

5. Geraldine Farrar, *Such Sweet Compulsion* (New York: The Greystone Press, 1938), p. 25.

6. "Seduit par les dons musicaux de premier ordre que possedait la petite candidate ... il volut s'occuper lui-meme des progrès de la jeune fille en qui il devinait une future tragédienne lyrique." "Madamoiselle Geraldine Farrar," no publication, n.d., n.p., included in Scrapbook 1907–1908, n.p. (found in the Farrar Collection at the Library of Congress).

7. Oscar Thompson, *The American Singer: A Hundred Years of Success in Opera* (New York: The Dial Press, Inc., 1937), p. 251.

8. Scrapbook 1898, n.p.

9. In 1909, Miss Farrar repaid this sum to Mrs. Webb.

10. Scrapbook 1899, n.p.

11. Willa S. Cather, "Three American Singers," *McClure*, 42 (December 1913), p. 38.

12. Farrar, *Geraldine Farrar*, p. 47.

13. The Post Young Woman, "Thirty Minutes with Pretty Yankee Girl Who Now Flocks with World's Most Tuneful Songbirds," no publication, n.d., n.p., included in Scrapbook 1907–1908, n.p.

14. Emily M. Burbank, "Geraldine Farrar," *Century*, 75 (March 1908), p. 692.

15. Farrar, *Such Sweet Compulsion*, p. 213.

16. Farrar, *Geraldine Farrar*, p. 52.

17. Ibid., p. 54.

18. Geraldine Farrar, "Geraldine Farrar Tells Her Idea of Marguerite," no publication, n.d., n.p., included in Scrapbook 1911–1915, n.p.

19. K.S.C., no title, no publication, n.d., n.p., included in Scrapbook 1911–1915, n.p.

20. Farrar, *Geraldine Farrar*, p. 56.

21. L.S., "Im Opernhaus," no publication, n.d., n.p., included in Scrapbook 1901, n.p.

22. Farrar, "Geraldine Farrar Tells Her Idea of Marguerite."

23. "Koenigliches Opernhaus," no publication, n.d., n.p., included in Scrapbook 1901, p. 15.

24. H.N., "Koenigliches Opernhaus," no publication, n.d., n.p., included in Scrapbook 1901, n.p.

25. W.J. Henderson, "Music," *New York Times Magazine*, 20 February 1898, p. 8, col. 2.

26. No author, no title, no publication, n.d., n.p., included in Scrapbook 1906, n.p.

27. Quaintance Eaton, *Opera Caravan: Adventures of the Metropolitan on Tour 1883–1956* (New York: Farrar, Strauss and Cudahy, 1957), p. 127.

28. "Einen vollen Erfolg." "Theater und Musik," no publication, n.d., n.p., included in Scrapbook 1901, n.p.

29. Interpolation in English translation is this writer's. "Hochgewachsen, ungemein zierlich von Gestalt, anmuthig in den Bewegungen, aus drucksvoll in den Zügen des kindlichen Gesichtes—so trat sie gleich als etwas Besonderes, als eine Personlichkeit vor uns. Endlich einmal wieder eine Gestalt, die keine Schablonenfigur ist, endlich einmal wieder eine Eigenart.... Manche vortreffliche Sängerin sandte uns Amerika schon. Nennen wir nur die Albann und die Nordica, die süsse Stimmen besassen and grosse Kunstfertigkeit, mehr als augenblicklich noch die Farrar. Aber so für sich einzunehmen, so sich in unser Herz einzunisten, verstanden sie nicht, wie der neue Operngast das gleich mit der ersten Rolle fertigbrachte. Jede waren nur Sängerinnen, diese ist eine dramatische Künstlerin, ob sie schon noch Einiges zu lernen hat. Sie ist stets in der Rolle und in der Situation. Sie singt und spielt

keine Partie ab, sondern sie durchlebt eine Handlung." R.F., no title, *Norddeutsche Zeitung*, n.d., n.p., included in Scrapbook 1901, n.p.

30. "Wie est heisst, steht die Dame als Novize erst ganz am Anfang ihrer Buhnenlaufbahn. Ist dies wirklich der Fall, dann hatten wir es mit einem bedeutenden, echt dramatische Talent zu thun, denn es gab eigentlich nichts Unfertiges, Unreifes in der ganzen Darstellung dieser Margarethe, bei der die schauspielerische Ausarbeitung ebenso sicher erschien, wie die musikalische, rein gesangstechnische. Es gab sogar einige Momente von geradezu berucken Schönheit; den Höhepunkt erreichte der Gast mit dem Schluss des dritten Aktes, wo sich das Fenster öffnet and Gretchen, sich allein wahnend, ihre Sehnsucht nach dem Geliebten in das Mondlicht hinaussingt. Durchaus reinzvoll, fein belebt wurde die Scene vor dem Schmuckkastchen gegeben, hier stand die Kunst des musikalischen Vortrags im schönsten Ebenmass zu der schauspielerischen Gestaltung. Geraldine Farrar hinterliess den Eindruck einer individuell veranlagten Natur, einer kunstlerischen Eigenart." E.E.T., "Koenigliches Opernhaus," no publication, n.d., n.p., included in Scrapbook 1901, n.p.

31. No author, no title, German Times, n.d., n.p. trans. Geraldine Farrar, quoted in Farrar, *Such Sweet Compulsion*, pp. 44–45.

32. "Fraulein Farrar ist noch keine Meisterin, aber sie ist ganz gewiss auch keine alltägliche Erscheinung; sie ist stimmlich, musikalisch and dramatisch ungewöhnlich begabt und besitzt Individualität." H.N., "Theater and Musik," no publication, n.d., n.p., included in Scrapbook 1901, n.p.

33. "Sie interessiert, weil sie sich frei von der Schablone halt und eigenen Eingebungen folgt. Man braucht nicht immer mit dem einverstanden zu sein, was sie macht, und wird doch zugeben können, dass eine künstlerische Absicht sie leitete. Allein es erfreut einen doch, dass die Künstlerin sich in die Rolle vertieft and dass sie auch beim Singen spielt." Ibid.

34. "Das war mir ganz neu, indess—nun meinethalben auch, denn warum nicht!" "Koenigliches Opernhaus," no publication, n.d., n.p., included in Scrapbook 1901, p. 151.

35. Geraldine Farrar and John J. Whitehead, Jr., "Coming Back and Looking Back," *Saturday Evening Post*, 14 April 1928, p. 19. Reprinted from the *Saturday Evening Post* 1928 The Curtis Publishing Company.

36. Carl Van Vechten, *Interpreters and Interpretations* (New York: Alfred A. Knopf, 1917), pp. 40–41.

37. Farrar, *Geraldine Farrar*, p. 5.

38. Gustav Kiesow, no title, no publication, n.d., n.p., included in Scrapbook 1901, n.p.

39. Farrar, *Such Sweet Compulsion*, pp. 46–47.

40. "Sie welkte dahin, wie eine vom Sturm des Lebens geknickte Blume." No author, no title, no publication, n.d., n.p., included in Scrapbook 1901, n.p.

41. "Sie schminkte sich ganz hoffnungsloss, so das auch ohne Husten-Anfälle and sonstige Anzeichen eines schweren Leidens das baldige Hinscheiden vorauszusehen war." "Koenigliches Opernhaus," no publication, n.d., n.p., included in Scrapbook 1901, n.p.

42. "Kunstwerk im Sinne einer edlen Uebereinstimmung von Darstellung und Milieu." "Kunst and Wissenschaft," no publication, n.d., n.p., included in Scrapbook 1901, n.p.

43. "Gigantischen Rembrandthut." No author, no title, no publication, n.d., n.p., included in Scrapbook 1901, n.p.

44. "Allzu jugendlich in den Formen, wie in der ganzen Erscheinung, wüsste sie nicht auch in ihrer Darstellung den freien, legeren Ton der feineren Demi-mondaine nicht recht zu treffen." "Kunst und Wissenschaft," no publication, n.d., n.p., included in Scrapbook 1901, n.p.

45. No author, no title, no publication, n.d., n.p., included in Scrapbook 1901, p. 8.

46. "Sie bringt vieles mit, was die Violetta erfordert, eine schlanke, geschmeidige, gewinnende Erscheinung, lebendiges, ungemein durchdachtes Spiel, das in ersten Akt schon das tragische Ende ahnen lässt." No author, no title, no publication, n.d., n.p., included in Scrapbook 1901, n.p.

47. "Sie benahm sich sehr natürlich, blieb immer im Bewusstsein der Situation, in der sie sich befand, and verstand es hierdurch fast noch mehr als durch ihren Gesang zu interessieren, ja zu fesseln," No author, no title, no publication, n.d., n.p., included in Scrapbook 1901, n.p.

48. "Koenigliches Opernhaus," no publication, n.d., n.p., included in Scrapbook 1901, n.p.

49. "The funniest Experience I Ever Had in Opera: A Symposium in Which Many Operatic Celebrities Have Taken Part," *Etude*, 40 (October 1922), p. 659.

50. "Man glaubte ihr nicht, dass sie fähig ware, sich den ihr unbequemen Anbeter Tonio mit der Peitsche vom Leibe halten konnen." E.E.T., "Koenigliches Opernhaus," no publication, n.d., n.p., included in Scrapbook 1902, n.p.

51. "War ihre Darstellung trotz aller ausseren Hast and Betriebsamkeit im ganzen temperamentlos." No author, no title, no publication, n.d., n.p., included in Scrapbook 1908–1910 and Later Photos, n.p.
52. No author, no title, no publication, n.d., n.p., included in Scrapbook 1909–1910, p. 74.
53. Geraldine Farrar and Mary F. Watkins, "No Means No," *Saturday Evening Post*, 21 November 1931, p. 72.
54. No author, no title, no publication, n.d., n.p., included in Scrapbook 1908–1910 and Later Photos, n.p.
55. Farrar, *Such Sweet Compulsion*, p. 99.
56. "Ihr Spiel war mir zum Teil nicht verständlich; es schien mir mehr auf grosse Bewegungen, auf grosse Linien von schlankem Schwung angelegt zu sein als auf die Sichtbarmachung innerer Vorgänge." No author, no title, no publication, n.d., n.p., included in Scrapbook 1902 n.p.
57. "Hatte das Publicum Recht oder die Kritik? Wir möchten uns in diesem Falle unbedingt für das erste entscheiden." E. v. R., "Fräulein Farrar als 'Julia,'" no publication, n.d., n.p., included in Scrapbook 1902, no. pg.
58. Farrar, *Such Sweet Compulsion*, p. 64.
59. Farrar, *Geraldine Farrar*, p. 61.
60. Geraldine Farrar and Rose Heylbut, "How Can We Best Serve Our Students," *Etude*, 56 (September 1938), p. 563.
61. Farrar and Whitehead, p. 128. Reprinted from the *Saturday Evening Post* 1928 The Curtis Publishing Company.
62. Ibid.
63. Ibid.
64. Henry T. Finck, *Success in Music and How It Is Won* (New York: Charles Scribner's Sons, 1913), p. 195.
65. Geraldine Farrar, "What Must I Go Through to Become a Prima Donna," *Etude*, 38 (June 1920), p. 368.
66. J.A. Haughton, "Opera Singers from the Golden Age," *Musical America*, 69 (February 1949), p. 304.
67. Farrar, "What Must I Go Through," p. 368.
68. Farrar and Whitehead, p. 19.
69. "Die Erscheinung der Künstlerin uns so interessiert, dass man sein Auge von ihr nicht abwenden mag, sobald sie da ist, und wenn sie nicht da ist, ihr Wiederauf treten mit ungeduldiger Spa nung erwartet." No author, no title, no publication, n.d., n.p., included in Scrapbook 1903–1904, p. 33.
70. "Als sie aus der Portechaise stieg, in..dem Festschmuck der Schonheitskönigin, ging ein glückliches Staunen durch das Haus." No author, no title, no publication, n.d., n.p. included in Scrapbook 1903–1904, p. 33.
71. Farrar, *Such Sweet Compulsion*, p. 55.
72. "Miss Farrar, exquise dans Manon." No author, no title, no publication, n.d., n.p., included in Scrapbook 1903–1904, p. 33.
73. "Frl. Farrar sah als Manon entzüchend aus und spielte die Rolle mit ganzer Hingabe." No author, no title, no publication, n.d., n.p., included in Scrapbook 1903–1904, p. 33.
74. No author, no title, no publication, n.d., n.p., included in Scrapbook 1903–1904, p. 33.
75. "Unter der Obhut den Gesangsmeisterin Lilli Lehmann, reift auch die Kunst der Stimmbehandlung zu sicherer Fertigkeit heran." No author, no title, no publication, n.d., n.p., included in Scrapbook, 1903–1904, p. 33.
76. Interpolation in English translation is this writer's. "Frl. Farrar ... hat in der Schule Lilli Lehmann's, die sie in letzter Zeit besucht, alles abgestreift, was sie von einer besten, wir können dreist sagen, der besten Koloratursängerin unseren Hofbühne noch trennte. Die Stimme hat sich so gekräftigt, dass sie den gewältigen Aufstrennungen dieser Partie bis zu letzten Ton gerecht wurde; ihr seltener Wohllaut sieht überall im Dienste eines künsterlerischen Empfindens; Intonation und Koloratur sind unfehlbar und auch die Krone mangelt nicht; das C und D der dreigestrichenen Ottave in Kraft and Glanz." No author, no title, no publication, n.d., n.p., included in Scrapbook 1903–1904, p. 33.
77. Farrar, *Geraldine Farrar*, p. 61.
78. "Il avait été frappé du velouté de cette voix dans les notes aiguës, de l'intelligence scénique de la cantatrice et de la personalité qu'elle réussissait à donner à ce rôle de Gretchen devenu banal." "Madamoiselle Geraldine Farrar," no publication, n.d., n.p., included in Scrapbook 1907–1908, n.p.
79. Harold Schonberg, "The Goddess that Was Geraldine Farrar," *New York Times*, 19 March 1967, Sect. II, p. 21, col. 4.
80. "Un sens remarquable de l'expression dramatique." "Les Theatres," *Le Figaro*, n.d., n.p., included in Scrapbook 1905, n.p.
81. "Unjust! Miss Farrar Cries," *New York Sun*, 1 March 1908, p. 6, col. 2.
82. In 1901, however, a Berlin critic did record that as Marguerite Miss Farrar's "two dark eyes glow supernaturally at the appropriate moment." "Zwei grosse dunkle Augen im rechten Moment förmlich geisterhaft hervorleuchten." No author, no title, no publication, n.d., n.p., included in Scrapbook 1901, p. 8.

83. "Das Weib, das dem Tannhäuser aus den Wollusthöhlen des Venusberges als Himmelstern den Weg nach oben wies." Richard Wagner, *Richard Wagner's Gesammelte Schriften*, ed., Julius Kapp (Leipzig: Hesse & Becker Verlag, 1914), I, 124.

84. "Freudig." Richard Wagner, *Tannhäuser* (Leipzig: Breitkopf and Hartel, n.d.), p. 143.

85. "Miss Farrar in Fine Voice," *New York Times*, 7 February 1907, p. 9, col. 3.

86. Philip Hale, "Impersonation of Elisabeth in Wagner's Opera at Boston Theatre Sympathetic and Charming Idealizing the Character," no publication, n.d., n.p., included in Scrapbook 1909–1910, p. 81.

87. Ibid.

88. Finck, *Success in Music*, p. 195.

89. "Das Schwierige fur die Elisabeth ist ... dass die Darstellerin den Eindruck der jugendlichsten and jungfräulichsten Unbefangenheit mache, ohne zu verrathen, ein wie sehr erfahrenes, feines weibliches Gefühl sie erst zur Lösung ihrer Aufgabe fahig machen konnte." Richard Wagner, *Gesammelte Schriften and Dichtungen von Richard Wagner*, (Leipzig: Verlag von E.W. Fritzsch, 1872), V, 202.

90. "Ja, kind, geh' du singen; inzwischen fress' ich was." Geraldine Farrar and Mary F. Watkins, "Diva's Decades," *Saturday Evening Post*, 16 January 1932, p. 92.

91. "Es genügt nicht mehr, auf die Bühne zu stehen and kunstgerecht zu singen; die neue Oper ... verlangt gebieterisch Mimik and Gebärdenspiel. Der Opernsänger soll mit dem ganzen Apparate des Schauspielers bewaffnet sein, seine Stimme darf da nur einen Teil, wenn auch der wichtigsten des Ganzen bilden. Diesen Anforderungen einer neuen Zeit gerecht zu werden, war Geraldine Farrar in hohem Grade berufen." No author, no title, no publication, n.d., n.p., included in Scrapbook 1906, n.p.

92. "Mlle Geraldine Farrar a fait de Zephrine une merveilleuse création. Elle a joué le personage avec une souplesse et une variété de talent réellement extraordinaires; elle lui a prêté une fébrilité, une tendresse, une ardeur d'une superbe intensité." "Les Theatres," *Le Figaro*, 27 April 1906, n.p., included in Scrapbook 1906, n.p.

93. Farrar, *Such Sweet Compulsion*, p. 112.

94. Ibid., pp. 86–87.

95. "Niemand ist auf den Brettern der Bühne natürlicher and ungezwunger wie sie, niemand versteht es hier besser, die Stimme durch die Sprache der halben Gebärden stärker zu unterstützen and zu ergänzen. Wir haben uns an die schauspielerische Bedeutung der Farrar allmählich so gewöhnt, dass wir sie als etwas Selbstverständliches hinnehmen.... Damit aber tun wir eine Künstlerin unrecht, die zu erstenmal mit einer unermüdlichen Durcharbeitung der Einzelzüge eine Gestalt auf die Bühne zu stellen weiss, wie wir solche bisher bei dem französischen Theater neidvoll bewunderten." No author, no title, no publication, n.d., n.p., included in Scrapbook 1908–1910 and Later Photos, n.p.

Chapter Two

1. Geraldine Farrar, *Geraldine Farrar: The Story of an American Singer by Herself* (Boston: Houghton Mifflin Company, 1916), p. 29.

2. Ibid., p. 84.

3. Geraldine Farrar, *Such Sweet Compulsion* (New York: The Greystone Press, 1938), p. 92.

4. Farrar, *Geraldine Farrar*, p. 86.

5. Farrar, *Such Sweet Compulsion*, p. 91.

6. Farrar, *Geraldine Farrar*, pp. 85–86.

7. Farrar, *Such Sweet Compulsion*, p. 97.

8. Ibid., pp. 96–97.

9. H. Howard Taubman, *Opera: Front and Back* (New York: Charles Scribner's Sons, 1938), p. 245.

10. William J. Henderson, Review of a Metropolitan Opera Performance of Puccini's *Tosca*, *New York Sun*, 3 December 1903, quoted in William H. Seltsam, ed., *Metropolitan Opera Annals* (New York: H.W. Wilson, 1947), p. 44.

11. Ena Makin, ed., and trans., *Letters of Giacomo Puccini: Mainly Connected with the Composition and Production of His Operas*, ed. Giuseppi Adami (Philadelphia: J.B. Lippincott Company, 1931), p. 16.

12. Farrar, *Such Sweet Compulsion*, p. 98.

13. Richard Aldrich, "*Roméo et Juliette* Opens Opera Season," *New York Times*, 27 November 1906, p. 9, col. 1.

14. "Three Debutants in *Roméo and Juliet*," *New York Herald*, 27 November 1906, p. 2, col. 1.

15. Henry R. Finck, *Success in Music and How It Is Won* (New York: Charles Scribner's Sons, 1913), p. 180.

16. No author, no title, no publication, n.d., n.p., Scrapbook 1907–1908, n.p.

17. Homer Ulrich, *Famous Women Singers* (New York: Dodd, Mead and Company, 1953), p. 72.

18. Review of a Metropolitan Opera performance of Gounod's *Roméo et Juliette* given

on November 26, 1906, *The Evening Sun*, 27 November 1906, n.p., quoted in Farrar, *Such Sweet Compulsion*, pp. 100–101.

19. Mabel Wagnalls, *Stars of the Opera* (New York: Funk and Wagnalls, 1907), p. 377.

20. Henry Krehbiel, Review of a Metropolitan Opera performance of *Roméo et Juliette* by Gounod, *New York Tribune*, 27 November 1906, n.p., quoted in William H. Seltsam, ed., *Metropolitan Opera Annals* (New York: H.W. Wilson, 1947), p. 171.

21. William R. Lester, "Geraldine Farrar's Voice Pleases; She's Too Active," no publication, n.d., n.p., included in Scrapbook 1907–1908, n.p.

22. Richard Aldrich, "*Roméo et Juliette* Opens Opera Season," *New York Times*, 27 November 1906, p. 9, col. 1.

23. Ibid.

24. "Music and Drama," *The Evening Post*, New York, n.d., n.p., included in Scrapbook 1906–1907, n.p.

25. Frederic Dean, no title, no publication, n.d., n.p., included in Scrapbook 1906–1907, n.p.

26. Ibid.

27. Ibid.

28. Philip Hale, "Actress of Indisputable Talent and a Lyric Singer with Delightful Voice-Other Singers Mediocre," no publication, n.d., n.p., included in Scrapbook 1906–1907, n.p.

29. No author, no title, no publication, n.d., n.p., included in Scrapbook 1918–1910, n.p.

30. Richard Aldrich, "Farrar and Chaliapine Knock Out Many *Faust* Traditions," *New York Times*, 7 January 1908, n.p., included in Scrapbook 1907–1908, n.p.

31. Henry T. Parker, "Bonci and Miss Farrar," *Boston Evening Transcript*, n.d., n.p., included in Scrapbook 1907–1908, n.p.

32. Geraldine Farrar and Mary F. Watkins, "Diva's Decades," *Saturday Evening Post*, 16 January 1932, p. 92.

33. Farrar, *Such Sweet Compulsion*, p. 72.

34. William J. Henderson, "*Tannhäuser* at the Opera," *New York Sun*, 7 February 1907, p. 9, col. 5.

35. Ulrich, p. 72.

36. "Dramatic and Musical," *New York Times*, 6 March 1900, p. 6, col. 1.

37. Charles Matz and Mary Jane Matz, "First Ladies of the Puccini Premieres," *Opera News*, 3 February 1962, p. 2 (New York: Benjamin Blom, Inc., 1971), p. 118.

38. Wagnalls, p. 375.

39. Farrar, *Such Sweet Compulsion*, p. 102.

40. Anne Homer, *Louise Homer and the Golden Age of Opera* (New York: William Morrow and Company, Inc., 1974), p. 259.

41. Matz and Matz, p. 24.

42. Geraldine Farrar, no title, *The Georgian* (Atlanta), n.d., n.p., included in Scrapbook 1910–1930, n.p.

43. Vincent Seligman, *Puccini among Friends*.

44. Makin, p. 168.

45. Farrar, *Such Sweet Compulsion*, p. 103.

46. Makin, p.168.

47. Mosco Carner, *Puccini: A Critical Biography* (New York: Alfred A. Knopf, Inc. 1959), p. 150.

48. Makin, p. 168.

49. "Puccini to Sail Tomorrow," *New York Times*, 28 February 1907, p. 9, col. 4.

50. "M'a tue." Makin, p. 168.

51. "Geraldine Farrar's Madam Butterfly an Artistic Delight," no publication, n.d., n.p., Montreal, included in Scrapbook 1907–1908, n.p.

52. Henry T. Parker, "*Butterfly* and *Lucia*," *Boston Evening Transcript*, n.d., n.p., included in Scrapbook 1909–1910, p. 80.

53. Ibid.

54. "Geraldine Farrar's Madam Butterfly an Artistic Delight."

55. Parker, "*Butterfly* and *Lucia*."

56. "Geraldine Farrar's Madam Butterfly an Artistic Delight."

57. Parker, "*Butterfly* and *Lucia*."

58. Ibid.

59. Sada Yacco was a renowned fin-de-siècle Japanese actress whom Puccini consulted on Japanisms when composing *Madama Butterfly*.

60. No author, no title, no publication, n.d., n.p., included in Scrapbook 1908–1910, p. 30.

61. "Madama Butterfly," no publication, n.d., n.p., included in Scrapbook 1907–1908, n.p.

62. "*Madama Butterfly* a Triumph." no publication, n.d., n.p., included in Scrapbook 1909–1910, n.p.

63. "Geraldine Farrar's Madam Butterfly an Artistic Delight."

64. "Geraldine Farrar's Butterfly" no publication, n.d., n.p., included in Scrapbook 1909–1910, p. 91.

65. Makin, p. 168.

66. William J. Henderson, "*Madama Butterfly* Sung," *New York Sun*, 12 February 1907, p. 9, col. 3.

67. "Farrar's Chicago Debut," (Chicago), no publication, n.d., n.p., included in Scrapbook 1907–1908, n.p.

68. Henderson, "*Madama Butterfly* Sung."
69. "Geraldine Farrar's Butterfly."
70. Taubman, p. 303.
71. Harriette Brower, *Vocal Mastery: Talks with Master Singers and Teachers Comprising interviews with Caruso, Farrar, Maurel, Lehmann and Others* (New York: Frederick A. Stokes Company Publishers, 1920), p. 20.
72. "Farrar in a Long Kiss," *New York Times*, n.d., n.p., included in Scrapbook 1909–1910, n.p.
73. These are the stage directions given in both the play's script and in the operatic libretto.
74. Dudley Glass, "'Mme. Butterfly' a Great Triumph for Miss Farrar," no publication (Atlanta), misdated 5 May 1910 instead of 7 May 1910, n.p., included in Scrapbook 1909–1910, n.p.
75. "Geraldine Farrar's Butterfly."
76. Carl Van Vechten, *Interpreters and Interpretation* (New York: Alfred A. Knopf, 1917), p. 48.
77. Miss Farrar was referring to Rosina Storchio, the first Madama Butterfly, and Emmy Destinn, the creator of that role at Covent Garden.
78. Frederick H. Martens, *Art of the Prima Donna and Concert Singer* (New York: D. Appleton and Company, 1923), p. 101.
79. The Post Young Woman, "Thirty Minutes with Pretty Yankee Girl Who Now Flocks with World's Most Tuneful Songbirds," no publication, n.d., n.p., included in Scrapbook 1907–1908, n.p.
80. Farrar, *Geraldine Farrar*, p. 94.
81. Geraldine Farrar, "Geraldine Farrar Tells What Mimi Means to Her," no publication, n.d., n.p., included in Scrapbook 1911–1915, n.p.
82. "Miss Farrar in *La bohème*," *New York Times*, 16 March 1907, p. 9, col. 4.
83. "A Repetition of *La bohème*," *New York Tribune*, 16 March 1907, p. 7, col. 5.
84. "A Double Bill at the Opera," *New York Tribune*, 23 March 1907, p. 9, col. 4.
85. Farrar, *Geraldine Farrar*, pp. 97–98.
86. Van Vechten, p. 47.
87. "Boito's' *Mefistofele* at the Metropolitan," *New York Times*, 21 November 1907, p. 9, col. 4.
88. Farrar, *Such Sweet Compulsion*, p. 111.
89. Henry T. Parker, "Bonci and Miss Farrar," *Boston Evening Transcript*, n.d., n.p., included in Scrapbook 1907–1908, n.p.
90. Ibid.
91. Ibid.
92. Wagnalls, pp. 376–77.
93. Henry T. Parker, "A Dull *Don Giovanni*," *Boston Evening Transcript*, included in Scrapbook 1907–1908, n.p.
94. Ibid.
95. "Miss Farrar as Zerlina," *New York Times*, 13 February 1908, p. 9, col. 4.
96. Parker, "A Dull *Don Giovanni*."
97. The original production of Verdi's *La traviata* in 1853 was given with costumes and decor of the Louis XIV period, thereby distancing the story and making it seem less immoral. For the next fifty years, it was traditional to employ seventeenth century costumes for all productions of this opera.
98. Henry Krehbiel, "Miss Farrar in *La traviata*," *New York Tribune*, 29 February 1908, p. 7, col. 4.
99. "Geraldine Farrar as Violetta," no publication, n.d., n.p., included in Scrapbook 1907–1908, n.p.
100. Richard Aldrich, "Miss Farrar as Violetta," *New York Times*, 29 February 1908, p. 7, col. 4.
101. Krehbiel, "Miss Farrar in *La traviata*."
102. "Geraldine Farrar an Ideal Mignon," no publication, n.d., n.p., included in Scrapbook 1907–1908, n.p.
103. Henry C. Lahee, *The Grand Opera Singers of Today: An Account of the Leading Operatic Stars Who Have Sung During Recent Years, Together with a Sketch of the Chief Operatic Enterprises* (Boston: The Page Company, 1912), p. 83.
104. Aldrich, "Miss Farrar as Violetta."
105. Parker, "Bonci and Miss Farrar."
106. "*Madama Butterfly* Draws Typical Matinee Audience," no publication, n.d., n.p., included in Scrapbook 1910–1930, p. 46.
107. Mary F. Watkins, "Geraldine Farrar 1928 Model: A New Portrait of an Old Favorite," *Woman's Journal*, 13 (February 1928), p. 1.
108. Willa S. Cather, "Three American Singers," *McClure's*, 42 (December 1913), p. 41.
109. Farrar, *Such Sweet Compulsion*, pp. 114–16.
110. Harold C. Schonberg, "The Goddess that Was Geraldine Farrar," *New York Times*, 19 March 1967, Sec. II, p. 21, col. 4.
111. Mary Watkins Cushing, *The Rainbow Bridge* (New York: G.P. Putnam's Sons, 1954), p. 173.
112. Schonberg, "The Goddess that was Geraldine Farrar."

Chapter Three

1. "The Opera Directorship," *New York Times*, 12 February 1908, p. 6., col. 4.
2. Geraldine Farrar, *Such Sweet Compulsion* (New York: The Greystone Press, 1938), pp. 114–21.
3. H. Howard Taubman, *The Maestro: The Life of Arturo Toscanini* (New York: Simon & Schuster, 1951), p. 116.
4. Farrar, *Such Sweet Compulsion*, p. 122.
5. Taubman, *The Maestro*, p. 122.
6. "New Carmen Sings at Metropolitan," *New York Times*, 4 December 1908, p. 11, col. 5.
7. William J. Henderson, Review of a Metropolitan Opera Performance of Bizet's *Carmen*, December 3, 1908, quoted in Irving Kolodin, *The Metropolitan Opera 1883–1966: A Candid History* (New York: Alfred A. Knopf, 1967), p. 202.
8. "New Carmen Sings at Metropolitan."
9. No author, no title, no publication, n.d., n.p., included in Scrapbook 1909–1910, p. 12.
10. Ibid., p. 13.
11. Ibid., p. 12.
12. Ibid.
13. Henry Krehbiel, "Music," *New York Tribune*, 4 December 1908, p. 7., col. 3.
14. "*Manon* Well Sung at the Academy," no publication, n.d., n.p., included in Scrapbook 1909–1910, p. 63.
15. Geraldine Farrar, "Caruso," *Theatre Arts*, 42 (January 1958), p. 91.
16. Kevin Brownlow, *The Parade's Gone By* (New York: Alfred A. Knopf, Inc., 1969), p. 420.
17. Geraldine Farrar, no title, no publication (Atlanta, Georgia), 4 May 1910, n.p., included in Scrapbook, 1910–1930, p. 7.
18. Henry T. Finck, *Success in Music and How It Is Won* (New York: Charles Scribner's Sons, 1913), p. 195.
19. J.B. Kennedy, "I Have Lived as I Liked," *Colliers* (9 April 1927), p. 39.
20. Ibid.
21. Farrar, *Such Sweet Compulsion*, p. 2-54. During the last act of a 1905 Rio de Janeiro performance of Tosca, Madame Bernhardt had missed the mattresses laid down to cushion her fall in the suicidal leap from the parapet and had struck the bare stage floor with the full weight of her body upon her right knee. As a result of this accident, the leg had to be amputated ten years later.
22. Irving Kolodin, *The Metropolitan Opera 1883–1966: A Candid History* (New York: Alfred A. Knopf, 1967), p. 14.
23. Farrar, *Such Sweet Compulsion*, p. 129.
24. Algernon St. John-Brenon, "New Theater Scores a Hit," no publication, n.d., n.p., included in Scrapbook 1909–1910, p. 51.
25. No author, no title no publication, n.d., n.p., included in Scrapbook 1909–1910, p. 52.
26. Henry T. Parker, "Miss Farrar as Tosca," *Boston Evening Transcript*, n.d., n.p., included in Scrapbook 1909–1910, p. 66.
27. Ibid.
28. Ibid.
29. Karlton Hackett, "*Tosca*," no publication, n.d., n.p., included in Scrapbook 1909–1910, p.s.
30. Miss Farrar first employed this effective piece of stage business in the Saint Sulpice scene of Massenet's *Manon*. See Chapter II, p.
31. Parker, "Miss Farrar as Tosca."
32. "Geraldine Farrar as Tosca," no publication, n.d., n.p., included in Scrapbook 1909–1910, p. 56.
33. "Brilliant Audience Braves Storm to Welcome Miss Geraldine Farrar," no publication, n.d., n.p., included in Scrapbook 1909–1910, p. 70.
34. Ibid.
35. "'Tosca' a Farrar Triumph," no publication, n.d., n.p., included in Scrapbook 1909–1910, p. 94.
36. "The Real Tosca," no publication, n.d., n.p., included in Scrapbook 1911–1915, p. 19.
37. "Are Movies Popularizing Opera?" *Theatre Magazine*, 29 (May 1919), p. 297.
38. "*Tosca* Sung at the Metropolitan," *New York Times*, 12 December 1911, p. 9, col. 3.
39. William J. Henderson, "Geraldine Farrar's Tosca," *New York Sun*, n.d., n.p., included in Scrapbook 1909–1910, p. 58.
40. Ibid.
41. Parker, "Miss Farrar as Tosca."
42. Henderson, "Geraldine Farrar's Tosca."
43. Parker, "Miss Farrar as Tosca."
44. Henderson, "Geraldine Farrar's Tosca."
45. Richard Aldrich, "Puccini's *Tosca* at Metropolitan," *New York Times*, 23 November 1909, p. 9, col. 1.
46. "Farrar a Genius," no publication, n.d., n.p., included in Scrapbook 1909–1910, n.p.
47. S.C. Williams, "Miss Farrar's Tosca Highly Individualized," no publication (Boston), n.d., n.p., included in Scrapbook 1909–1910 and Earlier, p. 69.
48. "*Lohengrin* Given Fine Performance," *Musical America*, 27 November 1909, p. 1, cols. 1–2.
49. "Geraldine Farrar as Tosca," no publi-

cation, n.d., n.p., included in Scrapbook 1909–1910, p. 56.

50. Hackett, "*Tosca*."

51. "A l'adorable Farrar, que le soleil e'claire [sic], toujours votre route, ma jeune amie. Que le bonheur soit votre ange gardien, que toutes les harpes, toutes les lyres chantent toujours dans notre [sic] voix!" Sarah Bernhardt to Geraldine Farrar, no title, no publication (Atlanta, Georgia), 4 May 1910, n.p. included in Scrapbook 1910–1930, p. 7.

52. No author, no title, no publication, n.d., n.p., included in Scrapbook 1911–1915, n.p.

53. "The Real Tosca."

54. "A Caruso-Farrar *Tosca*," *Musical America*, 1 November 1913, included in Scrapbook 1911–1915, p. 28.

55. Letter to the author from Frederick Jagel, 2 December 1974.

56. Geraldine Farrar and John J. Whitehead, Jr., "Coming Back and Looking Back," *Saturday Evening Post*, 14 April 1928, p. 19.

57. H. Howard Taubman, Opera: *Front and Back* (New York: Charles Scribner's Sons, 1938), p. 117.

58. Ibid.

59. David Ewen, *Living Musicians* (New York: The H.W. Wilson Company, 1940), p. 115.

60. Farrar, *Such Sweet Compulsion*, p. 131.

61. Geraldine Farrar, no title, *Atlanta Journal*, n.d., n.p., included in Scrapbook 1911–1915, n.p.

62. "Gives to America New Opera Jewel," *New York Herald*, 29 December 1910, p. 8, col. 1.

63. Frederick H. Martens, *The Art of the Prima Donna and Concert Singer* (New York: D. Appleton and Company, 1923), p. 99.

64. Farrar and Whitehead, "Looking Back and Coming Back," p. 19.

65. No author, no title, no publication, n.p., included in Scrapbook 1910–1930, p. 81.

66. No author, no title, no publication, n.p., included in Scrapbook 1910–1930, p. 80.

67. Ibid.

68. "Live Geese Act in the Metropolitan," no publication, n.d., n.p., included in Scrapbook, 1910–1930, p. 76.

69. Ibid.

70. Martens, p. 100.

71. No author, no title, no publication, n.d., n.p., included in Scrapbook, 1910–1930, p. 81.

72. "*Königskinder* Again," *New York Times*, 20 January 1911, p. 8, col. 4.

73. Miss Farrar sang the role of Elisabeth in *Tannhäuser* only during the 1906–1907 Metropolitan opera season.

74. "Miss Farrar Talks of Her Newest Role," no publication, n.d., n.p., included in Scrapbook 1910–1930, p. 95.

75. Oscar Thompson, *The American Singer: A Hundred Years of Success in Opera* (New York: The Dial Press, Inc., 1937), p. 258.

76. Geraldine Farrar, *Geraldine Farrar: The Story of an American Singer by Herself* (Boston: Houghton Mifflin Company, 1916), pp. 106–107.

77. No author, no title, no publication, n.d., n.p., included in Scrapbook 1910–1930, p. 75.

78. No author, no title, no publication, n.d., n.p., included in Scrapbook 1910–1930, p. 94.

79. No author, no title, no publication, n.d., n.p., included in Scrapbook 1910 and Earlier, p. 97.

80. No author, no title, no publication, n.d., n.p., included in Scrapbook 1910 and Earlier, p. 86.

81. No author, no title, no publication, n.d., n.p., included in Scrapbook 1910 and Earlier, p. 97.

82. Henry Krehbiel, Review of Metropolitan Opera Performance of Humperdinck's *Königskinder*, *New York Tribune*, December 1910, n.p., quoted in Henry T. Finck, *My Adventures in the Golden Age of Music* (New York: Funk and Wagnalls Company, 1926), p. 334.

83. Thompson, p. 258.

84. No author, no title, *Musical Leader*, n.d., n.p., included in Scrapbook 1903–1904, n.p.

85. "Halt German Opera at Metropolitan," *New York Times*, 2 November 1917, p. 13, col. 3.

86. Quantance Eaton, *The Miracle of the Met: An Informal History of the Metropolitan Opera 1883–1967* (New York: Meredith Press, 1968), p. 186.

87. Helen Noble, *Life with the Met* (New York: G.P. Putnam's Sons, 1954), p. 93.

88. "Miss Farrar's Geese Unruly in *Königskinder*," *New York Herald*, 1912, n.p., included in Scrapbook 1911–1915, n.p.

89. No author, no title, no publication, n.d., n.p., included in Scrapbook 1911–1915, n.p.

90. "Bluebeard and the New Woman in an Opera," *New York Times*, 15 January 1911, Sect. 5, p. 12, col. 3.

91. Ibid., cols. 3–4.

92. Ibid., col. 4.

93. Ibid.

94. Ibid., cols. 4–5.

95. "Maeterlinck's *Ariane et Barbe-Bleue*, with Dukas' Musical Setting, Offers the Little

American Prima Donna an Opportunity to Embody in Her Person Some Interesting Symbolic Ideas," no publication, n.d., n.p., included in Scrapbook 1911–1915, n.p.

96. Ibid.
97. Richard Aldrich, "Opera of *Ariane* Superbly Presented," *New York Times*, 30 March 1911, p. 7, col. 3.
98. "How *Ariane* Came to Metropolitan," *New York Times*, 27 March 1911, p. 11, col. 1.
99. Ibid.
100. William J. Henderson, Review of Metropolitan Opera Performance of Dukas' *Ariane et Barbe-Bleue* on March 29, 1911, quoted in Irving Kolodin, *The Metropolitan Opera 1883–1966: A Candid History* (New York: Alfred A. Knopf, 1967), p. 225.
101. H.F. Peyser, "Dukas' Opera Last Novelty of Season," *Musical America*, 1 April 1911, p. 5.
102. Henderson, Review of *Ariane et Barbe-Bleue*, in Kolodin, p. 225.
103. Carl Van Vechten, *Interpreters and Interpretations* (New York: Alfred A. Knopf, 1917), p. 53.
104. Aldrich, "Opera of *Ariane* Superbly Presented," p. 7, col. 4.
105. Farrar, *Geraldine Farrar*, p. 107.
106. Richard Aldrich, "*Le donne curiose* Well Performed," *New York Times*, 4 November 1912, p. 14, col. 2.
107. No author, no title, Musical Leader, n.d., n.p., included in Scrapbook 1911–1915, n.p.
108. Kolodin, p. 231.
109. Richard Aldrich, "*Secret of Susanne* Abounds in Melody," *New York Times*, 14 December 1912, p. 15, col. 3.
110. Henry Krehbiel, "Farrar Fine as Susanna," *New York Tribune*, n.d., n.p., included in Scrapbook 1911–1915, p. 29.
111. Aldrich, "*Secret of Susanne* Abounds in Melody."
112. Van Vechten, p. 52.
113. Farrar, *Such Sweet Compulsion*, p. 116.
114. J.A. Haughten, "Opera Singers from the Golden Age," *Musical America*, 69 (February 1949), p. 277.
115. Thompson, p. 260.
116. Haughten, p. 277.
117. Gustav Charpentier, Preface to His Opera *Julien*, quoted in Richard Aldrich, "Charpentier's *Julien* a Sequel to *Louise*—More Parisian Life, Realistic and Symbolical," *New York Times*, 22 February 1914, Sec. VII, p. 5, col. 2.
118. Farrar, *Such Sweet Compulsion*, p. 132.

119. No author, no title, *New York Herald*, 27 February 1914, n.p., included in Scrapbook 1911–1915, n.p.
120. Farrar, "Caruso," *Theatre Arts,* p. 91.
121. *New York Herald*, 27 February 1914, n.p.
122. William J. Henderson, no title, *New York Sun*, 27 February 1914, n.p., included in Scrapbook 1911–1915, n.p.
123. Richard Aldrich, "Charpentier's New Opera, *Julien* Sung," *New York Times*, 27 February 1914, p. 9, col. 3.
124. *New York Herald*, 27 February 1914, n.p.
125. Aldrich, "Charpentier's New Opera, *Julien*, Sung."
126. Henderson, *New York Sun*.
127. Farrar, *Geraldine Farrar*, p. 109.
128. Aldrich, "Charpentier's New Opera, *Julien*, Sung."
129. *New York Herald*, 27 February 1914.
130. Farrar, "Caruso," *Theatre Arts*, p. 91.
131. Farrar, *Geraldine Farrar*, p. 109.
132. "New Carmen Sings at Metropolitan," *New York Times*, 4 December 1908, p. 11, col. 5.
133. Farrar, *Geraldine Farrar*, p. 110.
134. "Abandon Carmen Revival," *New York Times*, 26 March 1914, p. 11, col. 2.
135. Farrar, *Such Sweet Compulsion*, p. 133.
136. Ibid., p. 136.
137. Farrar, *Geraldine Farrar*, p. 110.
138. Farrar, *Such Sweet Compulsion*, p. 137.
139. Ibid.
140. Geraldine Farrar and Frederic Dean, "The Psychology of *Carmen*," *Bookman*, 42 (December 1915), pp. 414–415.
141. Ibid., p. 413.
142. Ibid., pp. 415–416.
143. Ibid., p. 416.
144. Ibid., p. 417.
145. Martens, p. 99.
146. Farrar, *Such Sweet Compulsion*, p. 138.
147. Martens, p. 99.
148. "But What About Miss Farrar's Carmen?" *New York Herald*, 20 November 1914, p. 7, col. 1.
149. No author, no title, no publication, n.p., included in Scrapbook 1915, n.p.
150. William J. Henderson, Review of Metropolitan Opera Performance of Bizet's *Carmen* on November 19, 1914, quoted in Irving Kolodin, *The Metropolitan Opera 1883–1966: A Candid History* (New York: Alfred A. Knopf, 1967), pp. 249–250.
151. Richard Aldrich, "New Production of Bizet's *Carmen*," *New York Times*, 20 November 1914, p. 9, col. 3.

152. Quantance Eaton, *Opera Caravan: Adventures of the Metropolitan on Tour 1883–1956* (New York: Farrar, Strauss and Cudahy, 1957), p. 141.
153. Louise Dooly, "Season's Greatest Audience Applauds Stars of *Carmen*," no publication (Atlanta), n.d., n.p., included in Scrapbook 1915, n.p.
154. Dudley Glass, "Farrar's Wonderful Carmen Sets Largest Audience Wild," no publication (Atlanta), n.d., n.p., included in Scrapbook 1915, n.p.
155. Thompson, p. 260.
156. Van Vechten, p. 51.
157. Ibid., p. 45; Thompson, p. 2.
158. Quoted from an interview granted to this writer by Sylvia Blein on March 1, 1975.
159. Henderson, Review of Bizet's *Carmen*, cited in Kolodin, p. 249.
160. Henry Krehbiel, "'*Carmen* Draws Throngs to Opera," *New York Tribune*, p. 1, col. 1.
161. Van Vechten, p. 51.
162. Aldrich, "New Production of Bizet's *Carmen*."
163. Farrar, *Such Sweet Compulsion*, p. 140.
164. Taubman, *Opera: Front and Back*, p. 54.
165. Richard Aldrich, "World's Premiere of *Mme. Sans-Gêne*," *New York Times*, 26 January 1915, p. 8, col. 3.
166. William J. Henderson, Review of Metropolitan Opera Performance of Giordano's *Madame Sans-Gêne* on January 25, 1915, quoted in Irving Kolodin, *The Metropolitan Opera 1883–1966: A Candid History* (New York: Alfred A. Knopf, 1967), p. 251.
167. Van Vechten, p. 45.
168. Aldrich, "World's Premiere of *Mme. Sans-Gêne*," p. 8, col. 3.
169. Farrar, *Geraldine Farrar*, p. 111.
170. Geraldine Farrar, "The Story of My Life," *Photoplay Magazine*, XV (March 1919), p. 104.
171. Farrar, *Such Sweet Compulsion*, p. 144.
172. Giulio Gatti-Casazza, *Memories of the Opera*, trans., Louis Biancolli (New York: Charles Scribner' s Sons, 1941), p. 200.
173. Taubman, *Opera: Front and Back*, p. 303.
174. Farrar, *Geraldine Farrar*, p.112.

Chapter Four

1. Jesse L. Lasky and Don Weldon, *I Blow My Own Horn* (Garden City, N.Y.: Doubleday and Company, Inc., 1957), p. 116.
2. Ibid., p. 117.
3. Cecil B. DeMille, *Cecil B. DeMille Autobiography* (Englewood Cliffs, N.J.: by Cecil B. DeMille Trust, published by Prentice-Hall, Inc., 1959) p. 140.
4. Geraldine Farrar, *Geraldine Farrar: The Story of an American Singer by Herself* (Boston: Houghton Mifflin Company, 1916), p. 112.
5. Geraldine Farrar, "The Story of My Life," *Photoplay Magazine*, XV (March 1919), p. 104.
6. Farrar, *Geraldine Farrar*, p. 112.
7. Geraldine Farrar, "The Story of My Life," *Photoplay Magazine*, XV (April 1919), p. 52.
8. Lasky and Weldon, p. 117.
9. DeMille, p. 141.
10. Ibid., p. 142.
11. Ibid., p. 143.
12. Geraldine Farrar, *Such Sweet Compulsion* (New York: The Greystone Press, 1938), pp. 168–69.
13. "Geraldine Farrar a Hit in *Maria Rosa*," *New York Times*, 8 May 1916, p. 7, col. 2.
14. DeMille, p. 145.
15. Farrar, *Such Sweet Compulsion*, p. 169.
16. Farrar, "The Story of My Life" (April 1919), p. 53.
17. Farrar, *Such Sweet Compulsion*, p. 169.
18. Samuel Goldwyn, *Behind the Screen* (New York: George H. Doran Company, 1923), p. 147.
19. Ibid.
20. DeMille, p. 145.
21. Ibid., p. 146.
22. "Lasky Stages Bullfight in Los Angeles for *Carmen*," *Motion Picture News*, 31 July 1915, n.p., included in the Paramount-Lasky File of the Library of Congress Film Collection.
23. "Geraldine Farrar in Temptation," *Moving Picture World*, 18 December 1915, n.p., included in Paramount-Lasky File of the Library of Congress Film Collection.
24. Instrumental and vocal selections from Bizet's *Carmen* also accompanied the film's showings in other large cities, such as New York, Philadelphia, and Chicago.
25. "Miss Farrar Sees Film Debut; Weeps and Get $10,000 Wrap," *New York Herald*, 2 October 1915, p. 12, col. 2.
26. "Miss Farrar Sees *Carmen*," *New York Times*, 2 October 1915, p. 11, col. 1.
27. "*Carmen* Battle Won by Lasky," *New York Tribune*, 1 November 1915, p. 11, col. 3.
28. "Miss Farrar a Fervid Carmen," *New York Herald*, 1 November 1915, p. 13, col. 1.

29. "Farrar a Tigress as Screen Carmen," *New York Sun*, 1 November 1915, p. 7, cols. 5–6.
30. "Choice of Carmens for the Movie Fans," *New York World*, 1 November 1915, p. 13, col. 1.
31. "Geraldine Farrar Seen But Not Heard," *New York Times*, 1 November 1915, p. 11, col. 1.
32. Lesley Mason, "*Carmen*," *Motion Picture News*, 13 November 1915, n.p., included in the Paramount-Lasky File of the Library of Congress Film Collection.
33. "Miss Farrar Sees Film Debut."
34. Lasky and Weldon, p. 118.
35. Joseph P. Kennedy, *The Story of Films* (New York: A.W. Shaw Company, 1927), pp. 183–84.
36. Goldwyn, p. 83; and a conversation with Mrs. Wilfred C. Bain on July 2, 1974, in which she related that as a young girl she was not allowed to attend the movies until Miss Farrar's appearance on the screen. Her parents were very strict and only consented because it was Geraldine Farrar, the famous diva, whose family they had known at Lake George, New York. And, Mrs. Bain' s mother felt that these films would aid in her daughter's cultural development. Each visit to the movie house was an exciting event, because they lived out of town and had to travel there and back in the family carriage.
37. "Farrar in Temptation," *New York Times*, 3 January 1916, p. 22, col. 4.
38. "Geraldine Farrar in *Temptation*."
39. "*Maria Rosa*," no publication, 8 May 1916, n.p., included in the Paramount-Lasky File of the Library of Congress Film Collection.
40. "Geraldine Farrar a Hit in *Maria Rosa*," *New York Times*, 8 May 1916, p. 7, cols. 2–3.
41. DeMille, p. 141.
42. Farrar, *Such Sweet Compulsion*, p. 172.
43. DeMille, p. 73.
44. Scrapbook 1915–1930s, n.p.
45. DeMille, p. 171.
46. Ibid.
47. The Screen Girl, "*Joan the Woman* Masterpiece of Screen," no publication, n.d., n.p., included in Scrapbook 1915–1930s, n.p.
48. Peter Milne, "*Joan the Woman*," no publication, n.d., n.p., included in the Paramount-Lasky File of the Library of Congress Film Collection.
49. Farrar, "The Story of My Life" (April 1919), p. 53.
50. "Farrar Scores Triumph in *Joan the Woman*," no publication, n.d., n.p., included in Scrapbook 1915–1930s, n.p., n.d.
51. Farrar, *Such Sweet Compulsion*, p. 174.
52. "How Geraldine Farrar Lost Fifty Pounds," no publication, n.d., n.p., included in Scrapbook 1915–1930s, n.p.
53. DeMille, p. 173.
54. Kevin Brownlow, *The Parade's Gone By* (New York: Alfred A. Knopf, Inc., 1969), p. 34.
55. Nell Brinkley, no title, no publication, n.p., included in Scrapbook 1915–1930s, n.p.
56. Geraldine Farrar and Mary F. Watkins, "Diva's Decades," *Saturday Evening Post* (16 January 1932), p. 94.
57. Farrar, *Such Sweet Compulsion*, pp. 174–175.
58. DeMille, pp. 174–75.
59. Farrar, "The Story of My Life" (April 1919), pp. 53–54.
60. Farrar, *Such Sweet Compulsion*, p. 173.
61. DeMille, p. 92.
62. "You Should Have No Difficulty in Getting Business on the Strength of Star's Name," no publication, n.d., n.p., included in the Goldwyn File of the Library of Congress Film Collection.
63. "*Joan the Woman* Opens in Los Angeles," no publication, n.d., n.p., included in Scrapbook 1915–1930s, n.p.
64. "*Joan the Woman* Film Triumph for Star," no publication, n.d., n.p., included in Scrapbook 1915–1930s, n.p.
65. "Farrar Triumphs as Maid of Orleans," *New York Sun*, 25 December 1916, p. 5, col. 1.
66. Milne, "*Joan the Woman*."
67. "Joan of Arc Made Lifelike by Miss Farrar for Screen," *New York Herald*, 25 December 1916, p. 7, col. 3.
68. "Joan Born in Opera," no publication, n.p., included in Scrapbook 1915–1930s, n.p.
69. The Gallerite, "*Joan the Woman* as Seen from the Gallery," no publication, n.d., n.p., included in Scrapbook 1915–1930s, n.p.
70. The Screen Girl, "*Joan the Woman* Masterpiece of Screen."
71. "Farrar Likes Aztec Role in *The Woman God Forgot*," *Moving Picture World*, 6 October 1917, n.p., included in the Paramount-Artcraft File of the Library of Congress Film Collection.
72. Farrar, *Such Sweet Compulsion*, p. 177.
73. E.T. Keyser, "*The Woman God Forgot*," no publication, n.d., n.p., included in the Paramount-Artcraft File of the Library of Congress Film Collection.
74. "Farrar in Spanish Film," *New York Times*, 29 October 1917, p. 11, col. 2.
75. Farrar, *Such Sweet Compulsion*, p. 177.

76. "Last of Farrar Films," *New York Times*, 17 December 1917, p. 11, col. 4.
77. Farrar, letter to Samuel Goldwyn, summer 1918, included in the Farrar Collection at the Library of Congress.
78. George T. Pardy, "*Woman and Puppet* Presents Farrar as Star," *Picture Trade Review*, 17 April 1920, n.p., included in Goldwyn File of the Library of Congress Film Collection.
79. "*The Woman and the Puppet*," *Motion Picture News*, 17 April 1920, n.p., included in Goldwyn File of the Library of Congress Film Collection.
80. Goldwyn, pp. 150, 154.
81. Ibid., pp. 150–51.
82. "Farrar Goldwyn Policy Approved by Picturegoers," *Moving Picture World*, 11 January 1919, n.p., included in the Goldwyn File of the Library of Congress Film Collection.
83. "Two Opera Stars in Silent Films," *New York Times*, 25 November 1918, p. 11, col. 3.
84. "Farrar Filmed in *Turn of Wheel*," *New York Times*, 2 September 1918, p. 7, col. 1.
85. "The Screen," *New York Times*, 28 April 1919, p. 13, col. 2.
86. No author, no title, *Chicago Tribune*, 27 April 1919, n.p., included in Scrapbook 1915–1930s, n.p.
87. "Melodramatic Romance Has Some Tense Situations and Is Well Presented," no publication, 4 May 1919, n.p., included in the Goldwyn File of the Library of Congress Film Collection.
88. "The Screen," *New York Times*, 5 April 1920, p. 20, col. 1.
89. Daniel Blum, *A Pictorial History of the Silent Screen* (London: Hamish Hamilton, Ltd., 1954), p. 195.
90. Goldwyn, pp. 154–155.
91. "The Screen," *New York Times*, 8 November 1920, p. 20, col. 2.
92. Goldwyn, p. 155.
93. Edward Wagenknecht, ed., *When I Was a Child: An Anthology* (New York: E.P. Dutton and Company, Inc., Publishers, 1946), p. 149.
94. Kennedy, *Story of the Films*, p. 183.
95. Goldwyn, p. 157.
96. "Farrar Triumphs as Maid of Orleans," *New York Sun*.

Chapter Five

1. Geraldine Farrar and Mary F. Watkins, "Diva's Decades," *Saturday Evening Post* (16 January 1932), p. 95.
2. J.B. Kennedy, "I Have Lived as I Like," *Colliers* (9 April 1927), p. 39.

3. "Farrar's Carmen Made Realistic," *New York Times*, 19 February 1916, p. 9, col. 4.
4. Ibid.
5. Frances Alda, *Men, Women and Tenors* (New York: AMS Press, 1971), p. 214.
6. Henry Finck, "Music," *The Nation* (24 February 1916), p. 232.
7. "Geraldine Farrar a Lively Carmen—Introduces a Wrestling Bout in Bizet's Opera," *New York Times*, 18 February 1916, p. 9, col. 3.
8. Henry T. Parker, "Mme. Farrar as Carmen," *Boston Evening Transcript*, 6 April 1916, n.p., included in Scrapbook 1915–1930s, n.p.
9. Ibid.
10. Ibid.
11. "Geraldine Farrar a Lively Carmen."
12. H. Howard Taubman, *Opera: Front and Back* (New York: Charles Scribner's Sons, 1938), p. 303.
13. Henry Krehbiel, "First Metropolitan Performance of *Thaïs*," *New York Tribune*, 17 February 1917, quoted in William H. Seltsam, ed., *Metropolitan Annals: A Chronicle of Artists and Performances* (New York: H.W. Wilson Company, 1947), p. 307.
14. Richard Aldrich, "Mme. Farrar Sings Massenet's *Thaïs*," *New York Times*, 19 February 1917, p. 9, col. 1.
15. William J. Henderson, "Geraldine Farrar Real Siren in *Zazà*," *New York Sun*, 17 January 1920, p. 11, col. 2.
16. Irving Kolodin, *The Metropolitan Opera 1883–1966: A Candid History* (New York: Alfred A. Knopf, 1967), p. 267.
17. William J. Henderson, Review of a Metropolitan Opera Performance of Massenet's *Thaïs* on February 26, 1917, quoted in Kolodin, p. 267.
18. Geraldine Farrar, "The Story of My Life," *Photoplay Magazine*, XV (March 1919), p. 102.
19. Henry Krehbiel, "First Metropolitan Performance of *Thaïs*," quoted in William H. Seltsam, ed., *Metropolitan Annals: A Chronicle of Artists and Performances* (New York: H.W. Wilson Company, 1947), p. 307.
20. "*Lodoletta* Charms at Premiere Here," *New York Times*, 13 January 1918, Sect. I, p. 16, col. 2.
21. James G. Huneker, "Opera," *New York Times*, 15 December 1918, p. 22, col. 2.
22. "Three Operas by Puccini Are Sung," *New York World*, 15 December 1918, p. 22, col. 3.
23. Huneker, "Opera."
24. Robert Sabin, ed., *The International Cyclopedia of Music and Musicians*, 9th ed.

(New York: Dodd, Mead and Company, 1964), p. 633.

25. James G. Huneker, "Opera," *New York Times*, 25 January 1919, p. 9, col. 4.

26. William J. Henderson, Review of a Metropolitan Opera Performance of Puccini's *Suor Angelica* on January 25, 1919, quoted in Kolodin, p. 279.

27. Huneker, "Opera," 25 January 1919.

28. Ibid.

29. Ibid.

30. Geraldine Farrar, *Such Sweet Compulsion* (New York: The Greystone Press, 1938), p. 253.

31. Huneker, "Opera," 25 January 1919.

32. Farrar, *Such Sweet Compulsion*, pp. 253–54.

33. Ibid., p. 150.

34. Helen Noble, *Life with the Met* (New York: G.P. Putnam's Sons, 1954), p. 93.

35. Mary Watkins Cushing, *The Rainbow Bridge* (New York: G.P. Putnam's Sons, 1954), p. 173.

36. Giulio Gatti-Casazza, *Memories of the Opera*, trans., Louis Biancolli (New York: Charles Scribner's Sons, 1941), p. 200.

37. Noble, p. 93.

38. Mary F. Watkins, "Geraldine Farrar 1928 Model," *Woman's Journal*, 13 (February 1928), p. 10.

39. William J. Henderson, an Article in the *New York Sun*, 920, n.p., quoted in Harold C. Schonberg, "The Goddess that was Geraldine Farrar," *New York Times*, 19 March 1967, Sec. II, p. 21, col. 5.

40. Farrar, *Such Sweet Compulsion*, p. 151.

41. David Belasco, Western Union telegram to Geraldine Farrar, January 16, 1920, included in the Farrar Collection at the Library of Congress.

42. Frederick H. Martens, *The Art of the Prima Donna and Concert Singer* (New York: D. Appleton and Company, 1923) pp. 96–7.

43. James G. Huneker, "Zazà as Geraldine Farrar," *New York World*, n.d., n.p., included in Scrapbook 1915–1930s, n.p.

44. Ibid., no publication, n.d., n.p., included in Scrapbook 1915–1930s, n.p.

45. Max Smith, no title, no publication, n.d., n.p., included in Scrapbook 1915–1930s, n.p.

46. Henderson, "Geraldine Farrar Real Siren in *Zazà*."

47. Henry Krehbiel, "Farrar's Zazà a New Version of Ugly Role," *New York Tribune*, 17 January 1920, p. 13, col. 1.

48. Ibid., cols. 2–3.

49. No author, no title, no publication, n.d., n.p., included in Scrapbook 1915–1930s, n.p.

50. "Dr. Straton Assails Undress on Stage," *New York Times*, 10 May 1920, p. 17, col. 7.

51. Quaintance Eaton, *Opera Caravan: Adventures of the Metropolitan on Tour 1883–1956* (New York: Farrar, Strauss and Cudahy, 1957), p. 148.

52. "Dr. Straton Assails Undress on Stage."

53. Kennedy, p. 40.

54. Geraldine Farrar letter to David Belasco, February 16, 1921, included in the Farrar Collection at the Library of Congress.

55. David Belasco letter to Geraldine Farrar, February 1921, included in the Farrar Collection of the Library of Congress.

56. Huneker, "Zazà as Geraldine Farrar."

57. Richard Aldrich, "Farrar Sings *Zazà* Revealed in Opera," *New York Times*, 17 January 1920, p. 14, col. 2.

58. Letter to this author from Frederick Jagel, February 12, 1974.

59. Farrar, *Such Sweet Compulsion*, p. 152.

60. Geraldine Farrar, *Geraldine Farrar: The Story of an American Singer by Herself* (Boston: Houghton Mifflin Company, 1916), p. 94.

61. Geraldine Farrar letter to David Belasco, February 16, 1921, included in the Farrar Collection at the Library of Congress.

62. David Belasco letter to Geraldine Farrar, March 31, 1921, included in the Farrar Collection at the Library of Congress.

63. Richard Aldrich, "The Opera," *New York Times*, 16 January 1921, p. 19, col. 2.

64. William J. Henderson, Review of a Metropolitan Opera Performance of Charpentier's *Louise* on January 15, 1921, *New York Sun*, n.p., quoted in Kolodin, p. 292.

65. Farrar, *Such Sweet Compulsion*, p. 154.

66. Kolodin, p. 342.

67. Richard Aldrich, "The Opera," *New York Times*, 1 December 1921, p. 15, col. 2.

68. William J. Henderson, a Review of a Metropolitan Opera Performance of Massenet's *La navarraise* on November 30, 1921, quoted in Kolodin, p. 305.

69. Henry T. Finck, *My Adventures in the Golden Age of Music* (New York: Funk and Wagnalls Company, 1926), p. 386.

70. Geraldine Farrar and John J. Whitehead, Jr., "Coming Back and Looking Back," *Saturday Evening Post*, 14 April 1928, p. 18.

71. Farrar, *Such Sweet Compulsion,* p. 242.

72. Ibid, p. 241.

73. An interview by this author with Miss Sylvia Blein, March 1, 1975.

74. Farrar, *Such Sweet Compulsion*, p. 162.

75. Farrar and Whitehead, p. 19.
76. Finck, p. 377.
77. "Shout Tosca! at Farrar—She Asks Admirers What Role They Wish to Hear Her Sing at Farewell," *New York Times*, 24 January 1922, p. 16, col. 2.
78. An interview by this author with Miss Sylvia Blein, March 1, 1975.
79. "Pigeon in Bouquet Shower on Farrar," *New York Times*, 11 April 1922, p. 22, col. 3.
80. "Farrar Quits Amid Tears and Cheers," *New York Tribune*, 23 April 1922, p. 1, col. 4.
81. "Hail Farrar Queen as She Sings Adieu," *New York Times*, 23 April 1922, p. 20, col. 4.
82. "Farrar Quits Amid Tears and Cheers," p. 3, col. 5.
83. Noble, p. 94.
84. John Briggs, *Requiem for a Yellow Brick Brewery: A History of the Metropolitan Opera* (Boston: Little, Brown and Company, 1969), p. 146.
85. "Farrar Quits Amid Tears and Cheers," p. 1, col. 4.
86. "Hail Farrar Queen as She Sings Adieu," p. 20, col. 4.
87. An interview by this author with Miss Sylvia Blein, March 1, 1975.
88. David Belasco letter to Geraldine Farrar, April 24, 1922, included in the Farrar Collection at the Library of Congress.
89. "Farrar Joins Belasco; Quits Opera for Good. Next Play to Be Ready for Her Next Year When She Ends Concert Tour. Nature of Drama Still a Secret," no publication, n.d., n.p., included in Scrapbook 1915–1930s, n.p.
90. "From Opera to Drama," *New York Times*, 29 April 1922, p. 14, col. 4.
91. Farrar and Whitehead, p. 124. Reprinted from the *Saturday Evening Post*, c 1928 The Curtis Publishing.

Chapter Six

1. Jane Grant, "Geraldine Farrar's First Aid to Opera," *New York Times Magazine*, 21 September 1924, p. 10, col. 1.
2. Ibid.
3. Farrar, *Such Sweet Compulsion*, p. 196.
4. Geraldine Farrar and Mary F. Watkins, "No Means No!" *Saturday Evening Post*, 21 November 1931, p. 8.
5. An interview by this author with Miss Sylvia Blein, March 1, 1975.

Chapter Seven

1. Letter to this author from Frederick Jagel, dated February 12, 1974.

2. Conversation of this author with Edward M. Waters, 1974.
3. In 1904 a French periodical had referred to "the velvet quality of that voice in the upper register" of Geraldine Farrar. Obviously she never forgot that lovely image and repeated it to Miss Williams who then shared it with all her students. (see note 78, p. 29)
4. From an interview by this author with Camilla Williams, 1995.
5. Ibid.
6. Harold C. Schonberg, "Link with the Golden Age," *New York Times*, 12 March 1967, p. 86, col. 6.

Appendix 1

1. No author, no title, no publication, n.d., n.p., included in Scrapbook 1909–1910, p. 74.
2. Frederick H. Martens, *The Art of the Prima Donna and Concert Singer* (New York: Appleton and Company, 1923), p. 91.
3. Geraldine Farrar, "Our Operatic Opportunity," *The Forum*, 60 (November 1918), p. 528.
4. Martens, p. 98.
5. Farrar, "Our Operatic Opportunity," p. 528.
6. "Geraldine Farrar Discloses Credo of Life," *Singing*, n.d., n.p., included in Scrapbook 1915–1930s, n.p.
7. Emily M. Burbank, "Geraldine Farrar," *Century*, 75 (March 1908), p. 692.
8. No author, no title, no publication, n.d., n.p., included in Scrapbook 1915–1930s, n.p.
9. Martens, p. 94.
10. Farrar, "Our Operatic Opportunity," p. 528.
11. Martens, pp. 89–90.
12. "What Geraldine Farrar Would Do If 'Broke,'" *Literary Digest*, 15 February 1919, p. 68.
13. Martens, p. 90.
14. Emily M. Burbank, "Geraldine Farrar: The Early Days of an American Prima Donna," *Putnam's Monthly*, 4 (May 1908), p. 206.
15. "Geraldine Farrar Discloses Credo of Life," n.p.
16. Geraldine Farrar and R.H. Wollstein, "What's the Matter with Our Music?" *Etude*, 48 (August 1930), p. 537.
17. Geraldine Farrar and John J. Whitehead, Jr., "Coming Back and Looking Back," *Saturday Evening Post*, 14 April 1928, p. 18.
18. Farrar and Wollstein, p. 547.
19. Geraldine Farrar, *Such Sweet Compulsion* (New York: The Greystone Press, 1938), p. 285.

20. Geraldine Farrar and Rose Heylbut, "How Can We Best Serve Our Students?" *Etude*, 56 (September 1938), p. 564.
21. Farrar, "Our Operatic Opportunity," p. 528.
22. Farrar and Heylbut, p. 564.
23. Ibid.
24. Farrar and Wollstein, p. 538.
25. Farrar and Whitehead, p. 18.
26. J.B. Kennedy, "I Have Lived as I Liked," *Colliers*, 9 April 1927, p. 39.
27. "Geraldine Farrar Talks of Her Work," *Express*, n.d., n.p., included in Scrapbook 1909–1910, p. 29.
28. Geraldine Farrar and Mary F. Watkins, "No Means No!" *Saturday Evening Post*, 21 November 1931, p. 9.
29. No author, no title, no publication n.d., n.p., included in Scrapbook 1910–1930s, p. 81.
30. No author, no title, no publication, n.d., n.p., included in Scrapbook 1915–1930s, n.p.
31. Farrar and Whitehead, p. 128.
32. Burbank, "Geraldine Farrar," p. 693.
33. "Farrar Deplores a Pernicious Fallacy," no publication, n.d., n.p., included in Scrapbook 1907–1908, n.p.
34. No author, no title, no publication, n.d., n.p., included in Scrapbook 1910–1930, p. 81.
35. Edward Wagenknecht, *Seven Daughters of the Theatre* (Norman, Oklahoma: University of Oklahoma Press, 1964), p. 171.
36. "Maeterlinck's *Ariane et Barbe-Bleue*, with Dukas' Musical Setting, Offers the Little American Prima Donna an Opportunity to Embody in Her Person Some Interesting Symbolic Ideas," no publication, n.d., n.p., included in Scrapbook 1911–1915, n.p.
37. No author, no title, no publication, n.d., n.p., included in Scrapbook 1909–1910, n.p.
38. Algernon St. John-Brenon, "Geraldine Farrar in Don Giovanni," no publication, n.d., n.p., included in Scrapbook 1907–1908, n.p.
39. Wagenknecht, *Geraldine Farrar*, p. 35.
40. Ibid.
41. No author, no title, no publication, n.d., n.p., included in Scrapbook 1909–1910, p. 74.
42. No author, no title, no publication, n.d., n.p., included in Scrapbook 1910–1930, p. 81.
43. Jane Grant, "Geraldine Farrar's First Aid to Opera," *New York Times Magazine*, 21 September 1924, p. 10, col. 4.
44. Martens, pp. 95–96.
45. Harriette Brower, *Vocal Mastery: Talks with Master Singers and Teachers Comprising Interviews with Caruso, Farrar, Maurel, Lehmann and Others* (New York: Frederick A. Stokes Company Publishers, 1920) p. 16.
46. Geraldine Farrar, "The Art of Acting in the Movies," *Vanity Fair*, 11 (November 1918), p. 92.
47. Farrar and Heylbut, p. 56.
48. Martens, p. 94.
49. Sue Roberts, "From the Inside Looking Out," no publication, n.d., n.p., included in Scrapbook 1915–1930s, n.p.
50. "Unjust! Miss Farrar Cries," *New York Sun*, 1 March 1908, p. 6, col. 1.
51. Roberts, n.p.
52. Geraldine Farrar, "The Story of My Life," *Photoplay Magazine*, XV (February 1919), I, p. 90.
53. Farrar, "The Art of Acting for the Movies," p. 92.
54. Farrar and Heylburt, p. 563.
55. Geraldine Farrar and Mary F. Watkins, "Diva's Decades," *Saturday Evening Post* (16 January 1932), p. 92.
56. Geraldine Farrar, "The Girl Who Wants to Sing," *Ladies Home Journal*, 31 (October 1914), p. 29.
57. The Post Young Woman, "Thirty Minutes with Pretty Yankee Girl Who Now Flocks with World's Most Tuneful Songbirds," no publication, n.d., n.p., included in Scrapbook 1907–1908, n.p.
58. Farrar, "The Girl Who Wants to Sing," p. 29.
59. Farrar and Wollstein, p. 538.
60. Richard Aldrich, "Miss Farrar as Violetta," *New York Times*, 29 February 1908, p. 7, col. 4.
61. Farrar and Whitehead, p. 19.
62. No author, no title, no publication, n.d., n.p., included in Scrapbook 1909–1910, p. 74.
63. Wagenknecht, Geraldine Farrar, p. 34.
64. Homer Ulrich, *Famous Women Singers* (New York: Dodd, Mead and Company, 1953), p. 73.
65. Letter to this author from Frederick Jagel, dated February 12, 1974.
66. Conversation of this author with Mary Ludington, November 1974.

Select Bibliography

Alda, Frances. *Men, Women and Tenors*. New York: AMS Press, 1971.
Belasco, David. *The Theatre Through Its Stage Door*. New York: Harper and Brothers, 1919.
Blum, Daniel. *A Pictorial-History of the Silent Screen*. London: Hamish Hamilton, 1954.
Briggs, John. *Requiem for a Yellow Brick Brewery: A History of the Metropolitan Opera*. Boston: Little, Brown and Company, 1969.
Brower, Harriette. *Vocal Mastery: Talks with Master Singers and Teachers Comprising Interviews with Caruso, Farrar, Maurel, Lehmann and Others*. New York: Frederick A. Stokes Company, 1920.
Brownlow, Kevin. *The Parade's Gone By*. New York: Alfred A. Knopf, 1969.
Carner, Mosco. *Puccini: A Critical Biography*. New York: Alfred A. Knopf, 1959.
Cushing, Mary Watkins. *The Rainbow Bridge*. New York: G.P. Putnam's Sons, 1954.
DeMille, Cecil B. *The Autobiography of Cecil B. DeMille*. Ed. Donald Hayn. Englewood Cliffs, NJ: Prentice-Hall, 1959.
Eaton, Quaintance. *The Miracle of the Met: An Informal History of the Metropolitan Opera 1883–1967*. New York: Meredith Press, 1968.
_____. *Opera Caravan: Adventures of the Metropolitan on Tour 1883–1956*. New York: Farrar, Strauss and Cudahy, 1957.
Ewen, David. *Living Musicians*. New York: H.W. Wilson, 1940.
Farrar, Geraldine. *Geraldine Farrar: The Story of an American Singer by Herself*. Boston: Houghton Mifflin, 1916.
_____. *Such Sweet Compulsion*. New York: Greystone Press, 1938.
Finck, Henry T. *My Adventures in the Golden Age of Music*. New York: Funk and Wagnalls, 1926.
_____. *Success in Music and How It Is Won*. New York: Charles Scribner's Sons, 1913.
Garden, Mary, and Louis Biancolli. *Mary Garden's Story*. New York: Simon & Schuster, 1951.
Gatti-Casazza, Giulio. *Memories of the Opera*. Trans. Louis Biancolli. New York: Charles Scribner's Sons, 1941.
Goldwyn, Samuel. *Behind the Screen*. New York: George H. Doran Company, 1923.
Homer, Anne. *Louise Homer and the Golden Age of Opera*. New York: William Morrow and Company, 1974.

Kellogg, Clara Louise. *Memoirs of an American Prima Donna.* New York: G.P. Putnam's Sons, 1913.

Kennedy, Joseph P. *The Story of the Films.* New York: A.W. Shaw, 1927.

Kolodin, Irving. *The Metropolitan Opera 1883–1966: A Candid History.* New York: Alfred A. Knopf, 1967.

Krehbiel, Henry E. *Chapters of Opera: Being Historical and Critical Observations and Records Concerning the Lyric Drama in New York from Its Earliest Days Down to the Present Time.* New York: Henry Holt and Company, 1908.

Lahee, Henry C. *The Grand Opera Singers of Today: An Account of the Leading Operatic Stars Who Have Sung During Recent Years, Together with a Sketch of the Chief Operatic Enterprises.* Boston: The Page Company, 1912.

Lasky, Jesse L., and Don Weldon. *I Blow My Own Horn.* Garden City, N.Y.: Doubleday, 1957.

Latham, Alison, ed. *The Oxford Companion to Music.* New York: Oxford University Press, 2002.

Lehmann, Lilli. *How to Sing.* New York: Macmillan, 1916.

_____. *Mein Weg.* Leipzig: Verlag von G. Hirzel, 1913.

Lissfelt, J.F. *Basic Principles of Artistic Singing.* Boston: E.C. Schirmer Music Company, 1938.

Makin, Ena, ed., trans. *Letters of Giacomo Puccini: Mainly Connected with the Composition and Production of His Operas.* Ed. Giuseppe Adami. Philadelphia: J.B. Lippincott, 1931.

Mapleson, James Henry. *The Mapleson Memoirs: The Career of an Operatic Impresario 1858–1888.* Ed. Harold Rosenthal. London: Putnam and Company Ltd., 1966.

Martens, Frederick H. *The Art of the Prima Donna and Concert Singer.* New York: D. Appleton and Company, 1923.

Noble, Helen. *Life with the Met.* New York: G.P. Putnam's Sons, 1954.

Odell, George. *Annals of the New York Stage: 1891–1894.* XV. New York: Columbia University Press, 1949.

Sabin, Robert., ed. *The International Cyclopedia of Music and Musicians.* 9th ed. New York: Dodd, Mead and Company, 1964.

Sadie, Stanley and John Tyrrell, eds. *New Groves Dictionary of Music and Musicians.* 2d ed. New York: Oxford University Press, 2003.

Seligman, Vincent. *Puccini Among Friends.* New York: Benjamin Blom, 1971.

Seltsam, William H., ed. *Metropolitan Opera Annals: A Chronicle of Artists and Performances.* New York: H.W. Wilson, 1947.

Shaw, Bernard. *London Music in 1888–1889 as Heard by Corno di Bassetto (Later Known as Bernard Shaw) with Some Further Autobiographical Particulars.* London: Constable and Company Limited, 1937.

_____. *Shaw on Music: A Selection from the Music Criticism of Bernard Shaw.* Ed. Eric Bentley. Garden City, N.Y.: Doubleday, 1955.

Stanislavski, Constantin. *My Life in Art.* New York: Theatre Art Books, 1948.

Taubman, H. Howard. *The Maestro, the Life of Arturo Toscanini.* New York: Simon & Schuster, 1951.

_____. *Opera: Front and Back.* New York: Charles Scribner's Sons, 1938.

Thompson, Oscar. *The American Singer: A Hundred Years of Success in Opera.* New York: Dial Press, 1937.

Ulrich, Homer. *Famous Women Singers.* New York: Dodd, Mead and Company, 1953.

Van Vechten, Carl. *Interpreters and Interpretations*. New York: Alfred A. Knopf, 1917.
Wagenknecht, Edward. *Geraldine Farrar: An Authorized Record of Her Career*. Seattle: University of Washington Bookstore, 1929.
_____. *Seven Daughters of the Theatre*. Norman: University of Oklahoma Press, 1964.
_____, ed. *When I Was a Child: An Anthology*. New York: E.P. Dutton, 1946.
Wagnalls, Mabel. *Stars of the Opera*. New York: Funk and Wagnalls, 1907.
Wagner, Richard. *Gesammelte Schriften und Dichtungen von Richard Wagner*. Leipzig: Verlag von E.W. Fritzsch, 1872.
_____. *Richard Wagner's Gesammelte Schriften*. Ed. Julius Kapp. Leipzig: Hesse & Becker Verlag, 1914.
Williams, Camilla, and Stephanie Shonekan. *The Life of Camilla Williams, African American Classical Singer and Opera Diva*. Lewiston, NY: Edwin Mellen Press, 2011.

Index

Numbers in ***bold italics*** indicate pages with photographs.

Aarons, Alfred E. 130
Abbey, Henry 35
Abbott, Bessie *50*
Aida (role) *152*–153
Aida (Verdi) 5
L'Aiglon (Rostand play) 15
Albann, Emma *19*
Althouse, Paul 67
Amato, Pasquale *83*, 160
Ames, Winthrop 62
Amica (Mascagni) 29, 155
Amica (role) 29
L'Ancêtre (Saint Saën) 31, 155
Anderson, Marian 4, 132, *133*
Andrea Chénier (Giordano) 32, 155
Angela (*Le Domino noir*) 29, 32
Anisfeld, Boris 77, 115
Anita (*La Navarraise*) 121, 122, 123, 156
Ariane (role) 74, 75, 76, 77, 78, 89, 142
Ariane et Barbe-Bleue (Dukas) 74, 75, 77, 156, 171, 178

The Barber of Seville (Rossini) 14
Barnes, Dennis 11
Barnes, Henrietta (Farrar's mother) 11
Barrymore, John 90
Bates, Blanche *41*, 42
Belasco, David 1, 4, 6, *41*, *50*, 52, 90, 117, 118, 120, 121, 125, 127, 138, 139
Belasco, Mrs. David 95
Bel-Geddes, Norman 77
Bernhardt, Sarah 1, 15, 36, *51*, 52, 61, 62, 66, 98, 109, 135, 138
Biddles, George 132
Blein, Sylvia 3, 87
La bohème (Puccini) *28*, *50*, 130, 155, 156, 160

Camondo, Isaac de, Count 29, 32, 155
Capoul, Victor 8, 10, 14, 29
Cappiani, Louisa *12*, *13*, 14

Carmen (Bizet) 2, 26, 48, 58, 82, 87, 110, 111, 112, 129, 156, 160
Carmen (film) 90, 92, 93, 94, 95, 96, 98, 100, 105, 108, 157
Carmen (role/film) 90, 92, 93, 94, 95, 96, 97, 103, 106, 157
Carmen (role/opera) 1, 2, 9, 12, 59, 82–86, 87, 110, 111, 112, 123, 124, 138, 142, 156, 160
Carter, Mrs. Lesley 14, 36, 117, 119
Caruso, Enrico 1, 9, *28*, 38, *41*, 43, *50*, 57, 59, 61, *80*, 82, *83*, 110, 111, 160
Carvalho, Caroline 17
Catherine Huebscher (*Madame Sans-Gêne*) 87, 88
Cavalieri, Lina, *50*
Cecilie, Crown Princess, 27
Chaliapin, Feodor 9, 10, 32, 38, 40, 52
Charlotte (*Werther*) 62, 63, 82, 156
Cherubino (*Figaro*) 58, 59, 79, 142, 156
Cio-Cio-San (*Madama Butterfly*) *41*–49, 52, 58, *60*, 139, 156
Le clown (Camondo) 29, 32, 155
Concha Perez (*The Woman and the Puppet*) 159
Conried, Heinrich 34, 35, 52, 56, 57
The Countess Valeska (Stratz) 14
Crispano, Philip 70, 126
Crosman, Henrietta 90
Cushman, Charlotte 6
Cyrano de Bergerac (Rostand play) 14
The Czarina (Lengyel and Biro) 121

La Dame aux camélias (Dumas, fils play) 15
La Damnation de Faust (Berlioz) 29, 37, 52, 155, 156
Darclee, Hariclea 61
de Cordoba, Pedro 93, 95, 157
de Gogorza, Emilio 8
Delsarte, François *13*

183

DeMille, Cecil B., 2, 92, 93, 98, 101, 102
DeMille, William B. 92, 93
de Reszke, Jean 5, *12*, 34, 35
Destinn, Emmy 58
The Devil Stone 103, 105, 158
The Devil's Disciple (Shaw play) 14
Dippel, Andreas 57, 58
Dolores de Cordova (*The Stronger Vow*), 106, 158
Dome, Zoldan 16
Le Domino noir (Auber) 29, 155, 160
Don Carlo (Verdi) 32, 155
Don Giovanni (Mozart) 23, 52, 155, 156, 160
Le donne curiose (Wolf-Ferrari) 78, 156, 160
Duquesne, Edmond 15
Duse, Eleonora 10, 15, 49, 128, 144

Eames, Emma 57, 61, 64
Easton, Florence 114
Elisabeth (*Don Carlo*) 32
Elisabeth (*Tannhäuser*) 29, 30, 31, 32, 40, *41*, 139, 141, 142, 155, 156
Ellis, Charles 124
Erlanger, A.L. 130

Farrar, Henrietta Barnes (Farrar's mother) *12*
Farrar, Mrs. (Farrar's mother) 11, *12*, 14
Farrar, Sidney D. (Farrar's father) 11, *12*
Father (Farrar's father) 11, *12*, 120, 130
Faust (Gounod) 5, 8, 14, 17, 18, 22, 26, 38, 39, 40, 48, 79, 139, 155, 156, 160
La Fille (*Julien*) 142, 156
Fiske, Mrs. Minnie Maddern 14, 90
Fitch, Clyde *50*
The Flame of the Desert 105, *107*, 159
Foley, C.J. 129
Fornia, Rita 79
Les fourchambault (Augier) 15
Frederick, Pauline 94
Fu-ji-Ko 1, 42

Garden, Mary 9, 10, 15, 77, 118
Gatti-Casazza, Giulio 57, 58, 76, 82, *83*, 89, 114, 115, 122, 124, 126, 130
Gay, Maria 58, 59, 82, 84
Gerryflappers *116*, 124, 125, 127
Gest, Morris 90
Gest, Mrs. Morris 95
Gilda (*Rigoletto*) 32, 155
Gilmour, Mrs. Howard G. 132
Goldwyn, Samuel 2, 94, 95, 105, 106, 108
Goose Girl (*Königskinder*) 1, *68*–74, 113, 141, 156
Grau, Maurice *12*, 14, 35

Graziani, Francesco 16
Griffith, David W. *99*
Gunsbourg, Raoul *28*

Hackett, James K. 14, 19
Hamlet (Shakespeare play) 15
Hari, Mata 31
The Hell Cat 105, 106, 148, 158
Henry, George 70
Homer, Louise *41*, 160
Humperdinck, Englebert 1, *68*, 69, 70, 71, 72, 73, 74, 156

Jagel, Frederick 2, 67, 120, 131, 132, 142
Jeritza, Maria 124
Jerry 117, 125
Joan the Woman 2, *99*–103, 105, 109, 148, 157
Julien (Charpentier) 79, *80*, 81, 82, 121, 122, 156
Juliette (*Roméo et Juliette*) 14, 17, 23, 24, 32, 33, 35, 36, 37, 38, 52, 75, 141, 142, 155, 156, 160

Kautsky, Hans 87
Kellogg, Clara Louise 6
Königskinder (Humperdinck) *68*, 69, 72, 73, 74, 120, 156

Lady Isabelle Channing (*The Flame of the Desert*) 159
Lasky, Jesse L. 2, 90, 95, 108
Leonora (*Il trovatore*) 24, 155
Lilla Gravert (*The Riddle: Woman*) 108, 159
Lodoletta (Mascagni) 113, 114, 156
Lohengrin (Wagner) 17
Long, Mrs. J.H. *12*
Louise (Charpentier) 9, 79, 156
Louise (*Julien*/role) 79, *80*, 81
Louise (*Louise*/role) 121, 122, 156
Lucia (Donizetti) 14
Ludington, Mary 142

Mackaye, Steele *13*
Macpherson, Jeanie 94, *99*, 100, 157
Madama Butterfly (Puccini) 35, *41*, 47, 48, 49, *50*, 58, 90, 120, 124, 130, 139, 151, 156, 160
Madama Butterfly (role) 1, 2, 4, *41*, 42, 44, 48, 49, 72, 89, 112, 123, 132, *133*, 141, 142, 151, 156, 160
Madame Sans-Gêne (Giordano) 15
Maddalena (*Andrea Chénier*) 32, 155
Mahler, Gustav 58
Manon (Massenet) 26, 58, 59, 155, 156, 160

Manon (role) 9, 27, *28*, 32, 58, 59, *60*, 113, 141, 142, 155, 156
Mansfield, Richard *13*, 14
Mapleson, James Henry 7
Marcia Manot (*The Devil-Stone*) 105, 158
Margarita (*L'Ancêtre*) 31, 155
Margherita (*Mefistofele*) 52, 156
Marguerite (*La Damnation de Faust*) 29, 37, 38, 55, 156
Marguerite (*Faust*) 2, 17, 18, *19*, 22, 29, 32, 38, 39, 40, 52, 58, 139, 141, *152*, 155, 156
Maria Rosa 92, 93, 97, 98, 100, 157
Marlowe, Julia 14, 54
Martin, Ricardo 67
Martinelli, Giovanni 120, 160
Martini, Madame 15
Massenet, Jules 27
Matterhorn, Charley 126
Maurel, Victor 8, 34
Mefistofele (Boïto) 52, 156, 160
Melba, Nellie 5, 7, 10, 14, 18, 24, 26, 34, 35, 135
Micaela (*Carmen*) 58, 59, 141, *152*, 156
Mimi (*La bohème*) *50*, 52, 53, 55, 58, 75, 103, 141, 151, 155, 156
Mother (Farrar's) 2, 11, *12*, *13*, 14, *21*, 34, 55, 130
Muele, Marie 18
Muriel Barnes (*Shadows*) 158

La Navarraise (Massenet) 121, 122, 123, 156
Nazimova, Alla 36
Nedda (*I pagliacci*) 23, 32, *50*, 55, 58, 82, 142, 151, 155, 156
Nethersole, Olga 14
Nordica, Lillian 14, 16, *19*, 34
Le nozze di Figaro (Mozart) 58, 156, 160

O'Neill, James 90
Orlanda (*La Reine Fiammette*) 114, 115, 156

I pagliacci (Leoncavallo) 17, 23, 42, 50, 155, 156
Patti, Adelina 5, 6, 7, 10, 18, 34, 138
Peel, Colonel 119
Plançon, Paul 37, 38
Poncha O'Brien (*The Hell-Cat*) 106, 158
Puccini, Giacomo 43, 44

Queen Grenalda (*The Devil Stone*) 105, 158

Rehan, Ada 14
Reid, Wallace 93, 100, 157, 158

La Reine Fiammette (Leroux) 114, 156
Rejane, Gabrielle 15, 118
Renée Dupree (*Temptation*) 95, 157
Ricordi, Giulio 43, 44
The Riddle: Woman 108, 159
Rigoletto (Verdi) 32, 155
Rioton, Marthe 9
Le Roi de Lahore (Massenet) 31, 155
Romany Love (Lehar) 130
Roméo et Juliette (Gounod) 14, 17, 23, 35, 155, 156, 160
Rosalie Dean (*Turn of the Wheel*), 106, *107*, 158
Rosaura (*Le donne curiose*) 78, 79, 156
Rousselière, Charles 35, 37, 38
Rudersdorff, Erminia *13*
Russell, James 123

Salome (R. Strauss) 9, 32, 132
Salvini, Tommaso 8, 9, 10
Sanderson, Sybil 15
The School for Scandal (Sheridan play) 14
Scotti, Antonio 41, 57, 160
Il segreto di Susanna (Wolf-Ferrari) 78, 156
Seligman, Sybil 44
Sembrich, Marcella 24, *50*, 53, 54, 57
Shadows 105, 158
The Sign of the Cross (film) 14
Sita (*Le Roi de Lahore*) 31, 155
Stanislavski, Constantin 8, 10
Straton, John Roach, Dr. 120
Strauss, Richard 32, 132
The Stronger Vow 105, 106, 158
Sunday, Billy 9
Suor Angelica (Puccini) 114, 156
Susanna (*Il segreto di Susanna*) 78, 79, 141, 156
Swartwout, Christine 4

Tamagno, Francesco 8, 34
Tannhäuser (Wagner) 8, 29, 31, 40, 49, 71, 155, 156, 160
Tecza (*The Woman God Forgot*) 103, *104*, 158
Tellegen, Lou 2, 98, *99*, 103, 105, 106, 123, 143, 149, 159
Telva, Marion 132
Temptation 92, 95, 97, 98, 100, 157
The Termagant (Parker and Carson) 14
Ternina, Milka 61, 64
Thaïs (Massenet) 112, 156, 160
Thaïs (role) 2, 112, 113, 142, 156
Tosca (Puccini) 53, 124, 130, 156, 160
Tosca (role) 1, 2, *60*–69, 103, 112, 124, 139, 142, 156, 160
Tosca (Sardou play) 15, 61, 62, 106

Toscanini, Arturo 58, *60*, *83*
Trabadello, Antonio 15, 16
La traviata (Verdi) 14, 17, 20, 23, 32, 52, 53, 155, 156, 160
Il trovatore (Verdi) 24, 155
Turn of the Wheel 105, 106, 144, 158

Ulric, Leonore 90
Urban, Joseph 77

Violetta 20, *21*, 22, 23, 32, 52, 53, 54, 55, 138, 141, 142, 155, 156
von Hochberg, Count 16, 17
von Rath, Frau Adolph 16

Webb, Mrs. Bertram 15
Werther (Massenet) 62, 63, 156
Wilcke, Eva 17
Wilhelm, Crown Prince 27, 58

Williams, Camilla 3, 132, *133*, 150, 151, *152*, 153, 154
The Woman and the Puppet 105, 106, *107*, 159
The Woman God Forgot 103, 105, 158
The World and Its Woman 105, 159

Yacco, Sada 47

Zazà (Berton, Simon, Belasco play) 14, 117, 119
Zazà (Leoncavallo) *116*, 117, 120
Zazà (role) 1, 2, *116*, 117, 118, 119, 120, 123, 124, 125, 139, 142, 156
Zephirine (*Le clown*) 29, 32, 155
Zerlina (*Don Giovanni*) 23, 24, *25*, 32, 52, 53, 59, 79, 139, 141, 155, 156
Zorika (*Romany Love*) 130
Zukor, Adolph 90

www.ingramcontent.com/pod-product-compliance
Lightning Source LLC
Chambersburg PA
CBHW032102300426
44116CB00007B/860